DESCARTES

DESCARTES:
THE PROJECT OF PURE
ENQUIRY

BERNARD WILLIAMS

Knightbridge Professor of Philosophy,
University of Cambridge

HUMANITIES PRESS · NEW JERSEY

This edition published simultaneously with Pelican Books in 1978 by
HUMANITIES PRESS INC.
Atlantic Highlands, New Jersey 07716

© Bernard Williams, 1978

First published by Penguin Books Ltd 1978

Library of Congress Cataloging in Publication Data

Williams, Bernard Arthur Owen
Descartes.
Includes index.
1. Descartes, René, 1596–1650
B1875.W56   1978   194   78–5023

ISBN 0–391–00563–4

Printed and bound in Great Britain by
Redwood Burn Limited, Trowbridge & Esher

CONTENTS

CONTENTS

TO

STANLEY AND CATHY CAVELL

PREFACE

THIS is a study in the history of philosophy rather than in the history of ideas. I use those labels to mark the distinction that the history of ideas is history before it is philosophy, while with the history of philosophy it is the other way round. In any worthwhile work of either sort, both concerns are likely to be represented, but there is a genuine distinction.

For the history of ideas, the question about a work *what does it mean?* is centrally the question *what did it mean?*, and the pursuit of that question moves horizontally in time from the work, as well as backwards, to establish the expectations, conventions, familiarities, in terms of which the author could have succeeded in conveying a meaning. This enterprise itself cannot be uncorrupted by hindsight. This is not just because the understanding we bring to the explanations is a later one, though that is true and important, much as playing seventeenth-century scores on seventeenth-century instruments according to seventeenth-century practice, admirable enterprise though it may be otherwise, does not produce seventeenth-century music, since we have necessarily twentieth-century ears. Beyond that, it is also true that our selection of the works that we take to reward this enquiry is governed by their subsequent history and our present situation; and within the works themselves, what utterances strike us and strike our historical curiosity is, again, governed in that way.[1] Yet what we are moved to, as historians of ideas, is an historical enquiry, and the *genre* of the resulting work is unequivocally history.

The history of philosophy of course has to constitute its object, the work, in genuinely historical terms, yet there is a cut-off point, where authenticity is replaced as the objective by the aim of articulating philosophical ideas. The 'horizontal' search

1. For this point, and for other helpful considerations, see John Dunn, 'The Identity of the History of Ideas', *Philosophy* XLIII (1968), 85–104.

for what Descartes meant will, if it is properly done, yield an object essentially ambiguous, incomplete, imperfectly determined by the author's and his contemporaries' understanding, for that is what the work – at least if it is now of any autonomous interest at all – cannot fail to have been. The present study, while I hope that it is not unaware that that is so, prefers the direction of rational reconstruction of Descartes's thought, where the rationality of the construction is essentially and undisguisedly conceived in a contemporary style. Here the musical analogy is, as an ideal, Stravinsky's *Pulcinella*, in which the melodic line is Pergolesi's, the harmony and orchestration Stravinsky's. The analogy is not exact, since the distinction between melody and harmony is (largely) given in the works of Pergolesi; in works of philosophy, what is the melody is itself determined, in some part, by subsequent philosophical experience. There is the genuine analogy, however, that the new work is broadly of the same *genre* as the original. This study is meant to consist, to a considerable extent, of philosophical argument, the direction of it shaped by what I take to be, now, the most interesting philosophical concerns of Descartes.

The argument is in twentieth-century terms; the judgement of interest is a twentieth-century judgement; it is absolutely certain that a work which was primarily historical would represent Descartes's concerns in a different way. Yet, for all that, I hope that the concerns represented in this way were concerns of Descartes, and that to speak of his having had the special kind of project that I have tried to articulate in this book relates illuminatingly to something historically and importantly true about his outlook.

The writing of this book has stretched over an absurdly long period, particularly because it was laid aside for a number of years. It has largely been rewritten more recently, and I hope that it is not too obvious that a few passages were written up to fourteen years before others. One result of these delays is that the work has had the chance of benefiting from my opportunity to give courses on Descartes during two separate and enjoyable visits to the U.S.A.: in 1963 at Princeton University, and in 1973 at Harvard. I should like to express thanks to colleagues and students in those departments of philosophy for many helpful discussions. I am grateful to many people who in print or in discussion have helped my understanding of Cartesian problems. I cannot thank them all, but I should like to mention David Wiggins and Chris Hookway, to whom I am indebted for discussion of several points. Neither they nor anyone else except myself is to be blamed for what appears. I am, in addition, grateful to Sheelagh Barnard for research assistance, and to Heather Stephens for the final typescript.

Cambridge, February 1977

BOOKS AND REFERENCES

THE standard edition of the works of Descartes is that edited by Charles Adam and Paul Tannery, in eleven volumes (twelfth and thirteenth volumes of biography, index, etc.), now reissued by Vrin (Paris) in association with the Centre National de la Recherche Scientifique (1964–75). This is known as 'AT'. References to this edition are made merely by volume and page, thus: 'VII 261'.

The first five volumes of AT are devoted to correspondence. There is a more complete edition of Descartes's correspondence by Charles Adam and Gérard Milhaud (Paris, 1936–63), but all the references to letters in the present book are made to AT.

AT presents works in French and in Latin, including the French translations of the *Meditations* and the *Principles*. A useful collection which is all in French, including some correspondence, is that in the Bibliothèque de la Pléiade (Paris, 1952).

The best-known and most comprehensive English translation of Descartes's philosophical writings is by E. S. Haldane and G. R. T. Ross, in two volumes (Cambridge, 1911, corrected 1934). It does not include any correspondence and omits substantial parts of the *Principles*. The translation is rather stiff, and not always accurate on points of philosophical detail. References to this translation are made in the style: 'HR1 63', 'HR2 206'.

Substantial selections from the Haldane and Ross translation, with some corrections, are presented in *The Essential Descartes*, ed. Margaret D. Wilson (New York, 1969). Other translations of selections include: *Descartes: Philosophical Writings*, tr. Norman Kemp Smith (London, 1952); and *Descartes: Philosophical Writings*, tr. Elizabeth Anscombe and Peter Thomas Geach (London and Edinburgh, 1954).

There is no complete translation of the correspondence. A useful selection is translated and edited by Anthony Kenny,

Descartes: Philosophical Letters (Oxford, 1970). References to this are made by page number preceded by 'K': 'K 116'.

In 1648 Descartes had a conversation with a young man called Burman, who visited him in Holland and discussed with him a series of well-prepared questions. We have Burman's notes of this conversation (V 146–79). They have been translated and annotated by John Cottingham: *Descartes's Conversation with Burman* (Oxford, 1976). References to this are made thus: 'C p. 26' (this emphasizes that the reference is to the page, not the section number, of Cottingham's edition).

The secondary literature on Descartes is, of course, enormous. For a bibliography up to 1960, see G. Sebba, *Bibliographia Cartesiana* (The Hague, 1964). Various secondary works referred to in the text are identified in the notes. Works to which several references have been made include the following:

W. Doney, ed.: *Descartes: A Collection of Critical Essays* (New York, 1967).

H. G. Frankfurt: *Demons, Dreamers and Madmen: the Defense of Reason in Descartes' 'Meditations'* (New York, 1970).

E. Gilson: *Discours de la Méthode, Texte et Commentaire* (Paris, 1925). A deeply informed and valuable work.

A. Kenny: *Descartes, A Study of his Philosophy* (New York, 1968).

Passages from: the *Regulae;* the *Discourse on the Method* and its accompanying *Essays;* the *Meditations,* the *Objections,* and the *Replies;* and *La Recherche de la Vérité,* are given by an AT reference followed by a Haldane and Ross reference, as: *II Rep.:* VII 140, HR2 38.

A few passages from minor works not appearing in HR have only an AT reference.

References to *letters* are given by recipient, date, and AT reference, followed by Kenny reference when there is one, as: to Regius, 24 May 1640: III 65, K 73–4.

References to the *Conversation with Burman* are given by AT reference, followed by page reference to Cottingham: V 178, C pp. 49–50.

The *Principles* and *The Passions of the Soul* are divided into short numbered sections, and references to these works are given only by number of book and section: *Princ.* i 64, *Passions of the Soul* i 44 (in fact the section numbers of the *Passions of the Soul* run continuously through its books).

All quoted passages have been translated by myself; my debts to other translators are considerable and no doubt obvious.

Chapter 1

DESCARTES

RENÉ DESCARTES was born on 31 March 1596 in a small town near Tours, now called la-Haye-Descartes, where the house of his birth can still be seen. His family belonged to the lesser nobility, his father and his elder brother both being magistrates at the High Court of Brittany at Rennes. His mother died in childbirth a year after he was born, and he said that he inherited from her a dry cough and a pale complexion, and for a long time he feared that he would die young. In 1604 he entered the Jesuit college of la Flèche at Anjou, which had been opened only that year. The Rector knew his family, and he was allowed his own room and to get up when he liked. The spirit of the school was intellectually more open than in most. Though Galileo had not then become the centre of controversy he was to become later, it is significant that a poem was declaimed there on 6 June 1611 in celebration of Galileo's discovery of the moons of Jupiter. Though Descartes, as he said, found little real knowledge in what he was taught except in mathematics, he was well disposed to the Jesuits, and the marked tendency he showed throughout his life to conciliate the Church expressed itself in the case of the Society with signs of genuine respect and gratitude. He left la Flèche in 1614, and took a Baccalauréat and a Licence in law at Poitiers in November 1616.

In 1618, wanting, he says, to see the world of practical affairs, he joined at his own expense an army led by Maurice of Nassau, son of William the Silent. It was a travelling rather than a military undertaking, and he was not involved in action. In 1618–19 he was in friendly association with Isaac Beeckman, eight years older than himself, who was a doctor of medicine from Caen. Descartes said that Beeckman had woken him up to scientific questions, and he dedicated to him a small treatise on music which he completed in 1618. He travelled in Germany.

On 10 November 1619 there occurred a significant event, perhaps at Ulm. In a *poêle*, or stove-heated room, he had some intellectual vision of a mathematical science, and the same night had three dreams, which revealed to him, as he interpreted them, a destiny to create a *scientia mirabilis*. He made a vow to Our Lady of Loreto to make a pilgrimage to her shrine, which he later did.[1] The exact nature of the daytime intellectual vision is not clear, but he formed in this period aims of clarifying the basic ideas and notation of algebra (Descartes invented the modern notation for powers), and of developing the relations of algebra and geometry, which was to issue in his laying the foundations of analytical geometry; and also the wider project of unifying all sciences of quantity under mathematics (the eventual form of this last project in Descartes's hands we shall be considering in Chapter 9).

Descartes travelled a good deal in the 1620s. During this period various sceptical views, sometimes associated with radically *libertin* outlooks, were current. There was a meeting in Paris in the presence of the Papal Nuncio, at which a figure called Chandoux (hanged in 1631 for counterfeiting) lectured against the Aristotelian philosophy. Descartes made a speech in reply, urging that the sciences could be founded only on certainty. Among those present was Pierre de Bérulle, head of the Oratory, who in a conversation afterwards made Descartes promise to devote himself to philosophy.

In 1628–9 he wrote some of a work called *Regulae ad directionem Ingenii, Rules for the direction of the Understanding.* Conceived on an ambitious plan, this was left unfinished and was published only in 1701. In it, many of Descartes's basic philosophical concerns are expressed or at least prefigured, and we shall have various occasions to refer to it. In general, it emphasizes the methodological aspects of Descartes's thought, and offers already the idea of a universal science of quantity,

1. Huyghens, commenting on Baillet's life of Descartes, said: 'That passage, where he tells how he had his brain overheated and capable of visions, and of his vow to N.D. of Lorette, shows a great weakness, and I think that it will seem much the same to Catholics who have freed themselves from bigotry' (V. Cousin, *Fragments philosophiques* (Paris, 1838), II, 158).

but lays less emphasis on the metaphysical issues which concern him in later works. It also emphasizes less the distinction between the purely intellectual powers of the mind and the corporeal imagination which was to become basic to Descartes's philosophy, an epistemological correlate to the dualism between the body and the intellectual soul.[2]

In 1628 Descartes went to Holland, where he lived, with brief interruptions, until 1649. The atmosphere in Holland in the early seventeenth century was comparatively liberal: the Dutch publishers Elzevier, for instance, were able to publish works of Galileo in the 1630s. It was chosen for its liberty by a number of thinkers, including some Frenchmen. One objected to the weather ('four months of winter and eight months of cold'), but Descartes preferred its climate to that of Italy. He had a number of intellectual friends. Despite his desire for a quiet life, he was involved in some academic and religious disputes, unpleasant and at one point rather threatening; in particular one between Gisbert Voet of Utrecht and Regius (Henri de Roy), professor of medicine, who pronounced himself a Cartesian, but whose teachings later attracted Descartes's criticism. One of the few details of Descartes's purely personal life which is known is that he had an illegitimate daughter, baptized 7 August 1635, whose name was Francine; her mother was called Hélène, and Descartes told Clerselier (IV 660) that the child was conceived in Amsterdam on 15 October 1634. His daughter died at Amersfort on 7 September 1640, and Descartes is said to have found this the heaviest blow of his life.

In March 1629, the phenomenon of parhelia, sun-haloes, was observed at Rome, and Descartes was asked his opinion of this. He formed the conception of a treatise on meteorological questions, and, more generally, on physics: it was to be called *Le Traité du Monde*, *Treatise on the Universe*. Shortly before it was to be published, in 1633, Descartes heard of the condemnation of Galileo by the Inquisition for teaching the movement of the earth, and he suppressed his *Treatise*. He was to incorporate

2. For detailed discussion of the relations between the *Regulae* and Descartes's later work, see L. J. Beck, *The Method of Descartes* (Oxford, 1952).

some of its material in later works, and the *Treatise* itself partly survives in the form of two works, the *Treatise on Light* and the *Treatise on Man*, which were not published until after his death. Some material which linked these two parts is missing, and a third treatise, on the soul, which is promised in the *Treatise on Man*, has never been found and was perhaps never written.

The fear of being censured by the Church undoubtedly had some distorting effect on Descartes's thought (we shall encounter effects of this in Chapter 9), through personal fear of criticism, and also from a desire to have his works adopted officially as manuals of instruction. (For his attitude at the time of suppressing the *Treatise*, see his letter to Mersenne of April 1634: I 270–73, K 25–7.) 'It is not my temperament to set sail against the wind,' he wrote to Pollot in 1644 (IV 73), and this was certainly true. It was later said by Cardinal Bossuet, hardly himself a radical figure, that Descartes was too worried about being condemned by the Church.[3] That his precautions were extreme is perhaps suggested by the fact that Mersenne was able to persist in strongly pro-Galilean statements, in the less favourable atmosphere of Paris.

The suppression of the *Treatise* led Descartes, however, to produce a different and in several respects more unusual work. It consisted of three essays; they are presented in the order in which they were written. The first is the *Dioptric*, dealing with problems of refraction and related matters, and including a formulation of what is now called Snell's Law, though Descartes appears to have discovered it independently of Snell. The second treatise is the *Meteors*, and the third, the *Geometry*, which lays the foundations of what is now known as analytical geometry. The set of essays is prefaced by a remarkable work, the *Discourse on the Method*.[4] The whole book was written in

3. For his care in getting the *Meditations* recommended to the Sorbonne, see his letter to Gibieuf of 11 November 1640 (III 237). His caution in strictly theological issues is illustrated by his letter to Mesland about the Sacrament, 9 February 1645 (IV 162, K 154).

4. This is the correct translation of the title, in full 'Discours de la Méthode pour bien conduire sa raison et chercher la vérité dans les sciences'. Cf. also the letter to Mersenne cited below (I 349) '. . . and I call the follow-

French, Descartes hoping, as did Galileo, by writing in the ver-
nacular to reach over the heads of pedants and monks to the
growing population of lay persons of good sense, free from
academic and theological prejudice, with whom his reasonings
might strike home. The style is very lucid and elegant, and has
always been admired as a model of the expression of abstract
thought in French. Descartes wrote to a Jesuit (I 560, K 46) that
it was so written that even women should be able to understand
it,[5] and he told Mersenne that he had called it a *Discourse*,
rather than a *Treatise*, on the Method, because his aim was not
to teach, but only to talk about it (I 349).

The *Discourse* also remarkably expressed Descartes's indi-
viduality. It was already a contrast with the practice of some
geometers that he presented the *Geometry* in his own name –
many preferred to offer their discoveries as additions to the
works of the ancients, Viète appearing as the 'French Apollonius', Snell as the 'Dutch Apollonius' and so forth. But far
beyond this, the *Discourse* offers an account of Descartes's enquiries and his attitude to them in a genuinely autobiographical
form. Montaigne had of course displayed an amused and
searching interest in himself, but in virtue of that spirit itself
had been distant and ironically reserved about philosophy or
systematic speculation. The *Discourse*, on the other hand, dis-
plays its author not so much as an object of human interest to
himself or others, but rather as an example – though a genuinely existing, particular, example – of the mind being rationally directed to the systematic discovery of truth.

The sophistication of this way of presenting philosophy is
much further developed in his masterpiece, the *Meditations on
First Philosophy*, the first edition of which was published in
1641. In this work, the 'I' of the writer is not so much the
historical Descartes as it is any reflective person working their

---

ing treatises *Essais de cette Méthode*' – the Method, of course, being Descartes's own, of which he takes the following essays to be products. The
title is often mistranslated 'Discourse on Method'.

5. Doubtless a fair comment on contemporary reading habits. Accusations
of sexism should be restrained, e.g. in face of his relations with Elizabeth:
see below.

way through this series of arguments. The *Meditations* are not a description but an enactment of philosophical thought, following what Descartes regarded as the only illuminating way of presenting philosophy, the order of discovery: an order of discovery, however, which is not just arbitrarily individual, but idealized, the fundamental route by which human thought should move from everyday experience to greater philosophical insight. The extreme skill with which Descartes realizes this scheme, and the subtlety with which the work is organized (something which emerges more and more on repeated readings), make the *Meditations* one of the most original achievements of philosophical literature.

It was, unlike the book of 1637, written in Latin, though it was soon translated into French.[6] It was published together with six (in the second edition, seven) sets of *Objections* from various writers, and Descartes's *Replies*. These documents, some more than others, shed valuable light on Descartes's views. The *First* set, from Caterus, a priest in Holland, Descartes collected himself: the aim was to impress the Sorbonne, particularly through the Jesuit Gibieuf. He then sent the *Meditations* themselves and the first set of *Objections* and *Replies* to Mersenne, with instructions to collect other objections – instructions which Mersenne characteristically exceeded. The *Second Objections* came from various theologians, and include some of Mersenne's own. The *Third* are from the English philosopher Hobbes; this was not Descartes's idea, an association with the heretic and materialist Hobbes being unlikely to help with the Sorbonne. Fortunately for Descartes, Hobbes was hostile. Unfortunately for us, the resulting exchange does not illustrate much, except truculent misunderstanding on Hobbes' part and impatience on Descartes's. Far superior, indeed best of all, as Descartes himself thought, was the exchange (the *Fourth*) with Antoine Arnauld, then only twenty-nine, the Jansenist priest whose famous book *De la Fréquente Communion* (1643) led to a long quarrel with the Jesuits, as a result of which Arnauld was in retreat, even in hiding, for twenty-five years. Mersenne went beyond his instructions for a second time

6. See note 1, p. 72.

in inviting comments from Pierre Gassendi, a prolix atomist writer, who had been annoyed at not having been mentioned in the *Dioptric*, and also from the mathematician Fermat, with whom there had already been controversy. Fermat kept quiet, perhaps for fear of renewing the quarrel, but Gassendi offered *Objections* (the *Fifth*) at great length, and later responded to Descartes's *Replies* (which take a rather laboriously sarcastic tone) with a yet vaster work, the *Instances*. Descartes was eventually reconciled with Gassendi, perhaps on his visit to France in 1647; it may also have been then that there was a dinner for Descartes, Gassendi and Hobbes given by Descartes's correspondent William Cavendish, Marquis of Newcastle (who in 1638 was made tutor to the future Charles II of England).

The *Sixth* set of *Objections* was from various geometers, philosophers and theologians of Mersenne's circle. In the second edition of the *Meditations* (1642) all these were joined by a *Seventh* set by Bourdin, a professor at the Jesuit College in Paris. Despite Descartes's general disposition to be agreeable to Jesuits, these *Objections* obviously (and justifiably) annoyed him, though they did elicit one or two useful clarifications about the Method of Doubt. The tone and content of Bourdin's reply so upset him that he wrote, and had published with the *Meditations*, a letter to another Jesuit, Dinet, who had been his instructor at la Flèche; in this letter (VII 563 ff., HR2 347 ff.) he also cited what he had suffered at the hands of the Protestants in Holland.

Further in his attempt to establish his philosophy as official Catholic teaching, he produced in 1644 a work in the form of a text-book, divided into books and articles, the *Principia Philosophiae*, the *Principles*. Three of its four books are largely concerned with what would now be called scientific rather than philosophical matters. He had said to Huyghens (31 January 1642: III 523, K 131) that his suppressed treatise would have already appeared, but he had been 'teaching it to speak Latin; and I shall call it *Summa Philosophiae*, so that it will be more familiar to the scholastics, who persecute it and try to smother it before its birth, the Ministers as much as the Jesuits'. This was the *Principles*, which thus contains a lot of the *Traité du Monde*; at the same time, Descartes hoped that 'it could be used in Christian teaching without contradicting the text of Aristotle'. This tortuous objective means (as we shall see in Chapter 9) that as a guide to Descartes's true opinions, the *Principles* has in places to be used with caution. The work was translated into French by the Abbé Claude Picot, a new enthusiast for Descartes's philosophy, who had been opposed to him but had been converted by the *Meditations*. A letter to him forms the Preface to the French edition.

Descartes dedicated the *Principles* to a friend, the Princess Elizabeth, who is first referred to in his correspondence in 1642. This remarkable woman had been born at Heidelberg in 1618. Her father was Frederick, Elector Palatine, who was crowned King of Bohemia in November 1619 but lost the crown at the battle of the White Mountain in 1620, and then lived in exile until his death in 1632. Her mother, widowed with ten children, was Elizabeth Stuart, the 'Winter Queen', daughter of James I of England and sister of Charles I: Descartes found himself with the unusual task of writing the Princess a letter of consolation on the execution of her uncle (22 February 1649: V 281). Elizabeth normally spoke French, knew English, German, Flemish, Italian and Latin, had some skill in mathematics, solving a difficult problem set by Descartes, and had an interest in astronomy and physics. She was a Calvinist, but disapproved of narrow Protestant bigots. She and Descartes wrote frankly to each other on a range of topics. Though Descartes's letters to her were published in 1657, Elizabeth refused publication of her letters to him, and asked for them back; copies were found, and they were published in 1879.

One subject that Elizabeth pursued in her correspondence with Descartes was the relation of mind and body, and the nature and control of the passions. Prompted by her discussions, Descartes wrote what was to be his last work, *The Passions of the Soul*, which was published in November 1649, though a manuscript had been sent already in November 1647 to Queen Christina of Sweden. The larger part of this work consists of a classification and description of the emotions:

though it contains some points of interest, this part has been ignored in the present study. The material on mind–body relations, however, is a principal text for this, notorious, aspect of Descartes's views.

In 1647 the French King awarded Descartes a pension, 'in consideration of his great merits, and of the utility that his philosophy and his long researches would bring to the human race', but he seems never to have received any of it, and merely had to pay out for the sending of the warrant. A more significant royal interest was that of Christina. She had been born in 1626, and had come to the throne in 1644 after a regency, in succession to her father Gustavus Adolphus. At this time she had the idea of bringing arts and letters to the North, and assembled about her a number of scholars. Descartes was approached through the French resident in Stockholm, Hector-Pierre Chanut, and urged to go to Sweden. He hesitated for a long time, and said to others that he had no desire to go to 'the land of bears'. However, he did leave in September 1649, and arrived in Stockholm at the beginning of October. (The pilot of the ship is supposed to have told the Queen that Descartes was a 'demi-god' in matters of navigation and so forth.) There were two audiences with Christina, and then she left him alone for six weeks. Descartes was lonely and unhappy. He was required, among other absurd employments, to write verses for a ballet (*La Naissance de la Paix*, concerned with the Peace of Westphalia and Christina's birthday). The Queen was away for the first half of January. Descartes had his picture painted by David Beck, a pupil of Van Dyck, and is said to have converted the painter to sentiments of religion during their conversations. He also drew up the statutes of a Swedish Academy – one rule he proposed was that no foreigners should belong to it. The Queen returned, and took up philosophy lessons, which took place three times a week at 5 a.m. She said later, when she became a Catholic, that these conversations had had some effect on her (she could hardly say less). Chanut's residence, where Descartes lived, was at some distance from the Palace. He had had, moreover, for years the habit of not rising until 11, spending the earlier hours reading and writing in bed. He caught pneumonia and died at 4 a.m. on 11 February 1650. His last words are alleged to have been *Ça mon âme, il faut partir.*

He was buried in Stockholm, but in 1666 his body was removed to France and buried in Paris at Sainte-Geneviève. It was the occasion of a banquet of anti-scholastic and anti-authoritarian tone. Three years before, his philosophy had been condemned by Rome. This image of Descartes as an anti-clerical and indeed anti-religious force, deeply contrary to his actual disposition, was to persist. In 1791 a petition was raised for his remains to be transferred to the Panthéon: 'Descartes, kept away from France by superstition and fanaticism,' etc. The project was not carried out at that time, because of political events; taken up again by the Directory, it was opposed by a *député* who was apparently a supporter of Newton, and allowed to lapse. He was finally reburied in Saint-Germain-des-Prés in 1819, where his tomb can be seen between those of two Benedictines.

Descartes was lofty, chilly and solitary, and cultivated a certain reserve and self-sufficiency in life and manner. 'Fermat est Gascon (a boaster), moi non,' he is reported to have said. He valued his financial independence, and his references in the *Discourse* to the need for funds for experiments should not be read as an appeal for himself. He refused the offer of a M. de Montmort to set him up in a château near Paris (an offer later accepted by Gassendi), and also declined a considerable sum from the Comte d'Avaux, sent to Holland for his experiments. He was touchy where his originality was in question, and his attitude to other well-known mathematicians was often condescending or hostile. He took pleasure in mystifying them. In sending Roberval the solution to the problem of finding the tangent to a figure called the 'garland', which Roberval failed to solve, Descartes propounded another curve, which he in fact knew to be equivalent, as he told Mersenne in confidence; 'I did it to make fun of him' (23 August 1638: II 336). It was a habit of the time to wrap one's discoveries up: rather later, Hooke concealed in anagrams his discoveries about the arch. Yet it seems paradoxical that Descartes should have deliberately left out simpler material from the *Geometry*, part of the book of 1637, which was supposed to be luminous to all. He was afraid that his originality would not be recognized if he made it too easy, and he took pleasure in the thought of the difficulties it would cause to geometers in France such as Fermat and the unfortunate Roberval (to Mersenne, 1 March 1638: II 28, 30; to Debeaune, 20 February 1639: II 511).

This sense of superiority to contemporary mathematicians co-existed with a belief that his ideas could be made plain to ordinary men of good sense. This seemingly rather odd combination of attitudes is more than an accident of Descartes's temperament. The early seventeenth century was only just beginning to develop the apparatus of scientific communication, the foundation of an international scientific community, which is familiar today. The tireless Abbé Mersenne acted as a post office between the many scientists, mathematicians and others that he knew: Fermat at Toulouse, Debeaune at Blois, Desargues occasionally at Lyon, Descartes in Holland. Meetings of Pascal, Gassendi, Fermat and others at Mersenne's cell played a part in the origin of the Académie des Sciences, not founded till 1666. With these imperfect communications, there went an imperfect sense of the need for them. Descartes found that he had no time to read Galileo's mechanics (cf. X 573), and he died without having heard of Kepler's laws of planetary motion, which were first announced in Paris, without attracting much attention, in 1639.

It is important that there existed no clear sense either of the size of the scientific task, or, on the other hand, of its possibility. On the one hand, sane and informed people could believe that once the right path had been found, basic understanding of nature and hence control of it would be very rapidly available. Francis Bacon admittedly had a rather distant, organizational, view of the subject – 'he writes philosophy like a Lord Chancellor' William Harvey said of him – but he was able to say: 'the particular phenomena of the arts and sciences are in reality but a handful; the invention of all causes and sciences would be the labour of but a few years'. Descartes himself entertained when he was young some extravagant hopes about the control of aging, which were modified by experience.[7]

7. See p. 258.

On the other hand, this unclarity about what might be involved in the knowledge of nature could equally give rise to
doubts whether it was possible at all. The traditional framework of scholastic teaching had provided a range of patterns for
'legitimating belief':[8] scripture and the interpretative authority
of the Church in religious matters; the force of other author-
itative texts; the application to these, with the help of common
observation and some traditions of experimental enquiry, of
sophisticated forms of logical argument. The Reformation had
questioned the traditional sources of religious authority, but
had not produced any consensus, and was not going to produce
any, on what others there might be. The controversies surrounding these issues helped to generate movements of scepticism, not only with respect to religion itself, but with respect to
other forms of supposed knowledge. If it were objected that
religious belief had no true foundation, defenders of Chris-
tianity could reply that things were no better with secular
beliefs.[9]

But there was a general doubt at work, about what powers of
the human mind were relevant to the discovery of ultimate
truth. Inasmuch as the medieval tradition relied on authority in
secular questions, in particular (though by no means universally) the authority of Aristotle, it had no fully coherent answer
to this question, which was bound to recur in the form of asking
what peculiar access to truth was possessed by Aristotle, who
was after all only another human being, if a very gifted one.
This idea occurs repeatedly in Galileo's *Dialogues concerning
the two Chief World Systems*; while Descartes is, significantly,
in a position to deploy a clearly developed and dismissive concept of 'history' to make a similar point:

8. The phrase is Ernest Gellner's: see his *Legitimation of Belief* (Cambridge, 1974).
9. This aspect of sixteenth and seventeenth century scepticism has been
particularly emphasized by Richard Popkin in his *The History of Scepticism
from Erasmus to Descartes* (revised edition, Assen, 1964). – I knew a sturdy
anti-clerical who called this apologetic resource 'poisoning the wells'.
Versions of it are still popular, though the beneficiary is often now social
science rather than religion.

... nor shall we come out as philosophers, if we read all the arguments of Plato and Aristotle, but can form no sound judgement on the matters in question: we shall have learned, not the sciences, but history. (*Reg.* iii: X 367, HR1 6)

In the Renaissance, a confusion of possible answers was generated to this question of what capacities could lead to knowledge. Many Renaissance thinkers, particularly in Italy, understood their task to be not just the establishment of knowledge about the classical past, but also the revival of the attitude to knowledge which existed in that past. But this understanding was itself surrounded by great uncertainty about what the powers of the ancients consisted in. Some of these writers perhaps did unwittingly recapitulate a feature of fifth-century BC Greek culture, of which it has been well said[10] that the Greek sophists (who lived before the fundamental logical discoveries of Plato and Aristotle) 'were prone to confuse the force of reason and the power of the spoken word'. Those sophists were fascinated by sceptical arguments, and originally invented some of the sceptical material which was known to the seventeenth century chiefly through the works of Sextus Empiricus (*c.* AD 200). This incapacity to tell the difference between the power of words and the force of argument (prevalent, then as now, in Paris) contributed to the sceptical disorientation which existed in Descartes's time. Having discarded the run-down traditional logic which then was current (for which Descartes sustained a life-long contempt), and the answers to sceptical argument provided by the Aristotelian tradition, adventurous thinkers were uncertain what dialectical weapons could counter scepticism.[11] But that lack was not the most important. If there are evident examples of real knowledge around, the fact that one lacks arguments to explain how such knowledge is possible is of purely philosophical – that is to say, very limited – interest. But the early seventeenth century lacked prototypes of

10. Edward Hussey, *The Presocratics* (London, 1972), p. 117.
11. Rebuttals of scepticism were of course frequent: see Popkin. Mersenne offered one in 1625, *La Vérité des Sciences contre les Sceptiques,* in particular against Charron.

such knowledge and also lacked settled belief about how to acquire it.

One ancient idea, variously reinterpreted in this period, was that the truth of things was hidden – in some versions, occult. Some Renaissance and post-Reformation conceptions offered as the image of one who knows, and who through knowledge has power over nature, the *Magus*.[12] Recent work has emphasized, perhaps exaggerated, the role of magical and occult ideas in the formation of the seventeenth-century scientific outlook.[13] For Descartes, it is the case that the truth about the natural world is hidden, but it is not occult, nor are occult powers needed to uncover it. It is hidden in the form of a mathematical structure which underlies sensible appearances. It is uncovered by systematic scientific enquiry and the use of the rational intellect. If there is magic in Descartes's system, it is in its old place, with God, the Incarnation and the Sacraments.[14]

But what was the rational intellect? In whom could it be found? Descartes's straightforward answer was that it was to be found in everyone, in such a way that anyone, or nearly anyone, given help in clear thinking and freed from prejudice, could pursue reasonings which would lead to truth in philosophy, science or mathematics. This line is particularly emphasized in the *Regulae*, where he says that no sort of knowledge can be more obscure in itself than any other, since all knowledge is of the same nature, and consists solely in the putting together of simple things known in themselves. These perfectly simple truths are known even to quite uneducated people, but the minds of many have been clouded by absurd scholastic form-

12. It is tempting to speculate that these ideas, like witchcraft, are connected with the fact that the weakening of traditional Catholicism led not to the banishment of magic, but to its losing its institutional identity. See Keith Thomas, *Religion and the Decline of Magic* (London, 1971).

13. A popular presentation is Arthur Koestler's *The Sleepwalkers* (London, 1959). This substitutes for the old activity of measuring everyone by Galileo the no less baseless (and in this case highly subjective) attitude of measuring Galileo by Kepler.

14. However, see p. 288 for a magical aspect of the intervention of the will. But if this is magic at all, it is to be noted that it involves no special art or mystery. If it happens at all, it happens for everyone.

ulations (*Reg.* xii: X 426–8, HR1 46–7; cf. also the Introduction to the *Recherche de la Vérité*: X 495–9, HR1 305–7). He carried such ideas into practice, teaching his servant mathematics, and strongly approving of the scheme of a M. d'Alibert to found a college to teach arts and sciences to artisans and others who wanted to learn. The same attitude is expressed in the hope which has already been mentioned, to reach an unprejudiced public by publishing in French (a hope which, as we have also seen, he tended to replace later with that of insinuating his theories into the clergy). It goes with his preferring, in general, the company of practical men, and the same sort of attitude motivated, so he tells us, the journeys he made in his youth. As he very reasonably says:

It seemed to me that I could find much more truth in the reasonings which each man makes about the matters which are of concern to him, and of which the outcome is likely to punish him soon after if he has made a mistake, than in those which a man of letters makes in his study, concerning speculations which lead to no result, and which have no other consequence for him except perhaps that he will be all the more vain about them the further they are from common sense, since he will have had to spend that much more intelligence and skill in trying to make them seem probable. (*Discourse* Part i: VI 9–10, HR1 86–7)

It is notable that several of Descartes's friends were ambassadors or other men of affairs, and it was such people who intervened to help him in his disputes with the university pedants in Holland.

What the unprejudiced mind can deploy is the power of reason, good sense, what Descartes calls 'the natural light', and apparently people possess it in equal measure. The *Discourse* famously begins:

Good sense is of all things in the world the best distributed: each thinks he is so well provided with it, that even those who are hardest to please in other things are not in the habit of wanting more of it than they have. (*Discourse* Part i: VI 1–2, HR1 81)

Yet even if Descartes sincerely believed that men could, when freed from prejudice, equally follow scientific reasonings, did he really believe that they were equally capable of producing them? The joke about everyone's satisfaction with his own good sense already indicates irony, and Descartes's attitude to his own and others' work suggests that he thought that while anyone, properly taught, could understand the truth – which could consist ultimately of nothing but longer or shorter chains of absolutely clear and simple reasoning – it nevertheless took at least one genius to discover it. Yet even allowing for that, there will be no question of a return to authority. Nothing will be rationally believed because it was discovered by Descartes, even if it takes Descartes to discover it. It will be believed because, when put before the unprejudiced mind, it compels assent by its own rational clarity.

The ambivalence of Descartes's attitude to such matters is mirrored also in there being, as we shall see in the next chapter, more than one way of taking his project of Pure Enquiry – as something to be done once and for all by him, or as something which others might also profitably attempt. But there is a good reason why, for Descartes, these issues could remain unresolved. The question of how many, other than himself, might be capable of making fundamental scientific and philosophical discoveries was not very important if none remained to be made. Descartes's faith was that the basic task, at least, was soon to be achieved. Though much, quantitatively, remained to be done, he hoped to have laid the foundations.

In laying 'foundations', philosophy played an essential role – or, rather, a number of roles, for, as we shall see,[15] there is more than one thing encompassed by Descartes's favourite metaphor. But while the role is essential, it is very important that, for Descartes, philosophy's part was very small, in relation to worthwhile knowledge as a whole. This is a book about Descartes's philosophy, and it is as a philosopher that Descartes is now principally known; but by his own conception of things that is an irony. The project we shall be studying is a philosophi-

15. For the project of Pure Enquiry as providing the foundations of knowledge, in different senses of that expression, see pp. 60 ff. For philosophy as the foundation of the conceptual scheme of physics (but not of all its premisses), see pp. 229–30, 253 ff.

cal project, but it was intended by Descartes to be preliminary to a larger enterprise of science, medicine and technology, which would confer practical benefits on mankind. It was a product of his historical situation that he could hope for his project to have these results. It was also a feature of his situation that he could conceive of that project (as we shall see) as conducted by a solitary thinker, as transparent to human reason, and as definitively revealing how knowledge is, after all, possible.

Chapter 2

THE PROJECT

THE most general of the rules of method which Descartes had explored in the *Regulae* are summarized in four rules which Descartes sets himself in the second part of the *Discourse on the Method* (VI 18–19, HR1 92). He resolves to:

1. Accept nothing as true which I did not clearly recognize to be so: that is to say, to avoid carefully precipitation and prejudice, and to accept nothing in my judgements beyond what presented itself so clearly and distinctly to my mind, that I should have no occasion to doubt it.
2. Divide each of the difficulties which I examined into as many parts as possible, and as might be necessary in order best to resolve them.
3. Carry on my reflections in order, starting with those objects that were most simple and easy to understand, so as to rise little by little, by degrees, to the knowledge of the most complex: assuming an order among those that did not naturally fall into a series.
4. Last, in all cases make enumerations so complete and reviews so general that I should be sure of leaving nothing out.

Taken in the abstract, these rules are hardly very illuminating, and one can see some ground for Leibniz's gibe that Descartes's rules of method were 'like the precepts of some chemist; take what you need and do what you should, and you will get what you want'.[1] But Descartes did not suppose that the *Discourse* explained his Method:

My aim is not here to teach the Method which each person should follow in order to conduct his reason well, but solely to show in what way I have tried to conduct my own. (*Discourse* Part i: VI 4, HR1 83)

and he wrote to Vatier that neither the *Discourse* nor its ac-

1. *Philosophischen Schriften von G. W. Leibniz*, ed. C. I. Gerhardt (Berlin, 1875–90), vol. IV, p. 329.

companying treatises adequately expressed the Method (22 February 1638: I 559 ff., K 45–6; the letter more generally sheds light on Descartes's attitude to the book of 1637). But it is not just a matter of one work or a particular set of essays failing to explain fully the Method – no purely abstract treatment could. It is very much part of his outlook that actual exposure to intellectual problems is necessary to give any content to such maxims; the words gain meaning only from the experience of dealing with scientific questions themselves.

One of the rules, however, the first, has a special status. In the *Regulae* there had been an injunction to 'reject all merely probable knowledge, and only to trust to what is perfectly known and cannot be doubted' (*Reg.* ii: X 362, HR1 3), but this appears as one piece of methodological advice among others. In Descartes's mature works, this rule comes to play a distinct and formative role. It is not that, any more than the others, it can provide enlightenment in the abstract, if one is not confronted with real intellectual problems. It is rather that the relevant problems can be the basic problems *of philosophy*, and it is a distinctive feature of this rule that when it is applied radically enough – more radically than it is in the context of the *Regulae* – it provides the basis of a critique of all knowledge and hence of a distinctively philosophical enquiry. The other rules play their part in that enquiry, as they do in any orderly intellectual project, but the first rule has the special capacity of generating it. It gives the distinctive character to Descartes's investigation of knowledge, and the method which, following this rule to its limit, he uses in that investigation is famously known as the *Method of Doubt*.

It is very important that the Method of Doubt is not the whole of Descartes's Method. It is not even the whole of his philosophical method, since, as we shall see, doubt introduces and forms the enquiry, but eventually makes way for a systematic vindication of knowledge, and an orderly reconstruction of it. But also, Descartes's enquiries are not solely, nor principally, directed towards philosophy. The philosophical enquiry is a very special undertaking, which not everyone should try (*Discourse* Part ii: VI 15, HR1 90), and which needs to be done, if at all, only once in a lifetime. If one is going to conduct one's thoughts properly, it is at least as important to exercise the senses and the imagination, as it is the pure understanding in metaphysical enquiries, as he tells the Princess Elizabeth (28 June 1643: IV 695, K 141). These are not merely pieces of advice about how to spend one's time, though they are that, and very sensible ones. They also make the point that the kind of enquiry involved in the vindication of knowledge is necessarily different from any other kind of enquiry. This is not at all because Descartes holds, as some modern views hold, that philosophy has a quite special subject-matter, or is in some other way quite discontinuous from the sciences; on the contrary he thinks, rightly, that philosophy and the sciences are continuous with one another, and he expresses one version of that idea in his image of the tree of knowledge, of which the roots are metaphysics, the trunk physics, and the branches, the other sciences (author's letter attached to the French translation of the *Principles*: IX–2 14, HR1 211). A philosophical enquiry differs from others, for Descartes, in being a specially radical kind of enquiry, and, as a consequence of that, peculiarly free both from assumptions and from certain sorts of constraint which apply in general to the search for knowledge: this is an idea which we shall be specially concerned with in following Descartes's project.

This project takes the form of undertaking exactly the same task as any other enquirer, namely that of *trying to find the truth*; but of undertaking that task, unlike other enquirers, from the very beginning. To do this, Descartes regards the Method of Doubt as the right instrument; more than that, he regards it as quite obviously the right instrument. The first question we have to consider, which will take some time, is why he thinks this as obvious as he does.

In the fourth part of the *Discourse* (VI 31–2, HR1 100–101) he writes:

> For a long time I had remarked that so far as practical life is concerned, it is sometimes necessary to follow opinions which one knows to be very uncertain, just as though they were indubitable, as was said above [he refers to the third part of the *Discourse*, VI 24, HR1

96, where he sets out a 'provisional ethic' to see him through philosophical enquiry]; but because I wanted to devote myself solely to the search for truth, I thought that it was necessary that I should do just the opposite, and that I should reject, just as though it were absolutely false, everything in which I could imagine the slightest doubt, so as to see whether after that anything remained in my belief which was entirely indubitable. So, since our senses deceive us sometimes, I wished to suppose that there was nothing which was as they make us imagine.

A similarly rapid transition to the Method of Doubt occurs in the *First Meditation* (V II 18, H R1 145):

Reason persuades me already, that I should withhold assent no less carefully from things which are not clearly certain and indubitable, as from things which are evidently false; so if I find some reason for doubt in each of them, this will be enough for me to reject them all. It does not follow that I should have to go through them one by one, which would be an endless task; if the foundations are undermined, anything built on top of them falls down by itself, so I shall attack directly those principles which supported everything I have up to now believed.

The method of doubting everything, until one reaches, if one can, something that cannot be doubted, is presented as a strategy, as a systematic way of achieving something which is Descartes's basic aim: this is to discover *the truth*.[2] It is clear

2. H. Frankfurt (*Demons, Dreamers, and Madmen*, New York, 1970) seems to cast some doubt on whether this was Descartes's aim, or at least important among his aims: see in particular pp. 24 ff. It may be that this is a way of making the point, which Frankfurt rightly emphasizes, that Descartes is concerned not just with acquiring knowledge, but with vindicating the possibility of doing so: for this, see below, p. 61. The question is complicated by Frankfurt's ascribing to Descartes a view of truth as coherence; this is not only totally implausible historically but destroys what I shall argue later in this chapter is the most fundamental motivation for the Doubt. But even apart from the view taken of the nature of truth, it is certainly perverse to deny that Descartes's enquiry was centred on truth; as the quotation from the *Discourse* just given, and the implication of the first sentence of the *First Meditation*, make clear; cf. also *Princ*. i 4, 'Because we desire to apply ourselves only to the search after truth, we shall in the first place doubt ...' It is worth mentioning also the (incomplete) dialogue which Descartes wrote perhaps after the *Meditations*, though its date is unknown, which rehearses the same themes, and which is called

from both these passages, and from their brevity, that he regards this strategy as straightforwardly and obviously the rational course to adopt if truth, and nothing but the truth, is to be his aim. But it is surely far from obvious: we constantly want the truth about various matters, but hardly ever demand the indubitable. The first question, then, is what reason Descartes has for regarding this unobvious strategy as straightforwardly the rational course.

It is sometimes suggested that he has no reason; that the pursuit of certainty, in the form of indubitability, is a prejudice on his part, a gratuitous philosophical ambition, conditioned perhaps by his being over-impressed by mathematics. The last point, at least, as an answer to the present question is plainly silly, since if we ask what it was about mathematics as a form of knowledge that appealed to Descartes, the reply is its possibility of attaining certainty (see his remarks on his education, *Discourse* Part i: VI 7, HR1 85; and cf. *Reg.* ii: X 365–6, HR1 5). Indeed, Descartes never supposes that mathematical reasonings as such possess indubitability; in the *Discourse* he immediately goes on from the passage quoted above to make the point that one can be mistaken in mathematical reasonings of any complexity (cf. also *Princ.* i 5). Some – very simple – mathematical propositions may turn out to possess the required kind of certainty, but then what makes them important for the enquiry is their certainty, not their being mathematical. So this line of explanation leads nowhere.

The strategy is to aim for certainty by rejecting the doubtful. To *reject* the doubtful here means, of course, to suspend judgement about it, or at most to treat it as false for the purposes of the argument, not to assert that it is false – something which, as Descartes pointed out to the 'cavilling' critic of the *VII Objections* (*VII Rep.*: VII 460–61, HR2 266–7), would be no less dogmatic than one's usual state of mind, and considerably less reasonable. This strategy is not merely arbitrary, relative to the

La Recherche de la Vérité, The Search for Truth. The key to understanding Descartes is rather to see why the search 'only for truth' *turns into* the search for the indubitable. – On Frankfurt's views see further pp. 198 ff.

way Descartes construes his task – to get away from it, one has to reject very basically Descartes's interpretation of the search for truth. While it may be ultimately misguided to set such a high standard, taking the search for truth as (in the first place, at least) the search for certainty, it is not a merely gratuitous distortion, as is often suggested; its motivation lies deep in a quite natural conception of enquiry.

To gain some insight into that motivation, it will be helpful to leave Descartes's own line of argument for a while, and examine in our own terms a very basic model of the search for truth. Our concern will be how the search for truth can, in terms of that model, naturally turn into the search for certainty; but we must start with a prior question – whether the search for truth should be taken as the search for *knowledge*. This step may seem quite trivial. Ordinary speech, after all, effortlessly expresses the thought that A wants the truth on the question 'is p true or not?' in the form of saying that A wants to know whether p. But perhaps ordinary speech is not to be taken too seriously in this point; on reflection, it is not all that obvious why one who wants the truth should want to *know*, at least if that innocent phrase implies that what he wants is to enter into a state of knowledge. So we should first see whether the apparent triviality is even true. If it is, then anything peculiar in Descartes's strategy will lie in a second step, from the search for knowledge to the search for certainty.

Let us take a person, call him 'A', who is in the most primitive situation of wanting the truth. He has no elaborate or reflective demands – it is not, for instance, that he wants to acquire or found a science (as Descartes does, or at least will want to do). He merely wants the truth on certain questions. Such questions can of course take many forms, 'when . . .?', 'who . . .?', etc.; we shall simplify, and take A as in each case wanting the true answer to a question of the form *whether p*. What exactly is it that A wants? What state does he want to arrive at? He wants, at the very least, to have a belief on the question whether p, and that belief to be true. That is to say, he wants at least to be in this state:

(i) if *p*, *A* believes that *p*, and if not *p*, *A* believes that not-*p*.

He wants *at least* to be in that state; why should he want any more?

Here it might be said: he must want more than this, for if he is merely in state (i), he will not *know* that his belief is true. But why should he want to? The objection makes it sound as though (i) will not satisfy his original desires, those desires being met only by the state

(ii) If *p*, *A* believes that *p*, and if not-*p*, *A* believes that not-*p*, and in either case *A* knows that his belief is true

which entails

(iii) If *p*, *A* knows that *p*, and if not-*p*, *A* knows that not-*p*.

But why should (i) not meet *A*'s original needs just as well as (ii) or (iii)?

This question is superficially like a very old one, raised in Plato's dialogue, the *Meno*: wherein lies the superiority of knowledge over true belief? It does not lie, as Socrates quickly points out to a confused Meno (97C), in knowledge's being always true – *true* belief is just as true as knowledge. Rather, Socrates suggests, knowledge – which he connects with systematic understanding – will not run away: a point which we may take in the sense more interesting for the theory of knowledge, that knowledge cannot rationally be rendered doubtful, rather than as the blankly psychological proposition (in any case, surely, very dubious) that one is more disposed to forget what one merely believes than what one knows. But our present question comes earlier in the whole matter than the one that Socrates answers in this way. Descartes is indeed, like Plato, interested in what would make a solid science, and he is also interested in beating off sceptics, but we are not yet concerned with these larger ambitions. Our present interest is just with *A*, the most unambitious enquirer, and what, if anything, makes his search for truth into a search for knowledge.

The basic point here, unlike Plato's, does not directly concern the intrinsic merits of state (i) as against states (ii) or (iii): it concerns the methods available to *A to get even into state* (i). *A* is an *enquirer*. This means, for one thing, that his desire with regard to the question whether *p* is a real desire, and not just a wish. Moreover, he has no reason at all to believe that just waiting and hoping will get him even into state (i); thus he must adopt purposive means to get into (i). Now if I want to acquire a collection of flints, and only prehistoric flints, one way is to collect a lot of flints, and then investigate which of them, if any, are prehistoric. This might be inefficient, compared with a method of acquiring them in the first place which made it more likely that any flints I acquired were prehistoric ones. But the analogous process with acquiring true beliefs would be not just inefficient, but incomprehensible. Since to believe something is to believe that it is true, to acquire a belief is already to assume an answer to the question of whether it is true. So a method which *A* uses as an enquirer to get into state (i) must be a method of acquiring beliefs which itself makes it likely that the beliefs *A* acquires by it will be true ones; or, equivalently, is such that he is unlikely to acquire beliefs by that method unless they are true.

This requirement on the method of acquisition is equivalent, in turn, to a requirement on *A*'s beliefs; that they should have a certain property which at this point remains rather vague, but which can be put, if roughly, as

... produced in such a way that one is unlikely to acquire beliefs in that way unless they are true.

Let us label this property '*E*'. It applies of course to someone's belief regarded as a state of that person, and not just to the proposition which he believes, since someone else's belief in the very same proposition might be unreliably acquired and so lack the property. The nature of the proposition, what kind of belief is in question, does, however, help to determine what is a reliable way of acquiring such beliefs. Many questions remain here, as for instance how 'ways' of acquiring beliefs are to be individuated, and how that issue is related to subject-matter. We shall come back to some of these questions shortly.

We can now add something to the original specification of

A's objective. As a purposive enquirer, he will try to use reliable means, so if he is successful, it will be the case that he ends up in this state:

(iv) if *p*, *A* believes that *p*, and if not-*p*, *A* believes that not-*p*, and in either case *A*'s belief has the property *E*.

Can we further say that (iv) is the state that *A*, wanting the truth about *p*, *wants* to end up in? With a certain mild caution, we can. *A* is a conscious enquirer living in a non-magical world, that is to say, one in which methods of enquiry are needed to arrive at state (i). This can be taken as already assumed in the background of his being an enquirer. Granted that he wants to arrive, and that he knows that he must arrive by enquiry, then he wants his enquiries to be reliable. While he need not consider at any great level of abstractness what the property *E* consists in (which would be not just to enquire, but to philosophize), we can put his two wants together and redescribe his end-state from the point of view of his wants. Let us now forsake some generality for the sake of brevity, and just assume that the truth about the question at issue is *that p*, so we can drop the hypothetical formulation we have been using up to now ('if *p* . . .; if not *p* . . .'); then *A*'s end-state, if he is successful, will be

(v) *A* truly believes that *p*, and his belief has the property *E*.

Moreover, with the caution already indicated, we can say that (v) is the state that the enquirer *A* wants to arrive at (on the assumption all the time that '*p*' is the true answer to his question: we are not involved in any issues of his *wanting it to be the true answer*, which is quite a different sort of matter).

We got to (v) by considering *A*'s methods of answering his question *whether p*. Not all *A*'s true beliefs would be or could be acquired as a result of consciously directed enquiry applied to specific questions, and there are very many sorts of reasons why this could not always be so; but similar considerations apply also to the enquirer's attitude to beliefs which are not so acquired. The flint-collector, to return to him, not only might go and collect flints, but might find additions cropping up in his collection which he did not himself plan. He might welcome these or not – in particular, with regard to how many of the flints were prehistoric, and he might take steps to stop the accretions if not enough of them had the desired properties. But once more we have the contrast with the flint example, that acquiring a belief and judging it to be true are not two separate things. So the belief-collector has a motive yet stronger than the analogous motive with the flint-collector, to make sure that beliefs which arrive without his noticing it have the required property E. So not only in seeking the truth on a specific question, does he seek to arrive at (v), but also, he wants more generally his beliefs to arrive by routes which make it likely that they are true; that is to say, he wants them to possess E.

Is (v) the state of A's *knowing* that p? If so, we will have shown how it is that in wanting the truth, A wants to know. (The relevant question, in fact, is whether (v) is a sufficient condition of A's knowing that p: we are concerned only with the question whether someone who has a true belief which has the property E, knows, not with such questions as whether everyone who knows has to have a belief.) We can see at once that if (v) is a case of A's knowing, then knowledge has fewer implications than some philosophers have thought. Thus, if A knows in (v), it does not follow that he knows that he knows: it must be possible to know without knowing that one knows. Equally obviously, it must be possible to know something without being, or even feeling, specially certain about it. Moreover, from the way that E has so far been introduced, there is no obvious necessity why A, in state (v), should have conscious reasons for believing p; it would be hard to show that any reliable method of acquiring true beliefs which an enquirer could use *had* to be one which involved his having conscious reasons for the belief – though, equally, it is not hard to see why many in fact will do so.

It would be wrong just to claim dogmatically that knowledge must have any of these various implications, and hence that (v), as so far characterized, is not sufficient for knowledge. It is fairly obvious, in fact, that the everyday concept of knowledge does not have the first two implications (that if one knows, one knows that one knows, and that one must be certain of what one knows); and one can construct examples which strongly suggest that it does not have the third implication, either, that one must have conscious reasons – for instance, someone who was reliably but unreasonedly right about someone else's feelings would quite naturally be said to know what that person was feeling. This is just everyday speech: but to establish accord with an absolutely minimal everyday conception of knowledge is all that is wanted *at this stage.* Of course, this does not exclude somebody's trying to show that this everyday conception is in fact inadequate. The point is that any such attempt should go on from this point to *derive* stronger conditions from the requirements of enquiry, or in some other model which he substitutes for that of purposive enquiry. If he can effect that derivation, he will in fact have grounded a stronger demand on knowledge, not just asserted (implausibly) that those demands are respected in the way we generally use the notion.

However, before we can claim that (v) is a sufficient condition of knowledge even in a quite minimum sense which accords with the least critical everyday use, we have to look a little more closely at the property E. That property concerns the way in which someone acquires a belief; but, as has already been mentioned, there are questions about how such ways are to be picked out. Our estimate of the likelihood of a 'way' yielding a true belief obviously depends on how the 'way' is individuated. Thus 'getting it out of a book' yields fairly small likelihood of true belief, 'getting it out of a book which is the official year-book', much more. Further, as one would expect in a matter involving notions such as likelihood, it is not necessarily the case that the more specific characterization yields the greater likelihood. Relying on an eye-witness is not bad, relying on a drunk eye-witness is not so good, relying on a drunk and malicious eye-witness is worse still, and relying on Smith, who is drunk, malicious and much else besides, is quite hopeless. This is not to deny that the statement 'relying on eye-witnesses is a moderately good way of acquiring (some kinds of) true belief' is true; for that statement does not entail 'each and every case of relying on an eye-witness is a case in which you are more likely to be right than wrong'. The question of whether you are in a particular case more likely to be right than wrong depends of course on a lot of other facts about that case – and that much is uncontentious, whatever theory of likelihood one adopts, and correspondingly whatever sense one ascribes to the expression 'likelihood of being right in a particular case'.

But now the way in which the property E has been introduced in thinking about the enquirer's activities does not force us, or even encourage us, to read its definition, in the light of these latest reflections, as

... produced in a way which, as fully and specifically characterized as possible, is such that it gave a good likelihood of the belief's being true on the particular occasion

– whatever exactly that means. The motivation for including E at all seems to have given us the basis only for reading it as

... produced in a way such that in general beliefs produced in that way are likely to be true.

But if this is really all there is to E, then we cannot regard (v) as a sufficient condition of knowledge even in a minimal sense, since it will let through a kind of case which certainly fails to be knowledge by any natural criterion at all: the kind of case, that is to say, in which someone uses a reliable method, and acquires a belief which is true, but where the use of the method played no part, or no appropriate part, in his success.[3] Thus B may believe that someone in his office owns a Ford. He believes this because he believes that Jones, who is in his office, owns a Ford. He believes this because he has heard Jones speak of his Ford, seen Jones getting out of a Ford, etc. But Jones does not in fact own a Ford; the evidences were coincidental, or the product of

3. Such cases, or at least those where conscious reasons are involved, are often called *Gettier examples*, from Edmund Gettier who drew attention to their importance in his article 'Is Justified True Belief Knowledge?' *Analysis* 23 (1963) (the mention of Jones' Ford is in common between the example which follows, and Gettier's (more complex) example). There is much recent literature on this and related questions: for the 'no false lemmas' provision referred to below, see Gilbert Harman, 'Knowledge, Inference and Explanation', *American Philosophical Quarterly* 5.3 (1968), p. 164.

deceit. Brown, however, who also is in the office, really does own a Ford, though *B* has no reason to think so; so *B* does have a true belief, in believing that someone in the office owns a Ford. But in these circumstances, surely, no one could say that he *knew* it, even though he had a true belief, and also used a perfectly decent method, common social observation together with valid inference.

What is wrong in such a case is that the truth of the belief and the use of the method are detached from one another. If we were trying to define knowledge, we would try to link them up in some appropriate and illuminating way. Our actual concept of knowledge seems to require something like a provision discussed by Harman, which we may call the 'no false lemmas rule': if we reconstruct the route to the true belief in the form of an explicit argument, then, if the true belief is to be knowledge, the conclusion must not essentially depend on any false proposition, as *B*'s belief that someone in the office owned a Ford essentially depended on the false belief that Jones owned a Ford. We are not here attempting a definition of knowledge, and I shall not pursue in detail the question of how truth and method have to be linked up in order to constitute knowledge, nor the question whether the 'no false lemmas rule' is the best way of expressing the requirement. What is of interest to us, however, is the motivation for having some such requirement in the concept of knowledge, and how that may relate to the motivations of *A*, our original truth-seeking enquirer.

If we ask for the point of the 'no false lemmas rule' or analogous requirement, we find it surely in this: when someone arrives at a true belief, as in the Ford case, by luck, there is a sense in which he might as well not have used the method in arriving at that belief. This is not to say that the use of the method played no part in his arriving at the belief – that is obviously not so. The point is that although he used a sound method, and arrived at a true belief, and although there may be features of his use of the method that played some part in his arriving at the belief, it was not the features of the method *that make it generally sound* that led on this occasion to his believing a true proposition rather than a false one. In these circumstances we can say that the truth of the belief is *accidental* relative to the method. It is a comprehensible feature of the common concept of knowledge that it requires that this should not be so, that the truth of the belief be non-accidental relative to the method or way by which it is produced. It is hard to spell out in detail the content of the requirement, but in general terms we can see that it is a requirement, and we can see the point of it.

Should A, the truth-seeking enquirer, have an interest in a similar requirement? Surely so. While what he wants are true beliefs, as a conscious enquirer in a non-magical world he has to commit himself to a policy of acquiring them in reliable ways. Accidentally true beliefs, though they might seem welcome merely as true beliefs, are in fact only a sub-class of beliefs to which his methods are irrelevant; relative to his strategies of enquiry, they might as well have been false, and this state of affairs he cannot want. So in the description of the state which, with due caution, we can say that A wants to arrive at, namely

(v) A truly believes that p, and his belief has the property E,

we can read E as

... *appropriately* produced in a way such that beliefs produced in that way are generally true,

where 'appropriately' means that the truth of the belief is not accidental relative to what it is about the way of its production which makes that a generally reliable way. Taken in this way, (v) surely is sufficient for knowledge. So starting merely from the idea of pursuing truth in a non-magical world, and so of the truth-seeker's using methods of enquiry we do arrive at the conclusion that the search for truth is the search for knowledge. The notion of knowledge, however, is very unambitiously used. In particular, it does not entail any kind of certainty or indubitability. Descartes's step to that is what will now concern us.

Sticking just to generally reliable methods, A will almost certainly have some false beliefs. If he reflects, he can know that he will almost certainly have some false beliefs, but, very obviously, he will not know which they are – if he did, he would not have them as beliefs. So the methods are not, and are known to A not to be, perfect, in the sense of yielding only true beliefs. But they may well be the best that A can employ – there may be no way in which A can significantly raise the truth-ratio among his beliefs, at least within the context of objectives which are just as important to him. There may be no method which radically excludes falsehood, and still yields any beliefs at all, or at least any non-trivial beliefs. Of course, A is committed to being correct, not to being omniscient: he wants (ideally) all his beliefs to be true, not (even ideally) to believe all truths. But he certainly wants to have some beliefs; and he wants to have them on matters of concern to him.

A typical situation is that the truth-ratio could be somewhat improved without giving up any classes of beliefs altogether, but that the cost of doing so would be too high, relative to other activities (including other activities of enquiry). A might be able fruitfully to enquire further into the reliability of a given method, or whether its application on a given occasion was appropriate, but such activities take time and effort, which it may not be sensible to spend in any given case; while it is impossible to spend them in every case. In actual life, investment of effort into enquiry turns importantly on what is at stake: we check the petrol tank more thoroughly before a drive across the Sahara than before a drive across town. Moreover, there is the important point for both practical and for more theoretical enquiries, that each of us is one enquirer among others, and there is a division of epistemic labour, so that what it is rational (in this economic or decision-theoretical sense) for Y to investigate in detail, it is rational for Z to take on Y's say-so.

All these are reasons why A in his everyday circumstances either cannot increase his truth-ratio or should not regard it as rational to try. *But for Descartes's enquiry none of these considerations applies.* Descartes very carefully presents himself as now in a situation where he is devoted solely to enquiry, and as having, so long as this exercise continues, no other interests. He stresses repeatedly, as in the passage from the *Discourse* quoted

above (p. 34), that his 'Doubt', his instrument of reflective enquiry, is not to be brought into practical matters: equally, no
values drawn from those matters affect the enquiry. The strategic rationality which guides the enquiry is to be entirely internal
to it: no questions about what, in a general economic sense, is
worth enquiring into or checking, are, within the confines of this
exercise, to count. Moreover, not only is he solely devoted to
enquiry, but he is the sole enquirer. He is to embody rational
enquiry, so to speak, to the exclusion of everything and every-
body else. With the exercise defined in these terms, then, so long
as one remains within it, most of the considerations that rationally weigh with everyday A against his trying to raise his truth-
ratio, merely lapse.

There remains the issue we mentioned first, of the extent to
which he *can* raise the truth-ratio and still retain any, or any
non-trivial, beliefs. The point here is that Descartes just does
not know in advance of his enquiry whether or not there are
substantial beliefs to be had by methods which do not bring
false beliefs as well. But if this is uncertain, then in so far as
truth and (we have seen) knowledge are his object, it is worth
while trying to find out. There are, importantly, two different
levels at which this can be said to be worthwhile. Let us call the
perspective from which all strategic considerations are laid
aside except those internal to enquiry and the search for truth,
the perspective of the *Pure Enquirer*; our original primitive
truth-gatherer, A, may be said to turn into the Pure Enquirer
when he loses all interests other than his interest in knowledge.
Now within the perspective of the Pure Enquirer, it is trivially
true that the exercise of trying to find methods which maximize
the truth-ratio is a worthwhile exercise, for within that perspective there is no worth but the worth of truth-pursual. But
there is of course a different question, addressed to Descartes or
any other actual man, of the worthwhileness of adopting for a
while the perspective of the Pure Enquirer, and this question
requires an answer from outside that perspective, in terms of a
wider worthwhileness to human life.

Deeper reasons for adopting this project or, alternatively, for
rejecting it, we shall come back to at the end of this chapter.

For the present, however, it can be said that it is not obviously an unreasonable undertaking. It might well be the case that devoting oneself for a while exclusively and intensely to trying to raise the truth-ratio would offer some large benefits for ordinary enquiry outside that exercise, yielding better methods for enquiry even when enquiry is constrained, as Pure Enquiry is not, by extrinsic considerations. Such results might be public property, the product of Descartes himself becoming briefly, once and for all, the Pure Enquirer. But there might be, alternatively or as well, a kind of result of this exercise which was not public property, but which made it worthwhile for various individuals, once in their life-time, to take this stance, the sceptical discipline of Pure Enquiry helping each in the better use of his reason. Descartes accepted both these ways of looking at the project. Neither of these quite coincides with a third way of looking at it, namely as defining a certain approach to a philosophical subject, the theory of knowledge – for some philosophers, indeed, defining that subject. How it can come to do that is the major thing we shall consider when we come back to this question at the end of the chapter.

The project of seeing things in the perspective of the Pure Enquirer, is, then, Descartes's temporary project, and we shall be following it for a good deal of this book. In that perspective, it is rational to try first for a method of acquiring true beliefs which is totally free from error, and that must be a method which is error-*proof*. No method can be error-proof which allows a state of affairs in which the method has been correctly applied but has produced a belief which is nevertheless false. So the Pure Enquirer must look for a method whose correct application guarantees truth. Moreover, since he is concerned with true *beliefs*, it is no good specifying such a method merely in the abstract, as for instance a method specified merely as: 'accepting valid deductions from true premisses'. No finite enquirer, armed with that method and nothing else, could improve on a practice of accepting what *seemed* to be valid deductions from what *seemed* to be true premisses, and that practice can certainly generate error. What is needed is an error-proof method which is epistemically effective. This comes to the requirement that the beliefs which the method generates should be *certain*. At this point we can say that the search for truth, which is also (as we have seen) the search for knowledge, has turned into the search for certainty. It has done so because the pursuit of certainty is the only possible road for the *pure* search for truth, the project of improving the truth-ratio which is not constrained by any other limitations at all.

The Pure Enquirer starts from a situation in which he has beliefs: beliefs which have been acquired in ways which he knows are not error-proof, so he knows with virtual certainty that some of his beliefs are false. Seeking, from his present perspective, to raise the truth-ratio to the absolute maximum, the first step is to preserve, out of his present beliefs, any that are genuinely certain, and the way to do that is to set aside the ones that are not. After doing that, the Pure Enquirer can then see how much and what he is left with, and judge from that how the pure project of truth-gathering is proceeding. This is the Method of Doubt, and exactly as Descartes claims in the *Discourse*, it is a rational consequence of adopting the perspective of one who wants to devote himself *solely* to the search for truth.

But it is easier to introduce the notion of certainty at this point than to be clear about what it is. How exactly is 'certainty' to be taken? One line of approach here is to assume that in looking for beliefs that will be certain, one is looking for a *kind of proposition* – a kind which, when believed, must constitute true beliefs. The simplest definition of such a kind of proposition would be this: a proposition which is such that if someone believes it, then it logically follows that his belief is true. I shall call such a proposition *incorrigible*.[4] Acquiring beliefs which are incorrigible in this sense must be a sufficient condition of the Pure Enquirer's getting what he basically wants, truth, since anything incorrigible which he believes will be true. Moreover, the notion of incorrigibility is, unlike the bare concept of truth, a cognitive concept (it essentially involves a reference to belief), and in this respect shares an important feature with the notion

4. For a more accurate account of incorrigibility, the use of the term 'proposition' and related matters, see Appendix 1.

of certainty. It is tempting to think that incorrigibility is a species of the certainty which the Pure Enquirer wants. However, we should be cautious about this, since it is not altogether obvious that 'collect incorrigible beliefs' is an epistemically effective maxim – perhaps the Enquirer could be deceived about which beliefs are incorrigible. This is a kind of difficulty which cannot be disposed of here. In various versions, it continually stalks Descartes's enquiry: we shall face it more fully in the next chapter (see below, p. 86), and shall not really deal with it until Chapter 7.

Another point – a more encouraging one, perhaps – is that incorrigibility might be only one species of certainty. There may be beliefs which are certain without being in this way incorrigible, and in that case it will not of course be a condition of the Enquirer's gaining certainty that he accept only propositions which are incorrigible. We shall come to a suggestion of this kind very soon. But however that may be, at least this seems not an unreasonable way for the Method of Doubt to start off: by rejecting what is not incorrigible. It may be too harsh, but if it can be carried out, it cannot be too lax.

If the Method does start off in that way, it follows at once that large classes of propositions ordinarily accepted will have to be rejected. Take propositions such as 'I can see a table', 'I heard a clap of thunder'; add to them propositions such as 'a table is over there' or 'that was a clap of thunder', which do not themselves mention perception, but which we believe on the strength of perception and which claim the existence of publicly perceptible objects or states of affairs: call all of these 'perceptual propositions'. Then no perceptual proposition is in the defined sense incorrigible, since, where 'p' is any such proposition, 'A believes that p but "p" is false' does not express a contradiction. If we are rejecting everything but the incorrigible, all perceptual propositions must go.

But this immediately reopens the question whether we should be rejecting everything but the incorrigible. Perhaps that programme places the standards of certainty in the wrong place even for the demanding purposes of the Pure Enquirer? Take any perceptual proposition, such as 'I can see a table'. It is not incorrigible: but that says something only about a *class* of circumstances – all it means is that there could be *some* circumstances in which I believed that I was seeing a table, and that belief was false. But it does not follow that on any given occasion when I believe that proposition, it might on that occasion be false. The fact that the proposition is not incorrigible merely means that there are some occasions – for example, in a bad light, in an unfamiliar room, without my glasses – when I could believe wrongly that there was a table in front of me; but that undoubted fact does not mean that now, in good light, my wits about me and my glasses on, amid my familiar furniture, I can for all that properly think 'it is possible that there is no table there' or 'I might be wrong'.

In this respect, corrigibility is like contingency. The fact that a proposition is contingent – i.e. that it might (logically) have been false – does not entail that it might now be false. Descartes is sometimes accused of having mounted the Method of Doubt, or at least its application to perceptual and similar matters, on a confusion in that respect about contingency; but this is a mistake about Descartes. He is dealing with corrigibility, not contingency (his first important incorrigible truths will in fact be contingent). Moreover, he does not suppose that there is an immediate move even from the corrigibility of a proposition to its uncertainty in each given case. The Pure Enquirer needs further thoughts to arrive at that, and they occur in a transition which Descartes makes very clearly in both the *Discourse* Part iv and in the *First Meditation* (and also in the *Recherche de la Vérité*: X 510 ff., HR1 313 ff.). The transition is from the occasional errors of the senses, to the question of dreaming. The sort of error that consists in mistaking the shape of a distant tower – to take one of Descartes's examples – does not convey the possibility of error to each case of seeing a tower, still less to each case of perceiving anything; the 'errors of my dreams' may do so.

Descartes now believes (at least as firmly as he believes anything else about his history) that he has often, when dreaming, believed with the fullest possible conviction of truth, things which were false; and at the time, there was nothing that made him doubt them. Errors of the kinds he considered before, dependent on bad light, distance, illness, are resistant to generalization because, for one thing, reflection on the conditions of observation could arouse suspicions *at the time*: since he is now fully reflective and on his guard, he can establish that this is not an occasion of the special misleading conditions – that is to say, the doubt does not generalize to the present case. But, he suggests, since dreams take you in completely, reflection does not give you a grip within the situation for distinguishing it at the time as special: the discovery of error is here totally and unqualifiedly retrospective. But if that is so, what is there about the situation now which guarantees that it will not be followed by retrospective correction? The dream-doubt can be generalized as the previous doubts could not. An important aspect of this is that it can be generalized as to subject-matter. The previous sorts of error apply to particular classes of object or condition: refraction (so far as common errors of perception are concerned) affects the appearance of sticks in water and a few other things; jaundice, so it is said, affects apparent colour. But anything I can perceive, I can dream that I perceive. Confronted with an apparently bent stick, experience of refraction-illusions can put me on my guard – it is a special feature of the situation that it is an apparently-bent-stick situation, i.e. possibly a refraction-illusion situation. But since I can dream anything I can perceive, any situation, so far as its apparent constituents are concerned, could be a dream situation; and since dreams are marked, often, by total conviction, conviction which, moreover, often remains even if I raise the question of whether I am dreaming, the fact that I am and remain totally convinced that this is now not a dream situation makes no contribution, either, to genuine certainty that it is not one. So any given situation apparently of perception could be a dream situation: but if it is a dream situation, then my apparent perceptions are not veridical, and my perceptual beliefs about it are false. So on any given occasion, it is not certain that my perceptions are veridical; any given situation *could* be illusory.

It is not easy to assess the strength of the dream argument. (It is perhaps worth remarking that G. E. Moore, who robustly, or at least obstinately, affirmed his certainty that he was on a particular occasion seeing a material object, entered as the one *caveat* to this, the possibility that he might be dreaming.[5]) Rather than hold up the progress of Descartes's argument at this point, I have relegated more detailed discussion of the dream argument to an appendix (Appendix 3). I shall assume for the next part of the argument that Descartes has adequately convinced us, through the dream argument, that on any given occasion of apparent perception one could be mistaken. We shall see soon in fact that Descartes in any case uses the dream argument only as a temporary staging-post on the road of doubt: he will eventually leave it behind. Suppose we allow, then, that on any given occasion of supposed perception I might be mistaken, since I might be dreaming. We must emphasize that this is not just a question of the perceptual propositions in question being corrigible: that is certainly true, but it is not enough to make each situation dubitable, and Descartes does not suppose that it is enough. Nor, equally, is it just a matter of the proposition 'I am not dreaming' being corrigible, which is also not enough. The point is that, over and above that general consideration, no given occasion can select itself as an occasion on which I could not possibly be dreaming.

The idea that I *might*, on a given occasion, be mistaken involves the notion of what is often called *epistemic possibility*, a possibility relative to what one knows. The thought 'I might be mistaken' is, in such contexts, the thought 'for all I know, I am mistaken'; and this, of course, in line with the high standards of the Pure Enquirer in his search for exceptionless truth, is to be read as 'for all I know with absolute certainty . . .'. This is also how we should take the formulation which uses explicitly the notion of possibility: 'it is possible that I am mistaken'.

But, however we take the notion of possibility, epistemically or otherwise, one thing that is quite clear is that there is no valid inference from 'of any given x, it is possible that it is F' to 'it is possible that all x's are F'. Thus, in some sense of 'possible', of any given man it is possible he is a younger brother, but in no

5. 'Proof of an External World', in *Philosophical Papers*, ed. H. D. Lewis (London, 1959), p. 149.

sense of 'possible' is it possible that all men are younger
brothers. Thus, taking 'possible' epistemically: I might be unin-
terested in people's sibling relationships, so any given man
could be, for all I know, a younger brother, but I know, and for
certain, that not all men are.

Descartes certainly arrives at the end of the Doubt with the
conception that it is epistemically possible that *all* supposedly
perceptual judgements are mistaken,[6] and that the external
world, the supposed object of all such judgements, may not
exist at all. Even if we grant him the distributive proposition
that any given such judgement may be mistaken, it would certainly be a fallacy for him to infer from that the collective
claim that they all may be. But we shall see that he does not
need to commit this fallacy to arrive at his conclusion, and that
in fact he does not do so. He progresses from the universal
possibility of illusion to the possibility of universal illusion, but
he does not try to infer the second from the first.

Apart from that, however, it is notable that there are certain
respects in which his enquiry will proceed in very much the
same way even if he does not draw the collective conclusion at
all. Descartes, as Pure Enquirer, refrains from assenting to each
belief in which he detects the possibility of doubt. If he refrains
from each such belief, and every perceptual belief contains,
severally, the possibility of doubt, then he refrains from all of
them, without necessarily having to believe that they are all
false, or indeed that they could, all, be false. Consider an
analogy. Two men are in a forest, in which there are various
species of fungi. One of them believes that all these fungi are
poisonous. The other believes that some, but not all, of the
fungi are poisonous, but he cannot tell which are and which are
not. He reasonably adopts the policy of not eating any fungus
which is possibly poisonous. He will refrain from eating any,
which is also the course of action adopted by the first man. So

6. It is worth noting the consequence that the strict contradictory of a
perceptual judgement is not itself a perceptual judgement. The everyday
negation of 'there is a table in front of me', to the effect – very roughly –
that what is in front of me is not a table, is only a contrary of the original
judgement, and they could on Descartes's supposition both be false.

the courses of action coincide, though the beliefs from which they stem are different. In fact Descartes does hold the strong, collective, proposition about perceptual judgements, but the fungus analogy suggests that he does not have to do so, in order consistently to pursue the Method of Doubt with similarly radical effect.

The fungus analogy also illustrates the central characteristic of Pure Enquiry. A feature of the fungus case is this: the course of action adopted by the second man is obviously reasonable only if certain things are taken for granted – for instance, that there is something else to eat. If there is nothing else to eat, it is less obviously reasonable. And if there is nothing else to eat, even the first man's course of action is reasonable only if he prefers death by starvation to death by poisoning. And whether there is anything else to eat or not, the reasonableness of any course of action presupposes the value that the agent puts on staying alive. Analogously, a man who believed that some, but not all, perceptual beliefs were mistaken, did not know which were which, and based on that a strategy of not accepting any of them, would be a man who was in fact adopting certain valuations: he would place an indefinitely large disvalue on error, and would prefer to have no beliefs rather than to have a false one. As a posture in everyday life, this would be totally absurd, as Descartes frequently points out (for an example close to the present one, see a letter to 'Hyperaspistes', August 1641: III 398, K 110). But as a posture of the Pure Enquirer, it is not absurd, but follows directly from the nature of the project: if he *can* secure beliefs which are totally free from falsehood, then so much the better for the project of maximizing the truth-ratio, which is exclusively his project.

What would be an objection to the procedure, and would destroy the analogy with the fungus case, would be if it were impossible even to *doubt* a given perceptual judgement except in a context of assuming some other perceptual judgements to be actually true; in that case, the cumulative rejection procedure could not move ahead, or could do so only in some much more complicated and qualified way. We shall come to one aspect of that objection in a moment. More generally, however, this is a form of objection to the Method of Doubt as a whole – that there is no standpoint from which the Pure Enquirer could comprehensibly carry out his project. In that very general role I shall come back to it at the end of this chapter.

In fact, Descartes does not merely treat perceptual judgements to the Doubt one by one; he is prepared to entertain the collective hypothesis that they may all be false. This is not a mere (and invalid) derivation from the level we have already reached. It is a new step, marked by a new development – the introduction, in the *Meditations*, of the fiction of the *malin génie*, the 'malicious demon', 'of the highest power and intelligence, who devotes all his efforts to deceiving me' (I *Med.*: VII 22, HR1 148).

The introduction of this fiction is a device to provide considerations which will help combat the psychological force of habitual prejudice, and to provide those 'reasons' which, being as we are, we need to help us in sponging out the old picture and starting again, as he expresses the task in the *Recherche de la Vérité* (X 508, HR1 312). It helps, not only by giving a psychological push to doubts whose direction is already established, but by stimulating the mind to identify more things which can be, by the Pure Enquirer's standards, doubted. It provides one with a thought-experiment which can be generally applied: if there were an indefinitely powerful agency who was misleading me to the greatest conceivable extent, would *this* kind of belief or experience be false?[7] The model is of an agency which acts purposively and systematically to frustrate human enquiry and the desire for the truth. This model strikes very deeply at our assumptions: how deeply, is illustrated by the consideration that in the contemporary application of games-theory to the rationality of enquiry, a 'game against nature' is from the beginning identified with a one-person game. The model of the malicious demon is of the game against nature

7. For a non-supernatural version of the same test, see Peter Unger's ingenious book, *Ignorance* (Oxford, 1975). Any advantage that Unger's version might seem to gain, from its empirical elements, over Descartes's more abstract thought-experiment is, of course, illegitimate: under scepticism, we have no reason to believe that his imagined mechanism is even a mechanism.

being a two-person game, against an indefinitely well-informed and resourceful opponent. (This feature of it answers a question raised by Leibniz: why the demon, according to Descartes, had to be malicious.[8]) Under this test, the Doubt is extended, as well as to God and the past, to every judgement about publicly perceptible objects, including Descartes's own body: they are now, at this stage, collectively doubted.

At this point, where we reach the fully 'hyperbolical' doubt, as Descartes called it, we encounter a new kind of problem, which concerns the meaning of a proposition which the Doubt invites us to entertain. What is the content of the idea that, compatibly with other things seeming as they do, there might not be a physical world at all? If the hyperbolical doubt were arrived at merely by generalization from the particular doubts we considered before, it does not look as though there could be a coherent answer to this question. All the cases of error which the Doubt seized on in the earlier stages of the argument involved the use of some perceptions to correct others, and while we *might* be able to say, consistently with that, that we were not absolutely sure at any given moment that the present perception was veridical, we could not consistently say that no perceptions were. (This was the objection which, in part, we anticipated in discussing the fungus analogy.)

The dependence on other perceptions is just as obvious with the dream-doubt – which produced the half-way stage, of distributively general doubt – as it is with the more particular sorts of error which the Doubt seized on right at the beginning. 'How many times has it happened to me,' Descartes says in the *First Meditation* (VII 19, HR1 145–6) 'that I dreamed that I was in this place, that I was dressed, that I was near the fire, when all the time I was in bed with no clothes on.' But this claim rests on counting some previous experiences as veridical: those of waking up, and so forth. It relies also on some inferences from those experiences to other physical facts, as that before waking up he was lying in bed. If the hyperbolical doubt were correct, there would be no such facts, and the experiences supposedly of

8. See a letter to Foucher of 1676: *Philosophical Writings of Leibniz* (Everyman edn, London, 1934), p. 50.

waking up and so forth would themselves not have been veridical. It follows that the hyperbolical doubt is at least un-
happily expressed by the thought that perhaps we dream all the
time (as Descartes uncharacteristically puts it in the *Recherche
de la Vérité* (X 511, HR1 314)); more importantly it follows
that the hyperbolical doubt cannot in any way be supported by
considerations drawn from taking these experiences as veridical, nor can it rest in any way on his knowing that he has, in
the past, dreamed.

It does not: the ultimate radicalization of the Doubt takes
something from the previous levels, but it does not rest, self-
defeatingly, on the familiar facts which were put before us
at those levels. Those facts were used first of all to loosen our
prejudices; the final radical doubt undercuts those familiar facts
altogether. What it takes from them is something suggested by
reflection on them – a certain picture of what veridical perception is. In the *Sixth Meditation*, retrospectively considering
the dream-doubt, Descartes says (VII 77, HR1 189): 'as I do
not believe that the things which it seems to me that I perceive
when asleep, *proceed from objects outside myself*, I did not see
why I should believe this any the more, concerning those things
which it seems to me that I perceive when awake.' Descartes
regards it as self-evident that if I have veridical perceptions,
then I have experiences which are caused by things outside
myself. This idea – let us label it the 'causal conception of
perception' – is built into the hyperbolical doubt. It follows from
it that every perceptual judgement implies some one proposition to the effect that there are things outside oneself which
cause one's experiences. If this proposition is doubtful, then
every perceptual judgement is doubtful. In doubting that proposition, we will have applied the Doubt to them all at once,
not piece-meal; as Descartes indeed said that he would in the
passage I quoted at the beginning (p. 35).

What is the status of the causal conception of perception? If
it is dubious that there are objects 'outside' oneself, in the sense
that this conception requires, must it not be at least as dubious
that one's ordinary judgements of perception imply that there
are? This is the way that a follower of G. E. Moore might argue

at this point: if some commonsense judgements which we ordinarily believe with a high degree of conviction are said to imply some very general or philosophical proposition Q, and Q is doubtful, then we should regard this as a ground for criticizing the supposed implication, not for criticizing our ordinary judgements on the strength of the doubtfulness of Q. Descartes himself never in fact doubts the causal conception of perception: he regards the causal element as straightforwardly part of the concept of perception, in the sense of that term in which we perceive such things as tables. He also believes, in fact, though he does not use the belief at this stage, that everything 'outside myself' is known only through the medium of *ideas*, which represent reality, and are themselves the immediate objects of the mind's cognition (to Gibieuf, 19 January 1642: VII 474, K 123; *III Rep.*: VII 181, HR2 67–8); it is ideas that, in perception, are caused by external objects. This goes beyond a minimal causal conception of perception, and in carrying this weight of philosophical theory seems indeed open to grave doubt. On the other hand, it seems equally hard to deny that *some* causal element is part of the concept of perception. The real question is whether the minimal sense in which some causal element is undeniably part of the concept of perception is enough for Descartes comprehensibly to deploy it, in the hyperbolical doubt, against all our ordinary perceptual judgements together. We shall get a clearer idea of Descartes's own views after we have seen, much later, what Descartes takes *me* to be, and hence what he takes *outside me* to be.[9]

Whatever exactly the status and content of the causal conception of perception, the way in which Descartes uses it against ordinary perceptual judgements in the hyperbolical doubt importantly illustrates his Method. It helps to reveal, in particular, the significance of some of his images for the Method of Doubt: the building or foundations metaphor, which occurs frequently and is most elaborately deployed in the *Seventh Replies*; and the apple barrel image which is used in the same *Replies* (VII 481, HR2 282), by which the Method is likened to that of a man who takes all the apples out of a barrel one by

9. See further pp. 239–40 and 284–6.

one, inspects them, and then puts the sound ones back. The point of this procedure is said to be to prevent any bad ones there may be from turning the sound ones bad. But falsity in beliefs, unlike badness in apples, is not actually infective: nothing can make a true belief false, not even another false belief. The idea must be, rather, that one false belief can be the condition of my acquiring or retaining many other false beliefs, through its logical relations to them. There are several ways in which this could work: thus I might, in some holistic adjustment of my beliefs to produce a coherent whole, misguidedly adjust my beliefs to some false assumption, and thus make everything worse. Another possibility is that conclusions may be deduced from false premisses: in this case, the falsehood is not of course necessarily transmitted (since conclusions validly drawn from false premisses can be true), but if I arrive at truths, it will only be by luck. But most important for Descartes, in fact, is not this possibility, but its converse: that my beliefs may *imply* a false proposition, as all my perceptual beliefs imply, as he supposes, the possibly false proposition about objects outside oneself. This is the principal emphasis of the apple barrel image, and of the images in terms of building and foundations, for the Method of Doubt. Descartes's point at this stage is not, as is often supposed, that if we make the premisses certain, then valid deduction from them will give us a body of knowledge which is totally certain. It is rather that our beliefs cannot be certain so long as they *imply* or *presuppose* propositions which are uncertain.

In this respect, the Method of Doubt represents a programme of criticism. This is one sense, the weakest sense, in which the Method of Doubt can be regarded as an instrument for pro-viding 'foundations of knowledge'. However, at least two other undertakings can, in a stronger sense, go under that title. One is that of trying to find some limited set of propositions which will be certain, and from which all knowledge can be deduced. This is the sense in which Descartes is perhaps most widely supposed to have been concerned with the foundations of knowledge, but this supposition is a mistake. When Descartes eventually returns from the Doubt, and has reinstated the belief in a physical world, he will admit that we can know everyday propositions about that world, so long as we do not get muddled about their content,[10] but he does not suppose that 'I can see a table', for instance, can ever be deduced from certainties (for one thing, we remain liable to occasional error). A rather more plausible claim would be that Descartes hoped that all scientific, theoretical or organized knowledge of such things as the laws of nature would be deducible from evident axioms. But as we shall see in Chapter 9, it is far from clear that Descartes did believe this to be possible, either.

What is important to him, both with regard to personal bits of knowledge such as that I can see a table, and (more significantly) with regard to scientific knowledge, is that we should be able to know for certain the following: that if we conduct our methods of enquiry in ordinary life clear-headedly and rationally, we shall in fact come to know truths about the world, and our conceptions of the world will not be systematically distorted or in error. Showing that this is so is a basic aim of the Method of Doubt, and this gives a different sense to the search for the 'foundations of knowledge' – a sense by which what Descartes is looking for are foundations of the *possibility* of knowledge.

Here we come back at a more significant level to the question of how the Method of Doubt, and the project of Pure Enquiry in which it plays its part, are motivated. There is no question, we must always remember, of hyperbolical doubt playing any rational role within ordinary life: the Doubt is to be taken entirely seriously in the context of an enquiry about what can be most certainly known to us, he tells Gassendi, but 'one must bear in mind that distinction, which I have insisted on in various places, between the actions of life and the search for truth . . .' (*V Rep.*: VII 350, HR2 206; cf. *Princ.* i 1–3, and the letter of August 1641: III 398, K 110); and the existence of the external world is something which 'no one of serious mind ever seriously doubted' (*Synopsis* of the *Meditations*: VII 15–16, HR1 142–3). Within the project of Pure Enquiry, on the other hand, hyperbolical doubt follows naturally. The question which we

10. For the force of this qualification, see pp. 234–5.

now have to take further concerns the significance of the project of Pure Enquiry itself. I have already referred to some benefits which might be hoped for from the undertaking, and which could already provide a rationale for it. They were all of a kind which suggested at most that the project might be, once in a life-time, or perhaps once in one person's life-time, a good idea. They did not suggest that the project might be in any sense an intellectual necessity. But if the project can be seen as providing foundations of the possibility of knowledge, this naturally implies that without it there is a doubt about the possibility of knowledge, a doubt which the project, if successful, could allay. The doubt about the possibility of knowledge will be a sceptical doubt, and seen as a response to this, the Method of Doubt takes on the form of *pre-emptive scepticism*, which serves the aim of answering sceptical doubts by taking them as far as they can be taken and coming out on the other side. If the project of Pure Enquiry is seen, as some philosophers have seen it, as defining a whole subject, the theory of knowledge, this is because it is supposed that unless the project can be carried out, there will be no answer to scepticism, and there will remain something unclear or suspect about the possibility of knowledge altogether.

It is clear that if the project of Pure Enquiry can succeed, then knowledge is possible. At least, this becomes clear if we spell out fully something which has been only implicit in the description of the project up to this point: that if the Enquirer can come to the recognition of some certainties, then that recognition must be able to generate on-going states of knowledge, which will be capable then of staying with him, both within the course of Pure Enquiry itself, and after that into ordinary life. This clearly must be a feature of the project's success, if the project is going to be any real cognitive use; while the requirement is obvious, it will turn out to have important consequences, which will concern us in Chapter 7.

If the project can be carried out, then, knowledge is possible. But the idea we have now come to requires the converse, that *only* if the project can succeed will knowledge be shown to be possible. Why should anyone believe that? Once again, it is important that this should not be seen as a purely gratuitous demand, a merely obsessional concern with an artificial scepticism. I think also that it is a mistake to see it just as an extra aspiration for knowledge, a supererogatory ideal for it which the Western world, at least, has set before itself.[11] We should rather suspect that there is something in the notion of knowledge itself which invites this response, which makes it seem that unless the project of Pure Enquiry can succeed, it is doubtful whether there is any knowledge at all. What is it about knowledge that makes it seem problematical?

There might seem to be a very simple answer to this question, resting on a point we have already noticed: that if P implies Q, then if Q is doubtful, P must be doubtful. (We may call this the 'Dubiety Principle'.) From this, it might look like a short step to a further principle (which we may call the 'Ignorance Principle') that if P implies Q, and we do not know Q, then we do not know P; and from this it seems reasonable to infer that if what we take to be knowledge has any implications which we have not yet explored and tested, it is not in fact knowledge. But the step to the Ignorance Principle is not valid.

The Dubiety Principle itself is sound, if it is taken to mean: if P implies Q, and there is good reason to doubt Q, then there is good reason to doubt P. Let us add an axiom to the effect that if there is good reason to doubt P, then no one knows P; or – as it may more recognizably be put – if there is good reason for A to doubt P, A does not know P. This axiom I in fact believe to be too strong; but many theorists of knowledge have accepted it, including Descartes, and it is significant that the point I am now making will go through even if we do accept it. The Ignorance Principle will follow from these premisses only if we further assume that there is good reason to doubt any proposition which we have not explored and tested; and there is absolutely no reason to assume *that* – unless perhaps one has already assumed the position of the Method of Doubt, which is what the argument was supposed to be justifying. In fact, it is clear that the Ignorance Principle is quite unacceptable; since any

11. See for instance Leszek Kolakowski, *Husserl and the Search for Certitude* (New Haven, 1975).

proposition has infinite implications, no finite mind could know (as the Principle requires) all the implications of anything it knows.

Knowledge does have a problematical character, and does have something in it which offers a standing invitation to scepticism. Attempts to uncover this just in terms of the relations between the concepts knowledge, doubt, certainty and so forth seem nevertheless to fail, and characteristically to rely, like the last argument, on thoroughly implausible or question-begging assumptions. The source of the invitation lies deeper. What exactly it is, is a difficult question; I will try to sketch an approach which seems to me to lead in the direction of the source. This starts from a very basic thought, that if knowledge is what it claims to be, then it is knowledge of a reality which exists independently of that knowledge, and indeed (except for the special case where the reality known happens itself to be some psychological item) independently of any thought or experience. Knowledge is of what is there *anyway*. One might suppose this thought to be incontestable, but its consequences can seem to be both demanding and puzzling. Suppose *A* and *B* each claims to have some knowledge of the world. Each has some beliefs, and moreover has experiences of the world, and ways of conceptualizing it, which have given rise to those beliefs and are expressed in them: let us call all of this together his *representation* of the world (or part of the world). Now with respect to their supposed pieces of knowledge, *A*'s and *B*'s representations may well differ. If what they both have is knowledge, then it seems to follow that there must be some coherent way of understanding why these representations differ, and how they are related to one another. One very primitive example of this would be that *A* and *B* were in different places; another might be that they were both correctly predicting the movements of the planets, but by different, geometrically equivalent, systems. In either case, a story can be told which explains how A's and B's can each be perspectives on the same reality. To understand this story, one needs to form a conception of the world which *contains A* and *B* and their representations; *A* and *B* are not debarred from taking this standpoint themselves, but it involves their standing back from their original ways of representing these aspects of the world. But this process, it seems, can be continued. For if *A* or *B* or some other party comes in this way to understand these representations and their relation to the world, this will be because he has given them a place in some more inclusive representation; but this will still itself be a representation, involving its own beliefs, conceptualizations, perceptual experiences and assumptions about the laws of nature. If this is knowledge, then we must be able to form the conception, once more, of how this would be related to some other representation which might, equally, claim to be knowledge; indeed we must be able to form that conception with regard to *every* other representation which might make that claim. If we cannot form that conception, then it seems that we do not have any adequate conception of the reality which is there 'anyway', the object of any representation which is knowledge; but that conception appeared at the beginning as basic to the notion of knowledge itself. That conception we might call the absolute conception of reality. If knowledge is possible at all, it now seems, the absolute conception must be possible too.

What does that require? Here what was a natural, if very abstract, progression seems to have led to a basic dilemma. On the one hand, the absolute conception might be regarded as entirely empty, specified only as 'whatever it is that these representations represent'. In this case, it no longer does the work that was expected of it, and provides insufficient substance to the conception of an independent reality; it slips out of the picture, leaving us only with a variety of possible representations to be measured against each other, with nothing to mediate between them. On the other hand, we may have some determinate picture of what the world is like independent of any knowledge or representation in thought; but then that is open to the reflection, once more, that that is only one particular representation of it, our own, and that we have no independent point of leverage for raising this into the absolute representation of reality.

This is a very schematic account of a kind of problem which has constantly recurred in the history of Western thought. This formulation is influenced, of course, by philosophy since Descartes, and would not have been recognized by him; but we can see him as, in effect, attempting to transcend this dilemma, and trying to extract an absolute conception of reality from the process of Pure Enquiry. That attempt, and its failure, itself led to much that has developed subsequently in this line of thought (including this way of formulating what he was trying to do). The 'absolute conception' that Descartes himself offered will, I hope, emerge in the course of this study.[12] The present question, however, is how the implicit presence of the absolute conception, or rather the promise of it, within the concept of knowledge, helps to motivate Pure Enquiry. Pure Enquiry, as we have so far considered it, is the undertaking of someone setting aside all externalities or contingent limitations on the pursuit of truth; this ambition, I have already argued, is itself enough to generate the Doubt. But if we are to make an attempt to ground the absolute conception of reality which knowledge seems to call for, then the project of undercutting every conceivable source of error takes on a new importance. It is a matter not just of overcoming limitations on enquiry and hence of occasional error, as understood within the framework of our outlook, but of overcoming any systematic bias or distortion or partiality in our outlook as a whole, in our representation of the world: overcoming it, that is to say, in the sense of gaining a standpoint (the absolute standpoint) from which it can be understood in relation to reality, and comprehensibly related to other conceivable representations.

This motivation, which makes Pure Enquiry into a way of gaining the absolute conception, and hence showing that knowledge is possible, makes clearer something which was already present in Pure Enquiry as it has been treated up to now, namely that the pure search for truth seeks certainty against any *conceivable* doubt. It was already present, because it was involved in carrying to the utmost the objective of a method which should be errorproof. But we can now see a deeper

12. A particularly important aspect of the idea, which may help to make it clearer, relates to the distinction between primary and secondary qualities: see pp. 237–49.

significance in that objective and what it involves, for, from the point of view of seeking the absolute conception, the distinction between a source of error or distortion which is merely conceivable, and one which we take to be empirically effective, loses its importance. What we judge to be empirically effective is itself a function of what we believe, of our representation of the world, and must be undercut in the critical search for the absolute conception. (But may not even what is *conceivable* to us be a function of our peculiar representation of reality? This will in fact be a problem for Descartes, as we shall see in Chapter 7.)

It is often made a reproach to Cartesian scepticism that it deals in merely conceivable sources of error or distortion, not only in ones that we may have reason to think obtain. But this is absolutely central to its motivation, a motivation which (I have suggested) has its roots in the concept of knowledge itself. It is not a serious objection to the Cartesian programme to point out that philosophical doubt is not ordinary doubt, nor even that doubt, as an effective psychological attitude, is out of place in the philosophical context; Descartes willingly agreed to both these points. Nor is it enough just to claim that comprehensible criticism or suspension of belief must always rest on other undoubted assumptions (the point that we met before: see above, p. 57). This may be true, but without some larger theoretical backing it can be supported only by following the route of Pure Enquiry and showing what goes wrong with it. A serious level of criticism lies rather in argument for the contention that the deeper motivation for Pure Enquiry falls away, because there can be no absolute conception, and the search for the Archimedean point is based on an illusion.

This may be true – though in discussing it we must be prepared to distinguish two different questions, whether an absolute conception is possible, and whether that conception has to be grounded in *certainty*. Descartes, as I am interpreting him, implicitly assumed the connection of those two ideas, as have many others, but it may be that the search for certainty is only one approach to acquiring such a conception. There may be other approaches: that is a point we shall touch on again. But if there is no possible approach at all, and the whole notion of an absolute conception is an illusion, then it will be better if we can banish another illusion, that knowledge requires the absolute conception. If it does require it, and that conception is impossible, then knowledge is impossible, and we shall have to do with less. Many would claim that we are now familiar with the situation of doing with less than an absolute conception, and can, as modern persons and unlike the ambitious or complacent thinkers of earlier centuries, operate with a picture of the world which at the reflexive level we can recognize to be thoroughly relative to our language, our conceptual scheme – most generally, to our situation. But it is doubtful to what extent we really can operate with such a picture, and doubtful whether such views do not implicitly rely, in their self-understanding, on some presumed absolute conception, a framework within which our situation can be comprehensibly related to other possible situations. If we do have to make do with less, it is far from clear that anyone has a satisfactory idea of how much less, or of how to make do with it.

One last point should be made about Descartes's project: that it is radically first-personal. Some philosophers have supposed or presupposed that the most basic question of the theory of knowledge must take the form 'what can *I* know?', and Descartes is among them, perhaps first among them. It is an interesting and delicate question, however, at what point the first-personal bias, in any methodologically significant way, takes hold of Descartes's enquiry. He introduces the search for truth in first-personal style in both the *Discourse* and the *Meditations* (the 'I' of the *Discourse* is more determinately the historical Descartes than is the soliloquizer of the *Meditations*), but this is not yet very heavily committal: the questions asked in the enquiry might, for all that, be of the form 'what is true?' or even 'what is known?'. On the other hand, Descartes certainly ends the Doubt in what he takes to be a radically first-personal situation, within the world of his own ideas, seeking a route to a world outside that. Is there anything in his process of enquiry itself which determines that transition?

We have already noticed, in considering the doubts about perception, a strong assumption which Descartes makes, to the effect that all one's knowledge of anything is mediated by ideas, states of one's mind, and that assumption of course strongly contributes to, if it does not already constitute, his eventual 'egocentric predicament'. The mere undertaking of a search for truth cannot by itself commit him to that assumption.[13] However, when the search for truth takes the special form of Pure Enquiry, the nature of the enquiry does seem to import a distinctively first-personal element (although it may still not come to anything as strong as Descartes's assumption). Since Pure Enquiry seeks to maximize the truth-ratio among one's beliefs by looking (at least in the first place) for an exceptionlessly truth-producing method of acquiring beliefs, it involves critical reflection not just on the content of one's beliefs, but on one's methods of acquiring them. The question becomes for the first time not just 'what is the case?' but 'what can I know is the case?', and this second type of question, unlike the first, mentions oneself; to answer it requires reflection, not just on the world, but on one's experience of the world. It seems then that *some* first-personal form is implicit in Pure Enquiry from the beginning, and it is implicit in it merely as being a reflective and self-critical enterprise – it does not have to be defined as a search for the foundations of knowledge in any of the senses stronger than that for the first-personal structure to emerge.

If Pure Enquiry is the essential approach to the theory of

13. Jonathan Bennett has claimed that it does. Defining 'the Cartesian basis' as 'the intellectual situation in which one attends to nothing but one's mind and its states', he has argued (*Kant's Dialectic* (Cambridge, 1974), pp. 66–7) that we can derive the conclusion that 'the Cartesian basis is the foundation of all knowledge' from four 'almost trivial' propositions, of which the two most important are 'any intellectual problem which I have must, for me, take the form "what should I think about x?"' and 'My decision as to what to think about x must be based upon data which I have'. The first of these two is surely false, but in any case the argument requires at least the following further assumptions: (a) all knowledge can be regarded by somebody as 'my' knowledge, i.e. is some particular person's knowledge; (b) any such knowledge constitutes the answer to an intellectual problem which the knower reflectively has; (c) the data on which the answer must be based are states of the knower's mind. (a) is far from obvious (a point I shall touch on below); (b) is importantly false; (c) simply begs the question.

knowledge, and it has implicitly a first-personal form, then the theory of knowledge must have such a form. But here we have to remember how much we are assuming if we do take Pure Enquiry to be the essential approach to the theory of knowledge. We are assuming not only that any knowledge there is is some reflective person's knowledge; we are also assuming that a person who knows that P should be able to recover that knowledge in reflection and be able to assert, and justifiably assert, 'I know that P' – which requires in effect that if one knows, one must be able to know that one knows, a very strong requirement which the picture of the searcher after knowledge which we considered at the beginning gave us no reason to expect.

In these last considerations, I have been taking the 'first person' to mean the first person *singular*. Yet earlier I spoke of 'our' representations; why should 'we', even under Pure Enquiry, contract to 'I'? Might not Pure Enquiry be a collective enterprise? For Descartes, certainly, it is not; even if he conducts enquiry as our representative, he does it by himself. But perhaps that is not necessary; perhaps the bias to the first person might express itself just as well in the first person plural. There seems nothing in the idea of looking for 'the absolute conception', certainly, to determine otherwise: it is entirely natural to take 'our' representations to be collective representations, social products, shared by individuals in a society or cultural group. An obvious reply to such suggestions is that a group's knowledge or belief cannot be ultimate or irreducible – it must ultimately be individuals who are in such states, and to speak of the knowledge of a group, or of a society's representation of reality, must involve some kind of fiction. But even if there is some sense in which this must ultimately be so, it is not simply or straightforwardly so. It is not hard to think of ways in which what *we* know may be more than a simple sum of what each of us knows.[14] When we turn from knowledge to the activity, central

14. We surely need to get clearer about knowledge, and other such states, at the social or collective level, before we resort to Popper's 'third world' of knowledge which is neither social nor psychological, contains purely logical objects, and yet changes in time. See his *Objective Knowledge* (Oxford, 1973), especially chapters 3 and 4.

to Pure Enquiry, of self-criticism, it is very obvious that *our* self-criticism may essentially involve many selves. That fact in itself is enough to cast some doubt on the programme for the theory of knowledge which ties it to the first person singular.

Chapter 3

COGITO AND SUM

THE Method of Doubt, radically and generally applied, has left Descartes, it seems, with nothing. God, the world, his own body, the past, all seem to have succumbed to it; all might be illusions. Is there anything at all that he can know to be true, that can survive the process of doubt? At this point Descartes makes the reflection which brings the Doubt for the first time to a halt, and which sets him off in the opposite direction, on the path of positive knowledge.

I have convinced myself that there is nothing at all in the world, no heaven, no earth, no minds, no bodies; have I not then convinced myself that I do not exist? On the contrary: there is no doubt that I existed, if I convinced myself of anything. – But there is some deceiver, in the highest degree powerful and ingenious, who uses all his efforts to deceive me all the time. – Then there is no doubt that I exist, if he is deceiving me; let him deceive me as much as he likes, he can never bring it about that I am nothing, so long as I think that I am something. So after every thought and the most careful consideration, I must hold firm to this conclusion: that the proposition *I am, I exist*, must be true, whenever I utter it or conceive it in my mind.

This is a translation of what Descartes wrote, in the original Latin version, near the beginning of the *Second Meditation* (VII 25, HR1 150). But the French translation of the *Meditations* – which, the work of the Duc de Luynes, appeared in 1647 and had been seen and approved by Descartes[1] – presents a more complex version of the second sentence:

Certainly not: I certainly existed, if I convinced myself, or simply if I thought anything. (IX–1 19)

1. Descartes's first biographer, Baillet (*Vie de Descartes*, ii 171–3), says that the French version is actually preferable, because Descartes took the opportunity of the translation to introduce corrections and additions; see IV 194.

This emphasis brings out more strongly a connection which is already implicit, between Descartes's assurance that he exists, and his thinking. This connection is basic; but in the *Meditations* the claim that he is thinking is not itself offered as something of which he is certain – only the proposition 'I am, I exist' is explicitly said to be that.[2] In the famous words of the *Discourse*, however, his thinking is offered both as part of what is certain, and also as the ground, so it seems, of the assurance that he exists (Part iv: V I 32, HR1 101):

... I noticed that, while I was trying to think that everything was false, it was necessary that I, who was thinking this, should be something. And observing that this truth: *I am thinking, therefore I exist* was so firm and secure that all the most extravagant suppositions of the sceptics were not capable of overthrowing it, I judged that I should not scruple to accept it as the first principle of the philosophy I was seeking.

Cogito ergo sum, 'I am thinking, therefore I exist' – *the cogito* as it is often known – is not only the most famous but the most discussed of Descartes's sentences, and there has been much controversy about the ground of the certainty that it seems to possess; whether it is, as it seems to be, an inference; and what content can be found in the proposition 'sum', from which (as we shall see in the next chapter) Descartes is to extract quite ambitious metaphysical conclusions. Here we shall be principally concerned with the certainty of 'cogito' and of 'sum', and with the connection between them.

Since Descartes is prepared to regard 'cogito' and 'sum' as equally and independently certain, it is reasonable, in trying to explain or ground their certainty, to look in the first place for some characteristic which they both possess. Both possess the property introduced in the last chapter, of being *incorrigible*: if anyone believes that he is thinking, or again, that he exists, then necessarily he has a true belief. Moreover, they both have another property which is closely related to their incorrigibility, and contributes to it: each of them is *self-verifying*, in the sense

2. *Regulae* iii (X 368, H R1 7) offers as two *separate* propositions which can certainly be known to be true by the intuitive light of reason, *that one exists*, and *that one thinks*.

that if anyone asserts the proposition, then that assertion must be true.[3] The basis of this is particularly clear in the case of 'cogito', where it can be seen as the limiting case of a phenomenon displayed by other propositions. 'I am writing' will be true if I write it, but not if I say it; conversely with 'I am saying something'. 'I am making a public utterance' (in a rather strained sense of that sentence, perhaps) will be true whether I say it or write it, but not if I merely think it. 'I am thinking' is at the very end of that road: it will make a true assertion whatever mode it is asserted in, publicly or merely to myself. It can be true, of course, even if it is not *asserted* at all but merely if it is entertained or considered or doubted: for all of these are modes of thought, so the fact that I doubt or consider anything, and in particular, doubt or consider the proposition that I am thinking, will make it true that I am thinking. However, this by itself will not yet give me any true beliefs, since merely to consider or doubt something is not yet to believe anything. The Pure Enquirer will have a true or certain belief only when he advances to asserting something, for example that he is thinking, and here the self-verifying property of 'cogito' as asserted gives him inevitably a true belief. Since 'I am thinking', and also 'I exist', in this sort of way necessarily make true assertions, 'I am not thinking' and 'I do not exist' necessarily make false ones. They do not, however, make assertions that are *necessarily false*, in the sense of being logical falsehoods or self-contradictions. A logical falsehood is false in all possible states of affairs, its contradictory true in all possible states of affairs; but Descartes does not believe, either now or later in his reflections, that his thought or his existence are in any such way necessary features of the universe (we will see an important aspect of this in the next chapter, p. 109 ff). He might not have existed; but in any state of the world in which he did not exist, of course he could not then think, believe, assert etc. that fact. The denials of 'I am thinking' and 'I exist' are not logical falsehoods, but pragmatically self-defeating or self-falsifying – we might compare someone's saying 'I am absent' in a roll-call. Descartes himself

3. For a detailed discussion of epistemological concepts introduced in this chapter, see Appendix 1.

is not only committed to their not being logical falsehoods, but he is clear that they are not: '*I am, I exist*, must be true, *whenever I utter it or conceive it in my mind*.'

Several writers have emphasized this aspect of the incorrigibility possessed by 'cogito' and 'sum'.[4] It is with regard to this aspect that Hintikka has used the notion of a 'performatory' or 'performative' interpretation of the *cogito*. This term, however, can be seriously misleading. The main use of 'performative' in recent philosophy has been to cover certain uses of language by which the very act of uttering a sentence, in a correct context, constitutes the act to which the sentence refers: 'I hereby warn you . . .', 'I bid . . .', 'I promise . . .', are well-known examples. If the term 'performatory' is applied to the *cogito*, this might suggest, by a kind of analogy to these examples, that it is the very act of thinking the proposition that makes the proposition true. This might suggest, further, that the peculiar certainty that the thinker possesses about the proposition is the product of the fact that he has made it true – on the lines, perhaps, of Vico's favourite thought, *verum et factum convertuntur*, it is only what one oneself produces that one can know through and through.[5] But none of this can be on the

4. For various accounts of this kind, see e.g. A. J. Ayer, 'Cogito ergo sum', *Analysis* vol. 14 (1953–4), 17–33, and *The Problem of Knowledge* (London, 1958), pp. 45–54; John Passmore, *Philosophical Reasoning* (London, 1964), pp. 60–64; my own 'La Certitude du *cogito*', *Cahiers de Royaumont* IV (Paris, 1962), translated as 'The Certainty of the *cogito*' in W. Doney, ed., *Descartes, A Collection of Critical Essays* (New York, 1967); J. L. Mackie, 'Self-Refutation – a Formal Analysis', *Philosophical Quarterly* vol. 14 (1964), 193–203; G. Nakhnikian, 'On the Logic of cogito Propositions', *Nous* III (1969), 197–210. The term 'existentially inconsistent' has been introduced by J. Hintikka for the negations of these propositions, in his well-known article, '*Cogito, ergo sum*: Inference or Performance?', *Philosophical Review* LXXI (1962), 3–32, reprinted in Doney, op. cit., pp. 108–40, and see also *PR* LXXII (1963), 487–96; but his very unsatisfactory formulation of that notion has been well criticized by F. Feldman, 'On the Performatory Interpretation of the *cogito*', *PR* LXXXII (1973), 345–63.

5. For the importance of this thought in Vico's (profoundly anti-Cartesian) philosophy, see Isaiah Berlin, *Vico and Herder* (London, 1976), especially pp. 15 ff.

right lines. For while a sense might be defended in which I make it true that I am thinking, by thinking, there is no sense in which I make it true, by doing anything, that I exist; nor could Descartes have thought so, who, as we shall see later, emphatically insists that he could not be self-created. Now Hintikka does not himself seem to mean that the 'performatory' interpretation of the *cogito* involves the idea of *making these propositions true*; though he does rather misleadingly say that the relation of 'cogito' to 'sum' is 'rather comparable with that of a *process* to its *product*',[6] and also speaks of the 'act of thinking through which the sentence *I exist* may be said to verify itself'.[7] What he rather seems to mean is that it is the *indubitability* of 'I exist' which 'results'[8] from the act of thinking. But it is not clear how this is to be taken. If it just meant that Descartes could not recognize 'I exist' to be indubitable unless he thought it, this would not make any special point: he could not recognize any proposition to be indubitable without thinking it. Hintikka makes it clear that he means more than this. The idea is perhaps rather that the very act of thinking it *provides the grounds*, in some way, for recognizing 'I exist' as indubitable. This seems nearer to what is needed, but it also begins to narrow the gap between a 'performative' interpretation and some alternatives to it.

A distinctive mark of a 'performative' interpretation, as Hintikka discusses it, seems to be this, that it does not regard the *cogito*, in its fundamental form, as expressing a relation between *two* propositions. There is the one proposition, 'sum', of which Descartes becomes certain, but the other proposition, 'cogito', is not essential, as a reflexive thought of Descartes's, at all. What is essential is just that Descartes should be thinking, and it will be that thinking, and not a reflexive proposition recording it, which will somehow bring the indubitability of 'sum' before him. The *Meditations* formula, in which 'cogito' is not itself presented, will then be primary and more accurately express the nature of the *cogito*. But if we are to say that the

6. Doney, p. 122; Hintikka's emphasis.
7. Doney, p. 122.
8. ibid.

thinking is not just the occasion of recognizing 'sum' to be indubitable, but that it provides, in any sense at all, grounds for that recognition, it is hard to see how a full reconstruction of Descartes's thought can avoid expressing those grounds explicitly: that is to say, it will actually display the reflexive proposition 'cogito', and the *cogito* will involve two propositions. It does not follow from that that the relation between the two has to be one of inference; but it does remove one of the more compelling reasons one might have for denying that it was an inference, namely that the supposed premiss never appeared as a proposition at all.

We shall come back later to the question of whether the *cogito* can be an inference, and whether Descartes thought it was. Before that, however, we should look at a quite different aspect of the *cogito*, which involves a different way in which certainty comes into the matter. The 'self-verifying' property applied to both 'cogito' and 'sum'; and the fact that it applied to 'sum' in its own right contributed to the point we have just considered, that the role of 'cogito' as a proposition which is itself reflexively thought may seem not essential. We now turn to a different property related to certainty, and this, by contrast, undoubtedly requires the presence of a proposition other than 'sum' – out of the two, 'cogito' and 'sum', it is 'cogito' that it applies to. This property I will label 'being evident': that a proposition is *evident* (with respect to A) means that if it is true, then A believes it. It is, so to speak, the converse of incorrigibility, as I have defined that. A proposition can be both incorrigible and evident, as Descartes takes 'I am thinking' to be: in that case, A will believe it if and only if it is true. 'I exist', however, while it is incorrigible, cannot be assumed to be evident (in this special sense) at this stage, without anticipating the answers to many questions which will come later. It will turn out, eventually, to be in Descartes's view an evident proposition, because his existence will turn out to be that of an essentially (and constantly) thinking thing, so that his existence will be as evident as Descartes always takes his thinking to be. But he cannot assume yet that his existence is such that if he exists, he must believe that he does – it might be possible, as common-sense would suggest, for him to exist without believing anything.

As an *evident* proposition, 'cogito' is not just one peculiar item, but rather the representative of a large class of different propositions. It is an important point that in Descartes's usage the Latin verb *cogitare* and the French verb *penser* and the related nouns *cogitatio* and *pensée*, have a wider significance than the English *think* and *thought*. In English, such terms are specially connected with ratiocinative or cognitive processes. For Descartes, however, a *cogitatio* or *pensée* is any sort of conscious state or activity whatsoever; it can as well be a sensation (at least, in its purely psychological aspect) or an act of will, as judgement or belief or intellectual questioning. As he puts it in the more formal exposition of the *Principles* (i 32):

All forms of consciousness (*modi cogitandi*) that we experience can be brought down to two general kinds: one is cognition (*perceptio*), or the operation of the intellect; the other is volition, the operation of the will. Sensation, imagination and pure intellection are just various forms of cognition; desire, aversion, assertion, denial, doubt, are various forms of volition.

These various forms of *cogitatio* are not something that Descartes introduces only at a later stage of his philosophy. Already in the *Second Meditation* he is prepared to say, soon after the proof of his existence in the *cogito*, that he can be certain that a whole variety of purely mental operations must actually belong to him as he experiences them. He describes himself, on the strength of the *cogito* alone, as a 'thinking thing' (*res cogitans*) (VII 27, HR1 152); to this description we shall have to return later, but what matters for the present is the way in which Descartes is prepared to interpret this, which sheds some light on the meaning of the *cogito* itself. He goes on (VII 28, HR1 153):

What then am I? A thinking thing. What is that? One that doubts, understands, asserts, denies, is willing, is unwilling, which also imagines and feels.

This is quite a number of things, if they all belong to me. But why should they not? Am I not the being who is now doubting almost everything; who nevertheless understands something, and asserts this one thing to be true, who denies the others, who wants to know more, and does not want to be deceived, who imagines many things, sometimes against my will, and who is aware of many things as though they came by the senses? What is there in all this which is not just as true as that I exist – even if all the while I am asleep, even if the being who created me deludes me to the full extent of his power?[9] Can any of this be distinguished from my thought (*cogitatio*)? Can any of it be separated from myself? It is so self-evident that it is I who doubts, understands, and desires, that there seems no way in which it can be more clearly explained.

Further, it is also I who imagines; for even if (as I supposed) none of the things that I imagine is true, yet this power of imagination really exists and forms part of my thought. Finally, it is I who have sensations, that is to say, who is aware of objects as though by the senses, since indeed I see light, I hear noise, I feel heat. – But all these objects are unreal, since I am dreaming. – Let it be so; certainly it seems to me that I see, I hear, and I feel heat. That cannot be false; that is what in me is properly called sensation; and in this precise sense, sensation is nothing but thought.

In this passage, Descartes takes two important steps. First, he claims that there is a whole range of specific *cogitationes* of which he is certain. They are specific both as types of *cogitatio* – doubting, willing, imagining – and, further, in their content: he is doubting, willing or imagining some particular thing. In the previous discussion, we considered 'cogito' only in its unspecific form, 'I am thinking'; but Descartes is also prepared to include among his certainties such specific propositions as 'I am denying that I have a body' or 'it seems to me as though I can feel heat'. This is the first step. The second, instanced by this last example, is that among these *cogitationes* he is prepared to include some which he identifies as the purely mental element in experiences which earlier he treated as presupposing the existence of his body and the physical world, and hence to be ruled out by the doubt (VII 27, HR1 151). Now he is prepared to 'shear off' a purely mental experience, and call that 'sensation' (cf. *Princ.* i 66). He can be certain of the existence of this, he claims, merely

9. That is to say, the malicious demon: as Descartes explained to Burman (V 151, C p. 9), at this stage of his progress he is not yet clear that his creator is really God.

as a mental phenomenon, even though he remains in doubt whether such experiences are related to physical bodies through physical organs of sense.

All these kinds of *cogitatio* are accepted just as such, and their acceptance rests on no more than what was available at the moment of the *cogito*. Though Descartes refers to them only after he has proved his own existence, they are in a sense bound up with the 'I am thinking' part of the *cogito*: these *cogitationes* are part of what Descartes considers as self-evident when he says that the existence of his thought is self-evident. This makes a difference to the interpretation of the *cogito*. The unspecific proposition 'I am thinking' is, like 'I exist', self-verifying, and its incorrigibility can be traced to that; but 'I am uncertain whether God exists' or 'it seems to me as though I can see a red patch' are not self-verifying, and if they are incorrigible (as Descartes believes) then it is for a quite different sort of reason. One thing that helps to bring out the difference between this kind of proposition, and the self-verifying ones, is that these can be used to tell a lie. 'It all looks fuzzy', 'I feel cheerful', 'I believe what you say', can all in various ways be used to deceive, but 'I exist', and the others, for obvious reasons, cannot. The difference does not of course suggest that the evident kind of proposition is less certain than the self-verifying, but it illustrates how the basis of its certainty is something different.

Descartes takes those operations of the mind to be immediately obvious to the thinker, and the thinker to have immediate access to them. In our terminology, he regards some propositions about such states as both incorrigible and evident, and the states as being necessarily present to consciousness. It may seem artificial to treat matters such as this in the terminology of 'propositions': it may seem more natural merely to speak of the states that he is in, and of the fact that he is certain that he is in those states, and this is indeed how Descartes puts it in the *Second Meditation*. But the formulation explicitly in terms of propositions brings out something which is important and which is indeed implicit in Descartes's own treatment, that his certainty depends not just on what states he is in, but on how they are described. Take some state described as his having an experience *as of* seeing a table, or its seeming to him that he sees a table: then under that description, Descartes claims, he is certain of it. But that very same experience *could* be caused by the physical presence of a table, and if it is described in such a way as to imply that it is so caused – for instance, if it is described as the experience *of seeing a table* – then he is not certain of it. Similarly, if he claims that it seems to him now that he had dinner last night, then his claim will be certain, but if he describes that experience as *recalling having dinner last night*, then his claim, strictly taken, will not be, by the standards of the Doubt, certain. So, by Descartes's own provisions, there is no way of avoiding the point that the same experience or state can be characterized in different ways, and that how it is characterized is relevant to the possibility of certainty; it is this that forces on us the language of propositions. The most radical way in which this comes up we have already taken for granted: that these propositions are *in the first person*. If there were someone else to comment on Descartes's state of mind, they would refer to the same state in the third person as Descartes refers to in the first person, but their statements would not possess his certainty.[10]

What Descartes has acknowledged in this passage of the *Second Meditation* is that some (first-person, present tense) propositions about the mental life are certain. We have already partly interpreted that acknowledgement as involving the claims that these propositions about the mental life are both incorrigible and evident, and that the mental states are present to consciousness.

It will be worthwhile pausing here, before taking up further questions about 'cogito', 'sum', and the connection between them, to examine briefly some relations between these properties of *being incorrigible* and *being evident*, and to chart some larger claims about the mental which Descartes does, or will eventually make. Descartes's introduction of this class of propositions at this stage is, so to speak, the thin end of the wedge so far as his views about the mental life are concerned, and it is as well to be warned of the wedge's full size.

10. For more detailed discussion of 'proposition' here, see Appendix 1.

It is important, first, that the fact that these propositions are incorrigible does not entail, just in itself, that they are evident. It could be the case, in principle, that whenever I believed that I wanted a certain thing (for instance), I did want that thing, but nevertheless not the case that whenever I wanted something, I believed I did – the thought, on some occasions, might not occur to me at all. This possibility tends to escape notice because of the first-personal formulations that we are dealing with, which tend inevitably to imply that the matter has come up for me. But if we just consider what has to be the case for me to want something, then we can reflect that *that* could be the case without a belief in any way having occurred to me to the effect that it was the case. This will be so even if we agree (ill-advisedly, in fact) that propositions of the form 'I want *X*' are incorrigible.

It will also be so, whether or not we think that what has to be the case if I want something involves some conscious experience such as a feeling. Whether that is so or not is a separate question. In fact it is false that every want involves such an experience, but even if it did, it might still be possible for one to have that feeling without making any judgement, or forming any belief, to the effect that one had a certain want. An interesting case in this connection is pain. It would be generally agreed that pain is a conscious experience: one who is in pain feels something. Now it may, further, be true that a language user who is in pain will believe that he is in pain, unless perhaps he is in such a reduced state that he has lost effective hold on his language use. If one possesses and can use the concept *pain*, its application to oneself will be elicited by one's being in pain, and in this pains importantly contrast with wants. But non-language-users can be in pain (though Descartes, as we shall see in Chapter 10, denied it); they have no concept of pain they can apply to themselves, and to them we cannot in all seriousness ascribe, in addition to their pain, a belief that they are in pain.[11]

11. Some philosophers deny that anyone can be said to believe or, again, know that he is in pain; on the ground that '*A* believes that he is in pain' or '*A* knows that he is in pain' and their first-personal versions, 'have no standard use in the language'. With regard to knowledge, the claim is anyway

Further, the fact that some conspicuous group of propositions about the mental life are incorrigible or evident of course
does not mean that all such propositions are so, or that incorrigibility and evidence are necessary conditions of the mental.
There are many propositions, quite obviously about the mental
life, for which it is quite implausible to claim it: that one is in
love, for instance, or that one is not jealous, or that one can
bring to mind the colour violet. The list of supposed certainties
which Descartes gives in the *Meditation* already shows signs of
going too wide.

In particular, there are subconscious or unconscious mental
states or processes. We must get one difficulty out of the way
first: in the sense of 'evident' that I am using, a proposition
could even be *evident* and yet, in principle, refer to a state
which was unconscious. It will of course follow from its being
evident, by definition, that if one is in the state, one will believe
that one is; but to guarantee that the state is not unconscious,
one has to add a further requirement that that belief is not itself
unconscious. Similarly, one cannot just say that unconscious or subconscious states are mental states that one is in
without knowing that one is in them. How best to use these
notions, where and how to employ the concepts of unconscious
knowledge or belief, are not matters calling for verbal legis-
lation – they are questions of what will be the most fruitful
theory of such states. For Descartes's purposes, however, we
can agree to leave this particular problem on one side, and take
'belief' in the definitions of incorrigibility and the rest as relating to conscious belief.

Even allowing for that, there is nothing to stop there being a
mental state or process, propositions about which were *incorrigible*, but which could sometimes nevertheless be subconscious. A possible example of this combination is *noticing*.
On the one hand, it is quite plausible to claim that if one believes one has noticed something, then one has done so (though

---

false: the thought, concerning a suspected malingerer, that he knows
whether he is in pain, is entirely in place. But in any case it is a hopelessly
weak kind of ground.

one may be wrong in one's description of what one has noticed); but one can notice things subconsciously, i.e. notice them without consciously believing that one has, and without the noticing being an event in conscious experience.

If we take 'unconscious' processes, as opposed to 'subconscious' ones, to relate to processes *in the unconscious*, as postulated by some psychoanalytical theory, which will connect the notion of the unconscious with the notion of repression, then propositions about these processes cannot be incorrigible. It will not of course follow that they have been ruled out as mental processes. However, if there is some mental item, some propositions about which have already been accepted as incorrigible – let us say, for the sake of argument, wishes – then there is likely to be a real difficulty in saying also that some unconscious state is a wish in the same sense. If there is a difficulty about that, this will leave two options. One might perhaps have reason for saying that statements about unconscious states did not mean the same as corresponding statements about conscious states; one might have more reason, though, for saying that 'wish' (for example) did mean basically the same in conscious and in unconscious connections, but that people were wrong who, like Descartes, thought that propositions about wishes were incorrigible. Here again, what there will be reason for saying will be a matter of successful theory (for instance, on the question whether there is any class of wishes which could be marked off as conscious or as unconscious just in virtue of their content). That we do not as a matter of fact know what we have reason for saying here is evidenced by those philosophers who, having made a generalization about the incorrigibility of some class of mental propositions, so often add desperately '(except in Freudian connections)'.

The fact, then, that some propositions about the mental life are in the highest degree certain does not tell us all that much about the mental in general. But in fact Descartes will go on to hold that these characteristics apply quite generally: that it is a mark of propositions about the mental life that they are incorrigible and evident, and that mental states are fully available to consciousness.[12] (Signs of this are perhaps already to be seen in the generous list of psychological properties introduced in the *Second Meditation*.) There are indeed some mental states which we can accept as coming near to Descartes's model, as paradigms of privacy from others and of immediate access for the thinker. Above all, where *privacy* is the principal focus of the question, one paradigm is provided by certain episodic verbal thoughts and images – the kind of thing to which the old saying 'a penny for your thoughts' particularly applies. Pains and other bodily sensations, which have particularly been discussed by philosophers in these connections, present a slightly different contrast between the situations of subject and of observer. In the case of episodic thought, the contrast centres on the point that overt expression of thought or fantasy seems in the standard case to be an entirely voluntary matter; when such an episode occurs in my thought, it seems entirely up to me whether I give it any distinctive overt expression at all (of course this does not mean that whenever I express my thought – for instance, in expressing my opinion, or just in thinking out loud – there has to have been such an inner episode which I have chosen to express). In the case of pains, this is not the centre of the contrast: pains, or at least severe pains, tend to express themselves. In their case, the contrast which especially attracts the idea of privacy is another one, the difference between being in pain and believing that someone else is – a type of difference which is far less dramatic in the case of thoughts, and indeed may vanish.[13]

Although there are these paradigms of privacy – of more than one type, as I have suggested – it is vitally important that there is no useful or even viable concept of the mental or the psychological which takes these as the determining paradigm, and relegates everything else to some non-psychological category, to not being part of the mental life. Descartes's dichotomy of everything into the mental and the physical, and his equation

12. There is a minor problem about Descartes's view of innate ideas. See below, pp. 111, 134–5.
13. For this possibility, see further p. 298.

of the mental with the conscious, form jointly one of the most damaging, as well as one of the most characteristic, features of his developed system.

For the present, however, we are following Descartes as the Pure Enquirer in the search for certainty, and he does not need at this stage these extravagant conclusions about the mental. He just seeks some certainties, and in some first-personal, present tense, propositions about the mental life, as well as in the unspecific 'I am thinking', he finds some. But here an important question begins to surface. The terms we have been using, *incorrigible*, *evident*, etc., are of course our terms, not Descartes's. Descartes speaks of things that are certain, or indubitable, or – in a phrase which we shall repeatedly encounter – things that he 'very clearly and distinctly perceives' to be true. Such things, he supposes, will meet his need, and will stop the Doubt. But can a proposition's merely being incorrigible be enough to stop the Doubt? Or even the Pure Enquirer's seeing that it is incorrigible? Must he not, rather, be *certain* that it is incorrigible? – and whatever that certainty might consist in, it would not consist in another level of the incorrigible, since the claim that a given proposition is incorrigible or, again, evident is not itself incorrigible or evident.

These problems are not just difficulties for us and for our terminology. They are very important difficulties for Descartes's theory of knowledge, and for the construction of the Pure Enquirer's project. We shall not be in a position to discuss them adequately until later; until Chapter 7, in fact, where (and in Appendix 2) we shall look back and try to reconstruct the exact working of the rejection of the Doubt. For now, it is better to continue to use the concepts which have been introduced, which are at any rate closely related to certainty as Descartes wants it. Being incorrigible, or being evident, or being both, are not in fact enough for the indubitability that Descartes wants, but it is only later that we shall be in a position to see clearly what extra it is that he needs. Up to that point, we can discuss most of the issues, and in particular, some differences between different bases of certainty, adequately in these terms.

Descartes has, then, under the *cogito* two propositions ('cogito' and 'sum' themselves) which are self-verifying and incorrigible, and others ('cogito' and the specific psychological propositions) which are incorrigible and evident. Does he, for his future progress, need both sorts? The former sort (its interest to recent philosophers notwithstanding) is not essential to him; but the latter is, for two reasons. As we saw, he could, relying on its being self-verifying, acquire 'sum' as a certainty without the reflective proposition 'cogito' occurring to him at all; but without the reflective proposition he could not acquire *sum res cogitans*, which is essential in the coming step in his argument, and which he takes as including the more specific mental functions. Second, when at a later stage he proceeds from his own existence to the existence of something other than himself, he must essentially start from the contents of his own mind: there is nowhere else for him to start from. In particular, as we shall see in Chapter 5, he has to rely on knowing *that he has the idea of God*, and this proposition he regards as a certainty of the psychological, immediate access, sort.

It might be wondered whether he has to regard it in that light, or whether he might not, in fact, treat 'I have an idea of God' as self-verifying. Descartes's formal account of what *having an idea* is, is this:

> *Idea* is a word by which I understand the form of any thought, that form by the immediate awareness of which I am conscious of the said thought: in such a way that, when understanding what I say, I can express nothing in words, without that very fact making it certain that I possess the idea of that which these words signify. (*II Rep.*: def. II: VII 160, HR2 52)

Someone might argue: if one says 'I have an idea of God' and understands the meaning of those words, then (by this definition) what he says must be true. But if he does not understand the meaning of his words, then he is not asserting that proposition at all. So the proposition 'I have an idea of God' (or, indeed, the idea of anything else), if asserted, must be true, i.e. is self-verifying. Descartes in fact comes close to this conclusion in his answer to an anonymous objector (letter to Mersenne, July 1641: III 392, K 105). But there must be something wrong with this argument: it cannot be that one who says, for instance, 'I have no idea what a geodesic is' has said something pragmatically self-defeating – what he says could, quite clearly, be true. The answer to the argument is that statements to the effect that one has or lacks a certain idea are, in so far as they relate to words and their meanings, to be taken on the lines of statements in which words are mentioned rather than used. 'I have no idea what a geodesic is' will be, on this line, roughly equivalent to something like 'I do not know what "geodesic" means', and the assertion of that in no way presupposes its falsehood. Similarly, 'I know what "God" means', the (very rough) equivalent of 'I have an idea of God', is not self-verifying. It is an interesting and difficult question, what kind of self-knowledge is involved in the knowledge of propositions of this sort,[14] but it *is* a kind of self-knowledge, and Descartes needs that kind of knowledge to be able to proceed, eventually, beyond himself.

We can now turn to the question of whether the *cogito* expresses an inference; and, first, whether Descartes supposed that it did. Its form is trivially that of an inference, in the sense that it contains the word 'therefore'; and Descartes is happy to refer to it in inferential terms; for instance in the *Discourse on the Method*:

(seeing that) ... from the very fact that I was thinking of doubting the truth of other things, *it followed* very clearly and very certainly that I existed ... (Part iv: VI 32, HR1 101)

and again, in replying to a correspondent who, like many others, had pointed out that the argument of the *cogito* was anticipated by St Augustine:[15]

... it is a thing which in itself is so simple and natural, *to infer* that

14. Cf. *Must We Mean What We Say?* by Stanley Cavell, in his book of that title: New York, 1969.
15. For historical material on this point, see Gilson, *Commentaire*, pp. 295 ff. See also the admirable passage from Pascal quoted by Gilson (p. 299), which ends: '... this saying is as different in [Descartes's] writings, compared with the same saying in others to whom it occurred in passing, as a man full of life and strength is different from a corpse.'

one exists from the fact that one is doubting, that it could come
from the pen of anyone ... (Letter to Colvius, 14 November 1640:
III 248, K 84)

Yet the situation is more complex than these off-hand
remarks might suggest. Elsewhere, Descartes is very emphatic
that in some sense, at least, the *cogito* is not an inference:

When someone says, *I am thinking*, therefore *I am*, or *I exist*, he
does not conclude his existence from his thought as if by the force of
some syllogism, but as a thing which is self-evident: he sees it by a
simple inspection of the mind. This is clear from the fact that, if he
deduced it by the syllogism, he would already have to know this
major premiss: everything that thinks is, or exists. But on the contrary, he learns this proposition from what he perceives in himself,
that it is impossible that he should think, if he does not exist. For it
is the nature of our mind to form general propositions from the
knowledge of particular ones. (*II Rep.*: V II 140, H R2 38)

Two things at least emerge clearly from this statement. One is
that Descartes does not regard the *cogito* as a *syllogistic* inference, that is to say, an inference of the form 'All A's are B's; I
am an A, therefore I am a B'; though of course, since not all
inferences are syllogistic, the possibility remains open that the
cogito is some other sort of inference. The second thing that
emerges is that Descartes, in saying this, is not merely making a
psychological point – he is not merely saying that the experience
of grasping the *cogito* is that of an instantaneous insight, rather
than that of a mental passage from one proposition to another.
It is true that elsewhere Descartes is concerned with psychological aspects of logical inference; in the early work, the *Regulae*, he has a distinction between 'deduction' and 'intuition'
which is certainly psychological, since the question 'can I judge
of the validity of a complex piece of reasoning by intuition or
by deduction?' comes down to the question 'can I conceive the
whole chain of this reasoning in one act of the mind?'; and he
makes the point that familiarity with a piece of reasoning may
eventually enable one to see the whole thing intuitively, whereas
at first one could grasp it only by deduction, that is to say, step
by step. (For more on this, see Chapter 7, pp. 191 ff.)

However, it is clear that it is not merely this psychological distinction between intuition and deduction that Descartes is relying on in the passage just quoted about the *cogito*. The point that he is making is not just that he does not as a matter of fact conduct a syllogistic inference, but that he is in no position to, since such inference would involve relying on a premiss which he is in no position to know. What is rather less clear is what he supposes this impossibility to consist in. He says that the difficulty would be that he would have to presuppose a general 'proposition, but that he could only get to know this general proposition from the particular one which he perceives to be true in his own case. But this is a misleading way to represent the situation, since it makes it sound as though one arrived at the general proposition 'everything that thinks, exists' by some sort of induction based on observing that each particular thing that thinks also exists, which is absurd. Descartes regards the connection between thinking and existing as a necessary connection. He makes this clear even in the passage just quoted; for he says that what he observes in his own case is that it is *impossible* that he should think without existing, and this already imports the notion of necessity. But if it imports the notion of necessity, does it not import the notion of generality? For clearly it is not Descartes's view that this impossibility of thinking without existing could be peculiar to his own case – rather, in reflecting on his own case, he sees that in general it is impossible to think without existing. But if he supposes that he can grasp this general statement of impossibility at this stage, what becomes of his answer that the *cogito* cannot be a syllogistic inference because it would have to rely on a general proposition which he does not yet know to be true?

In my view, the answer to this depends on distinguishing between the syllogistic major premiss 'everything that thinks, exists', and the statement of impossibility 'it is impossible to think without existing' (or, what comes to the same thing, the statement 'in order to think, it is necessary to exist'). The first Descartes denies to be presupposed by the *cogito*; the latter he is prepared to admit as presupposed. And there is a reason behind this distinction. As he puts it in the *Principles*:

When I said that this proposition: *I am thinking, therefore I exist* is the first and the most certain that presents itself to one who conducts his thoughts in order, I did not for all that deny that it was necessary first to know what thought was, and certainty, and existence, and that in order to think it is necessary to exist, and other similar things; but, because these are notions so simple that in themselves they do not give us knowledge of any existent thing, I did not think that they had to be taken into account here. (*Princ.* i 10; see also a letter to Clerselier, June 1646, on what is meant by 'a first principle': IV 444–5, K 196—7)

Thus the point is that 'in order to think, it is necessary to exist' does not make any reference to anything existing in the world: it is a bare statement of necessity which can, on Descartes's view, be intuitively grasped. This property it shares with certain other statements, all of which Descartes is prepared to admit the mind can grasp, as abstract necessities, before it comes to know of anything actually existent in the world:

... when one says that it is impossible that one and the same thing should both be and not be at the same time; that what has been done cannot be undone; that one who thinks cannot fail to be or to exist while he thinks; and many similar things: these are merely (eternal) truths, and not things that are outside our mind ... (*Princ.* i 49)

The bare statement of necessity is thus all right as a presupposition of the *cogito*, since it makes no existential claim. Correspondingly, what is wrong with the syllogistic premiss 'everything that thinks exists' seems to be that it does make an existential claim; and while Descartes does not explicitly say this, it can perhaps be elicited from the denials and admissions already quoted. Moreover, this would be entirely in line with the traditional logic of the syllogism, since that logic does ordinarily presuppose that general propositions of the form 'All *A*'s are *B*'s' should refer to *A*'s that actually exist. On this doctrine, to assert anything of all thinking things would be to presuppose that there actually were some thinking things in existence, which Descartes is clearly in no position to presuppose; moreover, it would be paradoxical, since it is unclear what the premiss, so taken, would be saying, in asserting existence of things presupposed to exist. It is probably these points that he wishes to emphasize in preferring generally the statement of necessity, or 'eternal truth', to the syllogistic premiss form; together with the point, which is important to him, that the mind basically grasps eternal truths as they are presented in particular examples, rather than in an abstract formulation – which is not to deny that it grasps them *as general truths*.

It is this second point that Descartes seems to have stressed in the conversation he had with a young man called Burman who on 16 April 1648 came to question him on his philosophy. In that one place, however, Descartes admits that 'everything that thinks, exists' is presupposed by the *cogito* (V 147, C p. 4). Perhaps Burman (whose notes we rely on) made a mistake, or, very probably, Descartes did not always use these verbal forms strictly to mark the distinction. It is hard to reconcile the texts on any view, but the main point seems to me still to be that there is a real, and relevant, distinction between the 'eternal truth' and a standard syllogistic premiss.[16]

What is the content of the 'eternal truth'? It looks as though it is an application of a very general principle, that in order to do or be anything, or to have any predicate, it is necessary to exist – a principle which modern logic usually expresses in the form '$Fa \rightarrow (Ex)(x=a)$'.[17] In this form, the principle has nothing specially to do with thinking, nor with the first person. But the *cogito* has got something specially to do with thinking; and it

16. Cottingham, in his valuable edition of the *Conversation with Burman*, puts all the weight on the point about grasping general truths in particular cases, and denies any important distinction between the 'eternal truth' and the syllogistic premiss. This seems to me not to give enough weight to *Princ.* i 10, quoted above, in particular to Descartes's admission that 'it is necessary *first* to know ... that in order to think it is necessary to exist.'

17. Hintikka (Doney, pp. 113–14) denies that Descartes can invoke this principle without circularity. But the example which Hintikka invokes to illustrate the possible consistency of '*Fa*, but *a* does not exist' – 'Hamlet thought, but Hamlet did not exist' – is well answered by Kenny (p. 61); while Feldman (op. cit. pp. 355 ff.) has argued that any reconstruction of the *cogito* on Hintikka's own lines which is not trivial will itself rely on the principle.

also has something specially to do with the first person – the fact, pointed out by Kenny (p. 47), that Descartes also expresses *cogito*-like reflections in the third person, or, in the *Recherche de la Vérité* (X 515, HR1 316), in the second person, relates only to other persons' first-personal reflections, and does not subtract from the point that all the force of the reflection lies in its first-personal form. We can see how special features of thinking, and of the first person, co-operate in the *cogito* with the general principle.

The mere assertion or presentation of propositions of the forms 'he is *F*' or 'you are *F*' does not guarantee truths corresponding to 'he exists' and 'you exist': 'he' and 'you' might miss their mark altogether – there might be no one I was speaking about, or to. But assertion or thought involving 'I' seems not to be subject to this hazard: where there is assertion, or indeed any other genuine presentation, of a proposition involving 'I', there is some assertor or thinker for the 'I' to latch on to. Sometimes we are presented with sentences including 'I' where we cannot take seriously the application of 'I' – as with an ingeniously instructed parrot, or with the machine which says 'I speak your weight'. But in these cases, equally, we cannot take seriously the presented sentences as assertions or expressions of thought. So a peculiarity of the first person is involved in the *cogito*. As it can be expressed with reference to the English language: with regard to 'I', unlike other pronouns, the mere fact that it is used in genuine thought is enough to guarantee that it does not miss its mark.

But if that is so – why, in particular, 'I am thinking'? *Respiro ergo sum*, 'I am breathing, therefore I exist', would surely be just as good – a difficulty put to Descartes, in different forms, more than once. A quick answer to this would be that in the case of 'I am breathing' Descartes would not know the proposition to be true, since breathing and similar activities presuppose the existence of his body, a belief suspended in the Doubt; whereas 'I am thinking' can be known to be true, in virtue of the sorts of considerations we have already examined, such as its incorrigibility. But does the assertion *need* to be true? The principle we now have, with regard to the first person, is that if a proposition containing 'I' is genuinely asserted or thought, then 'I' cannot miss its mark. This does not require the proposition to be true, only to be genuinely thought: false thoughts require thinkers as much as true ones. So would it not do for Descartes to start by asserting or entertaining any proposition about himself, for instance the possibly false proposition 'I am breathing', and conclude from that that he exists?

In one sense, the answer is 'yes', but it is a sense which precisely illustrates the peculiarity of the *cogito*. For what he would draw his conclusion from in such a case would not be the content of the proposition regarded in the abstract, but rather from the fact that he was asserting, or entertaining, it; that is to say, from the fact that he was thinking it. So this line brings us back again to 'cogito' as the basic premiss: to entertain the proposition that one is breathing is just another *cogitatio*. The process which leads from *the thinking of* 'I am breathing' to 'I exist' will, if it is made fully explicit, actually display the reflexive proposition 'I am thinking . . .'. It will display it in the context 'I am thinking that I am breathing' (or '. . . about the possibility that I am breathing' etc.); and so will emerge, as we saw above (p. 80), as an incorrigible proposition of the psychological kind. This is very much what Descartes himself says in a letter of March 1638 (II 37; cf. also *V Rep.:* VII 352, HR2 207):

When one says 'I am breathing, therefore I exist', if he wants to conclude his existence from the consideration that breathing cannot go on without the breather existing, his conclusion is of no value, since he would have to have proved already that it was true that he was breathing, and this is impossible, if he has not already proved that he exists. But if he wants to conclude his existence from the belief or opinion that he has that he is breathing, in the sense that, even if this opinion were not true, all the same one sees that it is impossible that one should have it, unless one existed, then his conclusion is very sound, since this opinion that we are breathing presents itself to our mind before that of our existence, and we cannot doubt that we have the opinion while we have it. And to say in *this* sense 'I am breathing, therefore I exist,' is just the same as 'I am thinking, therefore I exist'. And if one is careful, one will find that all the other propositions from which we can in this way conclude our existence come back to this one . . .

But this line of argument also shows how, in a more basic sense, 'I am breathing' is really no replacement for 'I am thinking'. Since it is not the content of 'I am breathing', but the fact that I am thinking of it, which leads to the truth of 'I exist' – a connection which, reflexively spelled out, emerges as 'I am thinking "I am breathing"', therefore I exist' – we can see that the fact that 'I am breathing' is itself a first-personal proposition is not what is doing the work. In any sense in which 'I am breathing, therefore I exist' expresses the probative force of the *cogito*, so does 'it is raining, therefore I exist'. The first, unlike the second, constitutes a valid argument, but it is not the premiss of *that* argument which is doing the work. The work is done by a premiss which is produced by reflection on the point that I think 'I am breathing'; but, equally, it could be produced by reflection on the point that I think 'it is raining'.

The first-personal form, 'I am thinking', is essential; but what right to it has Descartes got? It has repeatedly been suggested, for example by the eighteenth-century philosopher and aphorist Georg Lichtenberg, that the most that Descartes could claim was 'cogitatur', 'there is some thinking going on' – like, in Lichtenberg's own comparison, 'there is lightning'. This idea, taken up by Ernst Mach, has recurred in a number of philosophies in this century, particularly of empiricist outlook. This is an important line of objection, and it may seem an attractive one, but more closely considered it turns out to share with Descartes his deepest error.

The objection is that in saying 'I am thinking' Descartes is saying too much. It assumes, that is to say, that there are two possible states of affairs, one more substantial than the other, which can be represented respectively as 'I am thinking' and 'thinking is going on', and that Descartes had no right to assert the more substantial rather than the less substantial. That is how those two states of affairs would be represented from the Enquirer's point of view; but the complaint against Descartes is that in asserting the more substantial rather than the less, the Enquirer is claiming more than he should about *what is objectively the case*, and this implies that the difference between the two states of affairs can also be represented from a third-personal point of view, as that between 'thinking is going on' and '*A* thinks', where '*A*' is a name, which could be used from a third-personal perspective, of whatever it is in the more substantial state of affairs that is doing the thinking. The point about what I am calling 'the third-personal perspective' is not of course that if the more substantial state of affairs obtained, there would actually have to be another person, still less another person who knew about it and could apply the name '*A*'. It is merely that, invited to grasp in the abstract the supposed difference between these two states of affairs, we grasp it in terms of there being, in the more substantial state of affairs, a thinker who could in principle be labelled '*A*', while in the less substantial state of affairs there is no such thinker.

It is not at all clear that we really can grasp this supposed difference in the abstract, but let us at least pretend that we make enough of it to continue. Suppose, then, that the following are true:

(T1) It is thought: *P*   (T2) It is thought: *Q*

Will it follow that the following is true?

(T3) It is thought: *P* and *Q*

However slight our grasp on the impersonal formulation, we must surely grant that T3 cannot follow: a distinct thought-content is involved in T3, and there is nothing in the occurrence of the two thought-events T1 and T2 to determine that *that* thought ever occurred at all. The thoughts T1 and T2 could be, as we might hopefully put it, 'separate'. But if thoughts can be, or can fail to be, 'separate' in this way, then a difficulty emerges for the impersonal formulation. It can best be illustrated if we extend the range of possible thought-events a little, to include that class of psychological phenomena which Descartes is at present accepting as described by the first-person forms 'I am doubting', 'I am willing' etc. While the present line of objection to Descartes will of course reject the 'I' from each of these, it has no reason to reject the idea that there are corresponding differences in the states of affairs which these forms (misleadingly) represent – differences which will have to emerge in properly impersonal representations of those states of affairs. So we shall need a class of 'non-I' or impersonal formulations, which we might put as: 'it is willed: *P*', 'it is doubted: *Q*?', etc.

We may now consider the following combination:

(T4) It is thought: it is not doubted whether *Q*
(T5) It is doubted: *Q*?

Is the thought reported at T4 true or false? Unless more is put in, nothing prevents its being straightforwardly made false, by the state of affairs T5. But granted what has just been said about T1, T2 and T3, it cannot be the case that the thought in T4 should have to be false just because of T5: we must want it to be possible that T5 be as 'separate' from T4 as T2 can be from T1. T5 can falsify T4, we will want to say, only if the doubt-event T5 is not 'separate' from the thought-event T4, or, one might say, if they both occur in the same thought-world (whatever that might turn out to mean).

The obvious reaction to this problem is to relativize the content of T4 so that it refers only to its own thought-world; to make it say, in effect

(T6) It is thought: it is not doubted here whether *Q*.

But the 'here' of T6 is of course totally figurative – nothing in the construction has given us places for these disembodied thoughts to occur at, let alone to serve as a basis for linking them up. So what might do better than 'here'? Further reflection suggests very strongly that, if the job can be done at all, there could be no better candidate for doing it than the Cartesian- 'I'. The content of the impersonally occurrent thought needs, it seems, to be relativized somehow; and there is no better way of relativizing it than the use of the first person. So the objector – assuming all the time that we can follow him at all – seems to have been wrong in saying that the *content* of the Cartesian thought should be impersonal rather than first-personal. However, this does not eliminate the possibility (if, again, we can understand it at all) that what is *objectively happening* is impersonal rather than substantial. That is to say, we have a reason now for preferring

(T7) It is thought: I am thinking

to

(T8) It is thought: thinking is going on;

but no reason so far for rejecting T7 in favour of

(T9) *A* thinks: I am thinking.

If the position we have now reached were the final one, the situation would be very odd. The objector would be wrong, it seems, about the required *content* of the Cartesian thought, but right about the state of affairs (or at least, the minimal state of affairs) involved in its being thought. It would follow from this that the first-personal content, even though it was correct and indeed requisite, might well represent a state of affairs which could not be described from the third-personal point of view as '*A* is thinking'. It would follow that Descartes could not make an inference from 'I am thinking' to 'I exist', if that, in its turn, were taken to represent (as Descartes takes it to represent) a state of affairs which could be third-personally represented as '*A* exists' ('there is such a thing as *A*'). It might then be unclear whether there was any sense at all in which 'I exist' could be got from 'I am thinking', but at any rate it would not express any substantial truth expressible in a third-personal form. The objection to Descartes seems to have failed at one level but succeeded at another; the result is that the relation between the two levels is very obscure, and we have lost our bearings on the connections between the thought-content 'I am thinking' and the state of affairs: *A is thinking.*

It is an uncomfortable position; but we do not have to, indeed cannot, remain in it. If we press further the same line of argument that got us this far, we shall find that the position has to be given up; but this does not mean the victory, after all, of Descartes over his objector, but rather the failure of them both. The device we have used to deal with the problems of 'separateness', that of relativizing the content of the impersonally occurring thoughts, only *appears* to be of help: by itself, in fact, it can achieve nothing at all. This can be seen if we compare the case of literal place. If someone seeks by relativization to save the following two statements from contradicting one another:

it is raining   it is not raining

he will achieve nothing by merely adding 'here';

it is raining here   it is not raining here

raise as big a problem as the first pair, unless we advance a stage further and make clear whether 'here' does or does not indicate the same place in the two cases. Thus

It is stated (thought) in place *A*: it is raining here
It is stated (thought) in place *B*: it is not raining here

yield statements which have a chance of both being true at once. Similarly with the figurative mental 'here', if we return to that for a moment: the relativized thought of T6,

it is not doubted here whether *Q*

does not in fact help by itself, because we have no way of specifying where, so to speak, 'here' is. So the relativization, if it is to do anything at all, cannot be confined to the content of thought-events; it must be attached, and in a third-personal, objective form, to the statements of their occurrence, so that T6 becomes rather

(T10) It is thought at place *A*: it is not doubted here whether *Q*.

But just as the 'here' in the content was totally figurative, and the best possible candidate for its replacement seemed to be the Cartesian 'I'; so some less figurative replacement is needed for 'at place *A*' in the statement of the thought's occurrence – and it is natural to conclude that nothing less than a personal name, or some such, will do as a replacement, so that T10 will give way to

(T11) *A* thinks: I am not doubting whether *Q*.

At this point we shall have returned completely to substantial formulations, and the programme of introducing impersonal formulations in their place will have finally collapsed.

The last step, however, may perhaps be too big. There might

possibly be some replacement for the figurative 'places' which served the purposes of effective relativization, but did not go so far as introducing a subject who thinks. If there is an effective replacement less ambitious than '*A* thinks', we shall still be left with some version of the problem about the relation between the 'I think' in the content of the thought, and what is objectively involved in the state of affairs which constitutes its being thought. The question whether there could be a replacement which fell short of '*A* thinks' is not one that I shall pursue further. The point is that *some* concrete relativization is needed, and even if it could fall short of requiring a subject who has the thoughts, it has to exist in the form of something outside pure thought itself.

The thought-event formulation we have been examining requires the notion of objectively existing thought-events, and in supposing that it can start out merely from the idea of thoughts as experienced, and from that achieve the third-personal perspective which is necessary if this notion is to apply, it shares a basic error with Descartes. There is nothing in the pure Cartesian reflection to give us that perspective. The Cartesian reflection merely presents, or rather invites us into, the perspective of consciousness. Descartes thinks that he can proceed from that to the existence of what is, from the third-personal perspective, a substantial fact, the existence of a thinker. The objection I have been discussing tries to find a fact which is less substantial; but that, too, will have to be capable of being regarded from the third-personal perspective if it is to be an objective fact, and the mere perspective of consciousness no more gives us a way of getting to that kind of objective fact, than it gives us a way of getting to Descartes's more substantial fact. This is not a verificationist point; the question is not about how anyone could come to know that various separate thought-events were occurring – it is a question about the coherence of the conception, of what it is one is invited to conceive.

If we have no help from anything except the pure point of view of consciousness, the only coherent way of conceiving a thought happening is to conceive of thinking it. So, sticking solely to the point of view of consciousness, we are forced back to a position in which there is, in effect, only one such point of view: events either happen for it, or they do not happen, and there is no way of conceiving of such events happening, but happening (so to speak) elsewhere. But this is what the objector, as much as Descartes, must need.

We shall come back to some of these matters in Chapter 10. Now, however, we return to the point that Descartes thinks he has reached just after the *cogito*. Having moved, as he supposes, from the existence of his own thought to the existence of 'an *I*' which has those thoughts, he now sets out to come to some conclusions about its properties. He will arrive at a striking conclusion; in following him, we should bear in mind the question, to what extent this conclusion is brought about by arguments which still at present lie before us, and to what extent it has already been determined in the pure reflection of the *cogito*.

Chapter 4

THE REAL DISTINCTION

BEING certain that he exists, Descartes next asks 'what is this "I"?' 'What am I?' 'I do not yet know,' he says, 'clearly enough what I am, I who am certain that I am; so that I must take the greatest care from the start not carelessly to take something else for myself.' He then rehearses the various things (*II Med.:* VII 25, HR1 150) that he might be tempted to say that he was. 'A rational animal' he rejects as an answer, since it could lead him only into a maze of further doubts, about the meanings of 'rational' and 'animal'; this point brings forward Descartes's rejection of the traditional scholastic philosophy (to which this phrase, as a definition of a man, famously belongs) as an instrument for the advance of knowledge. He goes on to consider various other notions, which have in common that they would identify him with some physical thing, either a body or a subtle spirit; these too he rejects, for he has no assurance of the existence of any physical thing. Similarly he rejects various faculties or abilities as belonging to this 'self' of his, as again implying the physical; these include even sensation, where this is regarded as implying the physical existence of a body. Following this path, he retreats once more to mere thinking, *cogitatio*; and here he finds an attribute that certainly belongs to him: 'this alone cannot be detached from me' (VII 27, HR1 150).

I am, I exist, [he repeats] that is certain; but for how long? For as long as I think; for perhaps it could happen, if I ceased to think, that then I should cease to be. I am admitting now nothing that is not necessarily true; I am, then, to speak precisely only a *thing that thinks* (*res cogitans, chose qui pense*), that is to say, a mind, an understanding, a reason ... What more? ... I am not that assemblage of limbs that is called a human body, or a tenuous and penetrating vapour spread through such limbs ... since I have supposed that all such things do not exist, and yet, without abandoning that supposition, I find that I do not cease to be certain that I am something. But perhaps it could be the case that these same things, which I suppose not to exist, are not in fact different from me, whom I do know? I know nothing of that; I can judge only of things that I know; I am not discussing that now; I have seen that I exist. But it is very certain that this notion and knowledge of myself, taken precisely enough, does not depend in any way on things whose existence is not yet known to me . . . (VII 27, HR1 151–2)

Exactly what, and exactly how much, does Descartes suppose himself to have shown at this stage of his progress? He concludes that he is 'a thing that thinks', that is clear enough – but how much does this claim? In particular, there are two pressing questions: first, is this supposed to mean that he is a thing whose essence it is to think – that he could not exist without thinking? Second, does the fact that he is a thinking thing exclude the possibility that he might not *also* be a corporeal thing? Concentrating merely on the passage that I have just quoted from the *Second Meditation*, the answer to both these questions might seem to be 'no'. 'No' to the first, since the most he says is '*perhaps* it could happen, if I ceased to think, that then I should cease to be', and he does not claim any certainty that this would be so. 'No' to the second, since he explicitly postpones the question, confining himself to saying, what is in itself none too clear, that 'this notion and knowledge of myself, taken precisely enough, does not depend in any way on things whose existence is not yet known to me'.

That 'no' is the correct answer to the first of these questions seems to be confirmed by the *Recherche de la Vérité*. The sequence of the argument follows (so far as it goes) fairly closely that of the *Meditations*. Here, again, Cartesian reflection leads to the conclusion that the '*I*' is a thing that thinks:

Thought alone is of such a nature that I cannot separate it from me . . . if I were not thinking, I would not know whether I was doubting, nor whether I existed . . . and it could even happen that if for an instant I stopped thinking, I might at the same time cease to be; so the only thing that I could not separate from me, which I know with certainty to be me, and which I can now assert without fear of error, is that I am a thing that thinks. (X 521, HR1 322)

Here again the emphasis seems to be on what the speaker knows, not on what more may be the case. This relates, indeed, to both our questions: all he knows is that he is a thing that thinks, and he only knows that he exists while he thinks. A little earlier in the *Recherche*, however, a bolder claim seems to be made. The speaker refers to

the certainty that I exist and am not a body; otherwise doubting of my body, I should at the same time doubt of myself, and this I cannot do, for I am absolutely convinced that I exist. (X 518, HR1 319)

This passage seems to return an affirmative answer to our second question; here certainty is claimed that I am not (also) a body, although the point reached in the Cartesian progress is no farther on than the *Second Meditation* (indeed, the *Recherche* goes no farther).

Now if this were just a matter of interpreting the *Recherche*, it would clearly be of no great importance. But there is a more serious problem within the *Meditations* themselves. Consider the following argument:

Since I know that everything that I clearly and distinctly conceive can be produced by God just as I conceive it, it is enough that I can clearly and distinctly conceive one thing without another for me to be certain that the one is distinct or different from the other, since they can come into existence separately, at least by God's omnipotence; and it makes no difference by what power this should come about, for one to consider the things as different. Now, from the mere fact that I know for certain that I exist and that I cannot see anything else that belongs necessarily to my nature or essence except that I am a thinking thing, I rightly conclude that my essence consists in this alone, that I am a thinking thing, a substance whose whole nature or essence is to think.[1] While it is possible (or rather, it is certain, as I shall say further on) that I have a body, which is very closely joined to me; nevertheless, since on the one hand I have a clear and distinct idea of myself, as purely a thing that thinks and is not extended, and, on the other hand, I have a distinct idea of the body as a thing that is extended and does not think, it is certain that

---

1. 'a substance . . . think' added in the French translation.

this *I*, that is to say my soul, which makes me what I am, is entirely and truly distinct from my body, and can be or exist without it. (VII 78, HR1 190)

This is the passage in which Descartes states the famous 'Real Distinction' between the mind and the body, which is one of the two things – the other being God's existence – that the title page of the *Meditations* claims that they will prove.[2] In this argument, it would seem that Descartes supposes himself to have proved both the things referred to in our two questions; since it is his essence to think, he could not exist without thinking, and again, his body is quite a separate and different thing from him and his mind (which are one). Now this passage occurs in the *Sixth Meditation*, very near the end of his progress; and consistently with our first impression that he does not claim this much in the *Second Meditation*, Descartes more than once emphasizes to objectors that the Real Distinction is not proved until this later stage. Thus to Hobbes, who remarks, in connection with the *Second Meditation*, 'it could be the case that something that thinks should be something corporeal', Descartes replies: 'I have not at all said the opposite, and in no way have relied on this as a foundation, but have left the matter entirely undetermined, until the *Sixth Meditation*, in which it is proved.' (*III Rep.*: VII 175, HR2 63; and cf. *II Rep.*: VII 129, HR2 30).

The problem, however, is this: is there anything in the argument for the Real Distinction, as produced in the *Sixth Meditation*, which could not equally well have appeared in the *Second*? If there is not, and if (as is so) Descartes supposes himself in that argument to have shown that he is essentially a thinking thing, and distinct from any body he has, we shall have to admit that the only reasons he has for these beliefs are reasons which were in fact available in the *Second Meditation*; though he himself seems anxious to stress that he was not in a position to reach these conclusions on the strength of the *Second Meditation* alone. But it is hard at first to see anything

2. In the second edition, 1642. The subtitle of the first edition, 1641, interestingly promises to prove the existence of God *and the immortality of the soul* – a doctrine never mentioned in the *Meditations*, but for which Descartes took the Real Distinction to lay the metaphysical foundations.

of importance in the argument for the Real Distinction which
was not available in the *Second Meditation*. It is interesting,
moreover, that the second quotation that I gave above from the
Recherche, while it corresponds in effect to the *Second Meditation*, is obviously a crude expression of the Real Distinction.
There is another passage, too, in which Descartes himself seems
to base the Real Distinction very directly on the *cogito*. Writing
to Colvius (14 November 1640), who (referring to the *Discourse*) had drawn his attention to the use of the *cogito* by
Augustine, Descartes replies that Augustine and himself do not
put the argument to the same use: 'I make use of it to make
known that this *I* that thinks is an immaterial substance, which
has nothing corporeal about it' (III 247, K 83–4). Yet, not only
in the reply to Hobbes, but repeatedly in his replies to other
objectors, Descartes insists that he does not determine that
'there is nothing corporeal in the soul', nor that mind and body
are really distinct, until the *Sixth Meditation* (*II Rep.:* VII 129,
HR2 30; *V Rep.:* VII 357, HR2 211; to Clerselier: IX–1 205,
HR2 133). Interpretation should certainly try to make sense of
this repeated insistence if it can.

What more is there in the final argument for the Real Distinction? Part of the answer, the lesser part, is that by the *Sixth
Meditation* he has a better concept of *body*: his body is referred
to there in terms of 'extension', a more refined conception of
matter which he has not reached at this point of the *Second
Meditation*, though he makes a step towards it later in the same
Meditation (see Chapter 8). This, as we shall see, plays some
role in the argument. More important than this, however, is the
role of God: certainly a further thing he has done by the *Sixth
Meditation* is to prove the existence of God (twice: see Chapter
5). But how is God involved? We must remove first a way in
which he is not involved. Since the Real Distinction is actually
explained by Descartes in terms of the idea of two things which
God at least could separate, it might be thought that this idea
will have no application until God has been shown to exist. But
this cannot be right. First, Descartes goes out of his way in the
passage quoted to say that it makes no difference 'by what
power this [separation] should come about, for one to consider

the things as different'. Second, and more basically, God's power cannot play an essential part in the notion of a real distinction, because of Descartes's other views about the power of God. Descartes believes that God's power is such that even logical truths and the *vérités éternelles* which appear to us as absolute necessities are the products of God's will (see letters to Mersenne, 15 April, 6 and 27 May 1630: I 145, 149–50, 152, K 11, 13–15; to Mesland, 2 May 1644: IV 118, K 151; to Arnauld, 29 July 1648: V 223–4, K 236; *VI Rep.*: VII 431–2, HR2 248). This being so, the fact that God could separate A from B could not in Descartes's view tell us anything about A and B at all, for God could create, if he so willed, anything apart from anything, including a triangle apart from three sides. By the criterion of what God can bring about, on Descartes's view of God's powers, everything is really distinct from itself. Hence if there is to be any content at all to saying of two things that they are really distinct, this must mean not just that God could separate them, but that we can conceive of what it would be like if God had separated them; which comes to no more than saying that we can conceive of them as separate, which is indeed what Descartes does in effect say, and this makes no reference to God at all.

It is thus misleading of Descartes to say (*IV Rep.*: VII 219, HR2 96–7) that the point turns on proving that God exists, 'that God who is capable of everything that I clearly and distinctly understand as possible' – an emphasis to be found also at the beginning of the crucial passage from the *Sixth Meditation*, given above (p. 104). The point should rather be about the validity of what he clearly and distinctly understands, and his insistence that the Real Distinction is proved only after the proof of God should stem rather from the idea that it is only after proving the existence of God that he can be sure that what he can conceive of as distinct will objectively be distinct; this being a particular application of a more general point which he appears sometimes to make, that only then can he be assured that what he can 'clearly and distinctly perceive to be so' will be true. He makes this point when he writes to Gibieuf (19 January 1642: III 478, K 125) that the objective truth cannot contradict our clear and distinct ideas about the Real Distinction 'otherwise God would be a deceiver, and we should not have any rule by which to assure ourselves of the truth'; and he states it plainly in a later passage of the *Fourth Replies* (*IV Rep.*: VII 226, HR2 101). This is the major part of what Descartes had in mind when he so insisted that the doctrine of the Real Distinction was to be found in the *Sixth*, and not in the *Second*, *Meditation*. But this answer involves a difficulty: since it is only by relying on the validity of clear and distinct ideas that he proves the existence of God, to rely on God for the validation of clear and distinct ideas seems to be arguing in a circle. This is the famous Cartesian Circle, of which he has repeatedly been accused.

Leaving aside the general difficulty of the Circle (which we shall examine in detail in Chapter 7), this answer does leave us with the problem of still finding virtually all the materials for the Real Distinction in the *Second Meditation*. For if what the *Sixth Meditation* adds is just the licence to proceed from subjective clarity to objective truth, then the basic *content* of these truths will have to have been provided already at the subjective level. It is not quite as simple as that, however, since, as we shall see, the step in this case is a rather special one, from subjective uncertainty *via* subjective clarity to objective possibility, which does change the conceptual content of what is being entertained. But that is all – the rest of the materials for the Real Distinction (apart from the refined conception of matter, mentioned earlier) has to be found in the *Second Meditation*.

What then are they? We may start with Descartes's doctrine that his essence is to be a thinking thing – a doctrine so closely linked to the doctrine that the mind is really distinct from the body that I shall, as I have already, discuss them together. This claim is tied up with the remarks, repeated almost verbally in the *Meditation* and in the *Recherche*, that thinking is the only thing that 'cannot be separated from himself'. The ideas are immediately and explicitly connected in the *Discourse*:

Then, examining with attention what I was, and seeing that I could pretend that I had no body, and that there was no world, nor any place in which I was; but that I could not pretend, for all that,

that I did not exist; and that, on the contrary, from the very fact that I could think of doubting the truth of other things, it followed very evidently and certainly that I existed; whereas, if I had only ceased to think, even if all the rest of what I had imagined were true, I should not have had any reason to believe that I existed; I knew from that that I was a substance whose whole essence or nature is only that of thinking, and which, in order to exist, has no need of any place, nor depends on any material thing. Thus this 'I', that is to say the soul by which I am what I am, is entirely distinct from the body ... (Part iv: VI 32–3, HR1 101)

Descartes's argument that his essence consists in thinking seems then just to be this: he can conceive of himself without a body but he cannot conceive of himself not thinking, so thinking is of his essence, but a body is not. In a sense, this is the argument, but the way in which it should be taken is not the most obvious way. The most obvious way of taking it would be to assimilate it to an argument such as the following: I cannot conceive of a plane triangle whose angles do not add up to two right angles, so this property is of the essence of a plane triangle. But the parallelism with that argument is specious, and if that is how Descartes's argument had to be taken, it would be invalid. If I say

(a) I cannot conceive of myself not thinking

this is true (if at all) in a way totally different from that in which

(b) I cannot conceive of a plane triangle whose angles do not add up to two right angles

is true. (b) is true in the sense that not merely can I not conceive of there being such a thing now, but I cannot conceive of there ever being such a thing; moreover, no one else could conceive of there being such a thing either: the thing is objectively and timelessly impossible, and that is why (b) is connected with a statement about the essence of a plane triangle, with what a plane triangle must necessarily be. But (a), if true at all, is true only in the sense that at this moment I cannot entertain the possibility that I am not thinking at this moment. It is not at all true that I cannot conceive of myself not thinking at another time, nor that others, if they can conceive of me at all, could not conceive of me as not thinking. It is not even true that I cannot entertain the idea that I *might not have been* thinking at this moment. But these further things would be necessary if (a) were to ground a statement of essence in a way parallel to (b).

There is a subtler error that might come into the argument at this point. In saying that one can entertain the idea of one's not thinking at another time, or the idea that one might not have been thinking now, one is implicitly taking a view of oneself from what I called in the last chapter the third-personal perspective – just as much as one explicitly does in invoking others' conception of oneself. If one sticks totally to the first-personal perspective, or what I called earlier the 'standpoint of consciousness', these possibilities evaporate. From that point of view, the only question about what a certain possibility would consist in is what it would be like *for me*, i.e. how it would seem to (my) consciousness, and in that sense the possibility of my not thinking would consist of nothing at all. But this consideration yields nothing about the essence of anything in Descartes's sense (nor, one may suppose, in any other). The essential property he arrives at is the property of an objective thing in the world – a thing to which, as I put it earlier, a name could in principle be given from the third-personal perspective; and that must allow one, equally, to entertain possibilities about it from that perspective. Either the *I* can be considered from the third-personal perspective, or it cannot. If it cannot, it is not a thing with an essence; if it can, the *cogito* cannot show, on the lines of the present argument, that its essence consists in thinking.

A further consideration shows that this line of argument cannot be what Descartes wants. (a) derives any force it has merely from a version of the *cogito*, that 'I am not thinking' is not something that I can truly think. But Descartes himself points out in the *Second Meditation*, as we saw in the last chapter, that 'I do not exist' is not something that I can truly think, either. (From the standpoint of consciousness again, my non-existence is not something *for me* – a consideration which encourages some not to believe in the possibility of their own death.) But if the fact that I cannot truly think 'I am not thinking' means that I cannot conceive of myself not thinking, and this in its turn means that my essence is to think; then the fact that I cannot truly think 'I do not exist' means that I cannot conceive of myself not existing, and this in its turn means that my essence is to exist. But Descartes believes that there is only one being whose essence is to exist, or whose essence is existence, and this is God (*V Med.*: see pp. 153ff.). Hence if his argument is as suggested, he could equally well prove that he was God. This is a conclusion he resisted.

In every way, the mere truth of (a), if it is true at all, is inadequate to prove the statement about essence. Most generally of all, since it rests only on the *cogito*, whose principle is that one cannot think without existing, it is not obvious how it could be converted to prove that it was an essential property of mine to think, for this involves saying that I cannot exist without thinking. Descartes does eventually want to say this, and he indeed connects it with the doctrine of essence[3]; but he cannot get it from these premisses. To found the argument for his essence on assimilating (a) and (b) is to confound the peculiar 'necessity' of 'I am thinking', which is true whenever I think it, with the absolute necessity of geometrical propositions which are true whether anyone thinks them or not; but this is a distinction to which Descartes was certainly alive, and which (as we have just seen) he needs if he is not to prove that he is God. Fortunately we do not have to ascribe this invalid line of argument to Descartes.

To see how he can be better interpreted, we should turn now to the very closely related argument for the Real Distinction. At first glance, the basic argument for this seems to involve a fallacy which is even grosser. The argument, in the *Second Meditation*, seems to come to this: I cannot doubt that I (as a mind) exist, but I can doubt that my body exists, therefore I (as a mind) and my body are really distinct. It is presented baldly like

3. See the letter to Gibieuf cited above, p. 107: III 478, K 125; also *IV Rep.*: VII 246, HR2 115, where Descartes makes it clear that we do not have to be conscious of all the mind's powers or potentialities – though mind is consciousness, not all properties of mind have to be properties *for* consciousness. For some bluff criticism of Descartes's position, see Locke *Essay* II. 1. 10 ff.: 'The soul thinks not always; for this wants proofs.'

this in the passage from the *Recherche* quoted above (p. 104). This uncomfortably resembles a fallacy recognized by Stoic logicians, which came to be known as the *larvatus* or 'masked man' fallacy[4]: I do not know the identity of this masked man; I do know the identity of my father; therefore this masked man is not my father.

This is in effect one of the objections brought against Descartes's argument by Arnauld in the course of his set of *Objections* to the *Meditations* – the most cogent and forcefully argued that Descartes received. Arnauld cites (*IV Obj.*: VII 201–2, HR2 83) the case of a man confronted with a geometrical figure, a triangle inscribed in a semi-circle: such a man might be certain that the triangle was a right-angled triangle, but uncertain that the square on the diameter was equal to the sum of the squares on the other two sides – yet this would in no way go to show that its being a right-angled triangle, and these relations holding, were 'really distinct' properties, having no necessary connection with one another. That is to say, one cannot infer from one's subjective state of certainty and uncertainty about two propositions, to the objective connection or lack of connection between them; but it is just such an inference that Descartes seems to be making about himself and his body, and which gives his argument its embarrassing resemblance to the masked man fallacy.

But Descartes does not suppose that the inference can be made from any arbitrary state of subjective uncertainty. To arrive at the Real Distinction, it is necessary first that I can remain uncertain about the existence of my body while certain of my existence as a thinking thing, *however carefully and clear-headedly I consider the situation*: that is to say, in Descartes's terminology, that I can clearly and distinctly conceive of myself existing without a body. We may perhaps be sceptical about whether he can perform this feat, but Descartes certainly supposes that he can: though assured of his own existence in the *cogito*, he supposes that the most careful scrutiny

4. See P. T. Geach, *God and the Soul* (London, 1969), p. 8. Geach ascribes the fallacy to Descartes.

will not reveal anything in the existence so disclosed which implies that he must have a body.

In the course of his reply to Arnauld, in which he distinguishes several points of difference between his argument and the geometrical example, he considers (*IV Rep.*: VII 220, HR2 97) how his argument is related to something else he had said, of which Arnauld had reminded him (*IV Obj.*: VII 200, HR2 82, referring to *I Rep.*: VII 120–2, HR2 22):

A real distinction cannot be inferred from the fact that one thing is conceived apart from another by means of an abstraction of the intellect which is considering the thing inadequately, but solely from the fact that each thing is understood apart from the other completely or as a complete thing.

Descartes denies that his conception of the *I* is the product of such an abstraction. He indeed says that he is not claiming, in the argument for the Real Distinction, adequate knowledge of himself, since adequate knowledge of a thing, strictly speaking, would imply knowledge of all its properties, which is in no way to be expected. But there is one sense in which his knowledge can be considered complete – it is knowledge *of a complete thing*: and a similar point is made in a letter to Gibieuf referred to above (19 January 1642: III 474 ff., K 123 ff.).

Kenny (*Descartes,* pp. 86ff.) pertinaciously pursues Descartes through a large number of his formulations with a charge of confusion on this point, arguing that, one way or another, he moved from the claim 'I do not know that there is a corporeal element in the *I*' to the claim 'I know that there is no corporeal element in the *I*'. But the question is not so much of a confusion or an illicit inference, as of a large claim by Descartes about what he can intuitively grasp. As the letter to Gibieuf makes clear, his idea is that he has a conception of himself as a thinking thing which does not presuppose any bodily thing in order to exist, and his conception is, in that sense, the conception of a complete thing.[5] If the conception of

5. For the generalization of this to the notion of *substance*, see below, p. 124 ff.

himself as a thinking thing did really presuppose body, then he would be able to detect this by careful mental inspection, since he equally has the idea of body (we can see here how the refined idea of body, attained only later in the *Meditations*, also plays a part). To the objection that there must be many consequences of his conceptions which he is not aware of, Descartes will agree, admitting also that they may involve ideas he does not have; but that is irrelevant, for in the present matter of determining the completeness of the thinking thing *vis à vis* body, he has all the relevant ideas. The objector may reply in turn that even if this is conceded, it does not avoid the difficulty, which rests rather just on the formal point that in saying that *no* consequence or presupposition of his conception of a thinking thing involves body, he is claiming a universal negative proposition, which is a rash thing for a systematic doubter to do. But if this is all that the objector has to offer, Descartes can well reply that in order for his thought to advance *at all*, he has to make at each stage an assumption of this form, namely, that no consequence of his thoughts is of the form *P and not-P*. The objection seems then just to come down to saying that Descartes may be wrong, which is less than compelling. However, Descartes's resistance to the objection has involved him in a strong claim, that his ideas of thought and of body are all the relevant ideas that bear on this matter: this is an assumption, near the heart of his procedure, which we shall come back to later in this chapter.

Descartes starts, then, with subjective uncertainty: he doubts whether he has a body, while certain that he exists as a thinking thing. The close inspection of the mind converts this into a subjective certainty: he can remain uncertain of the body however hard he thinks about himself, and this is because he has a clear and distinct conception of himself as a thinking thing which presupposes or implies no bodily property. There still remains a step to be taken from this to objective possibility. This is the step which Descartes thinks cannot be provided until the objective validity of clear and distinct ideas has been guaranteed, with the help (to a degree, and in a way, still to be determined) of God's benevolence. The objective possibility is: granted that my mind exists, it is still possible that my body should not, or (what comes to the same thing) it is a possible state of affairs that I should exist as a mind and that no body of mine should exist.

But even if we grant this step, have we arrived at the right place? Have we the materials for showing that mind and body are, in the relevant sense, really distinct? It depends, of course, on what that sense is. We have already seen that Descartes's favourite explanation of the notion, in terms of God's powers, is quite useless. We shall get a better view of what is involved if we read back from Descartes's completed views, from which we shall learn that mind and body are two totally different kinds of thing which, though they can be in mortal life closely linked with each other (we shall come to Descartes's views on this link in Chapter 10), cannot under any circumstances be the same thing. If X and Y are really distinct in Descartes's sense, then at least it follows that they are not the same thing, they are non-identical (cf. to Elizabeth, 28 June 1643: III 693, K 142–3). Indeed, Descartes's conclusion seems to be stronger than that: that they are necessarily non-identical, and could not under any circumstances be identical.

In order to reconstruct Descartes's argument at this point, and to save it from the charges of quite simple invalidity which have often been brought against it, we need to use an ancient distinction which has recently returned to fashion in philosophy, concerning the modal notions necessity and possibility. The distinction is between what are called in the traditional terminology *de dicto* modalities, which are properties of propositions or sentences, and *de re* modalities, necessities and possibilities which belong to a thing independently of how the thing happens to be picked out or characterized.

Suppose we say, opening the box: 'the animal in the box might have been a spider'. That may well express a genuine possibility, if it is taken, *de dicto*, as saying (in effect) that the expression 'the animal in the box' might have truly applied to a spider – that is to say, that some spider might have been in the box. But if we use the expression 'the animal in the box' just to pick out the animal that is actually in the box, and say of *that* animal that *it* might have been a spider, then it is far from clear, granted that animal is some other sort of creature, that what we say could be true. Suppose it is a lion. The idea that that very lion might have been a spider seems to express no genuine possibility at all; if there is no such possibility, then it may be plausible, further, to claim that anything which is in fact a lion is (*de re*) necessarily a lion. This is of course a very different thing from another *de dicto* item, the triviality that 'a lion is a lion' is a necessary statement. That says merely that necessarily, if anything is a lion, it is a lion, and that type of necessity holds with regard to any property at all: it is just as true that necessarily, if anything is blue, it is blue. The suggestion with regard to the property of being a lion would be that if anything is a lion, it is *necessarily a lio*n, and could not exist without being one; whereas of most blue things, and perhaps of all, it is true that they could exist without being blue, and so are not *necessarily blue*.[6]

It is the material of *de re* modalities that is needed to reconstruct Descartes's argument. In doing this, we must recall the other argument that we left hanging, for the conclusion that his essence is to be a thinking thing – all we have done for that so far is to discover an invalid version of it, not replace that with a valid version. If we allow Descartes the notion of a *de re* essential property – the notion of a property which expresses a thing's nature, and which the thing necessarily has however that thing is verbally picked out; if, further, he is given the premiss that the *I* proved to exist in the *cogito* is a thing which has some essential property; then we can reach the Real Distinction, and the conclusion that thinking is the essential property of the *I*, in one simple argument.

(1) I have some essential property.
(2) Any property which I might lack is not my essential property.

(2) follows immediately from the definition of an essential

6. The example is only for illustration. Descartes himself, as I understand him, did not think that *being a lion* or any other such property constituted a necessary attribute; for him, the only necessary attributes were thought and extension. See below, p. 219.

property; my essential property is a property which I necessarily possess, which I cannot exist without (cf. *IV Rep.*: VII 219, HR2 97). The sense of 'I might lack' here relates, of course, to an objective possibility, arrived at, as we have seen, through the objective validity of clear and distinct conceptions: it does not just mean 'what, for all I know, I lack'.

(3) I might lack every property except thought.

(3) is the supposed result of the thought-experiment of the *Second Meditation*, converted into an objective possibility. Hence,

(4) Thought is my essential property.

In addition, I have a pure conception of a body, and hence of *my* body; a conception first glimpsed in the latter part of the *Second Meditation*, developed in the *Sixth Meditation*, and equally converted into an objective notion: 'I have a distinct idea of the body as a thing that is extended and does not think . . .' (VII 78, HR1 190; quoted above, p. 104). Taking 'my body' to mean any body I may turn out to have, we can say at least

(5A) Thought is not the essential property of my body;

we can note, but shall not immediately use, the stronger claim

(5B) It is a necessary consequence of the essential property of my body that my body does not think.

(4) and (5A) together say that I have a property which my body lacks, namely that of *being essentially a thinking thing*. Here we see particularly clearly the importance of taking these necessities *de re*: '. . . necessarily a thinking thing' has to be taken as a predicate of the form '*Fx*'. So, by the basic logic of identity, the so-called 'non-identity of discernibles', we get

(6A) I am not identical with my body;

but presumably, if (4) and (5A) are true, they are necessarily true (thought could never be my body's essential property): so,

(6B) I am necessarily not identical with my body

which expresses the Real Distinction in its strongest form.

The implications of the Real Distinction for the relations of
mind and body we shall take up in Chapter 10. There are several questions raised immediately by the argument which we
should consider here. Leaving aside the transition from subjective clarity to objective possibility, even the subjective aspect
of the matter, the thought-experiment which lies behind (3),
may be found suspect. It emerges, of course, from the Doubt,
and as we should expect from that, 'I might not have a body' is
meant by Descartes as saying 'I might not have a body, even
though everything seems as it does' – i.e., even though it seems
to him, in all sorts of normal ways, that he does have a body.
One may object to that; but if one does, and finds doubt at that
level senseless or unacceptable, it is important that something
weaker will do for the argument to the Real Distinction in its
present reconstruction. Since it rests on the notion of an essential property, all that is necessary for (3) is that there should be
some possible circumstances (not necessarily the present ones)
in which I could exist without a body and without any other
property except thought. If I could exist disembodied at all,
with things perhaps seeming very different from the way they
seem now, the argument for the Real Distinction would still, if
one grants the rest, go through; that possibility by itself would
be enough to show that thought is my essential property, if I
have an essential property at all.[7]

But even if I can 'think away' my body, is it true that thought
is the only thing that I cannot 'think away'? Here we encounter
a new version of a difficulty that came up before with the invalid version of the argument to essence. If thought is a
property which, in an appropriate sense, I cannot lack, then
equally so, it seems, is existence itself: if a *de re* necessary
property of A is a property of A which it must have if it exists,
then existence is certainly such a property. It may be answered
that existence is not a property – but not by Descartes, who
thought that it was (*Princ.* i 56; and see below on the Onto-

7. I have argued elsewhere ('Are Persons Bodies?', in *Problems of the
Self* (Cambridge, 1973): see pp. 70–73), without using the notion of an
essential property, that the possibility of *becoming* disembodied, at any rate,
would imply a Cartesian account of persons.

logical Argument, pp. 154 ff.). We can say, rather, that existence will not do for the essence of the *I*, because the notion of an essence for Descartes is that which constitutes the nature of a thing, such that to come to know its nature is to know what it is; and existence in itself could give us no such knowledge (cf. *Princ.* i 42–3).

However, this way of putting it does not adequately express Descartes's position. It suggests that existence, unlike others among a thing's necessary properties, does not count as part of its essence because it is not informative or distinctive enough. But existence is not a property which, for Descartes, is in every case debarred from belonging to the essence of something: it belongs to the essence of God, and of God alone. The point is that it does not belong to the essence of any created or contingent thing. Now this is a point that Descartes is prepared to put also in the form of saying that existence is not a necessary property of anything except God (cf. Princ. i 15). When he says this, he does not of course mean by 'necessary property' merely what we have been taking it to mean, namely a property which a thing must have if it exists: in that sense, existence is trivially a necessary property of everything. He means a property *entailed by a thing's essence*: which (as we shall see when we come to discuss the Ontological Argument) supposedly has the much stronger consequence in the case of God's existence, that he is a *necessary existent*, i.e. that he would exist whatever else was the case.

In fact, if we say that in our very weak sense existence is a necessary property of everything, we shall not contradict anything that Descartes asserts: his denial attaches to a much stronger sense. However, we shall avoid confusion and be nearer to Cartesian usage if we take the term 'essence' as basic. We should not, to understand Descartes, define 'essence' as a particularly informative and distinctive sub-set of a thing's necessary properties; rather, a thing's necessary properties are to be understood as its essence and properties entailed by its essence. *Essence*, for Descartes, is the primary notion.

I have taken it also as the primary notion in the reconstruction of the argument for the Real Distinction, by making the first premiss of the argument the claim that the *I* must have some essential property. However, this may seem too close to the required conclusion to be illuminating. Stephen Schiffer has said of it, in an instructive analysis of Descartes's argument,[8] 'to suppose that such an assumption is being made should be for us a solution of last resort'. From the point of view of historical understanding, it must be said, it is far from clear why this should be a last resort; it may well be the case that the greatest measure of overall interpretative insight is given by a reconstruction in which this proposition indeed figures as an assumption. However, taking the argument just by itself, it can readily be granted that if a more interesting inference can be based on more basic premisses which Descartes would have accepted, this will be a significant result. Schiffer's own reconstruction, which I shall not try to quote in full, takes as a premiss that (leaving aside existence and duration) thought and extension (Descartes's refined conception of body) are the only two candidates for being a property of the *I* at all. The argument then proceeds by using intuitions which Descartes could readily have accepted, to the effect that nothing could change from merely thinking to being extended, for 'it' would then be a different thing; and that any 'one' thing which possessed both thought and extension would have to be two things.

But the first of these intuitions comes within an inch of claiming already that thought is an essential attribute, while the second is straightforwardly equivalent to the Real Distinction. The effect of Schiffer's approach is not, then, to produce a longer, more interesting, or less question-begging argument. It is rather to suggest that there is not much of an argument at all, and that the Real Distinction arises almost directly from a primary intuition of the two basic attributes, thought and extension, between which everything is divided and in terms of which everything is to be explained.

There is much to be said for this point of view. The intuition of the dualism is primary, and Descartes does not so much arrive at it by the progress back from the Doubt, as reconstruct the

8. 'Descartes on his Essence', *Philosophical Review* LXXXV (1976), 21–43.

world in terms of it. He does this gradually, however, and there is something to be said, if one is going to formulate an argument for the Real Distinction, for choosing the premiss (1) which I have chosen; it is a traditional formulation, which, as Descartes uses it, anticipates but does not yet embody the developed dualism, and that is a way in which Descartes characteristically expressed his new view of the world, certainly to his objectors and in some part – necessarily – to himself. In this reconstruction, the question-begging anticipations of the dualistic conclusions are not, however, avoided – they are at work in shaping the premisses. We have already seen one sign of this in the assumptions that go into interpreting the thought-experiment that lies behind (3), to the effect that Descartes has all the relevant ideas.

Let us now go back to the detail of the argument on p. 117. There, we moved from (6A) to the required conclusion (6B) by using the idea that if thought is not the body's essential attribute, it never could be. This seems sound enough. It might be wondered, however, whether there might not be a direct step from (6A) to (6B). The direct inference of (6B) from (6A) would rely on a disputable principle of modal logic:

(N) If A is non-identical with B, then A is necessarily non-identical with B.

Let us assume (N). Even if we do, it is at least doubtful that Descartes is in a position to apply it, and more than doubtful that even if he does, it will give him what he needs. If (N) is valid, it is so only if the expressions represented by 'A' and 'B' are understood *purely referentially*, just as picking out the item in question.[9] Thus if we infer from

9. Not a great deal turns for the present argument on this particular formulation of the conditions for applying (N); there exists a variety of proposals for analysing the undoubted ambiguity of sentences such as 'Harold Wilson was necessarily not the winner of the British General Election of 1970'. For detailed discussion of some disputed issues, see David Wiggins, 'The *de re* "must": a Note on the Logical Form of Essentialist Claims', in Evans and McDowell, eds., *Truth and Meaning: Essays in Semantics* (Oxford, 1976). – The point of the present argument is that Descartes cannot avoid invoking an essential property of any body he may have.

Harold Wilson was not the winner of the British General Election of 1970

to

Harold Wilson was necessarily not the winner of the British General Election of 1970

this will be valid only if 'the winner of the British General Election of 1970' is understood purely referentially, merely as a way of leading us to a particular person, i.e. Edward Heath: that *he* should be not only non-identical with Wilson, but necessarily so, is hardly surprising (what would the world have had to be like for those two persons to be one and the same person?). What would be surprising, and cannot follow, is that Wilson should necessarily have the property of having lost the Election of 1970.

If (N) is to be validly applied to (6A), then 'my body' has to be taken purely referentially, just as a way of picking out a certain item. But it is far from clear that Descartes is yet in any position to use that expression in that way. He has not yet, when conducting the argument of the Real Distinction, assured himself that he has a body: *a fortiori*, he has no idea *what* item it is, if any, which is his body. He is thus in no position to fix the reference of 'my body', as he would need to, if he were to use the expression purely to refer to or pick out a certain item.

More radically, there is a difficulty about what exactly the item would be. The most natural supposition would be that the item was a particular piece of matter. But this certainly will not give Descartes what he needs. Suppose that the reference is to a particular piece of matter, and that we christen this piece with the proper name '*M*'. Then what will have been shown is that Descartes, as a thinking thing, is not and could not be identical with *M*. But this does not exclude his being identical, at some other time, with some other piece of matter *MM*, which has so far not been referred to; and *MM* might at that time play the role of being Descartes's body – it is not necessary, and indeed not even true, that one and the same parcel of matter should at all times constitute Descartes's body. Hence it is compatible with the conclusion of the argument, as now conducted, that

Descartes should at some time be identical with some matter which at that time was his body. Clearly that is not compatible with the doctrine of the Real Distinction as Descartes understood it.

It may be said that what this shows is that the 'pure' reference of 'my body' cannot after all be to a piece of matter: it must be to a *body*, and if the identity of a body can differ from the identity of a piece of matter (as the previous argument assumes), then the reference will follow the identity of the body. But this will not help either. For nothing that Descartes believes at this stage (or, come to that, later) excludes the possibility that he might have at different times what were, by any physically based criteria at all,[10] two different bodies, as in reincarnation; and if that is possible, the same type of objection arises again.

What these arguments show is that if the Real Distinction is to be proved with the required generality, the expression 'my body' in (6A) and (6B) must be taken variably, to mean 'whatever it is that is my body' (this is, roughly, how the expression was introduced into the argument in the first place). But if this is so, it cannot be used in the purely referential way which is necessary in order to get, if one can get at all, from (6A) to (6B) via (N). The argument, as we have it so far, has this feature: while it proves that I, as a thinking thing, can never be my body, it does not prove that my body can never think. The body's essence is, indeed, not that of thinking; but must that exclude the possibility that it might also, though not essentially, think? Descartes does exclude that: he does so by relying on the strong premiss (5B), which in our reconstruction we have not so far used. (Once introduced, it will of course give us, together with (4), a very simple route to (6B).) The essence of body being, for Descartes, extension (for the sense of this, see Chapter 8), no

10. This reservation is necessary because Descartes claimed (to Mesland, 9 February 1645: IV 166, K 157) that the criterion of identity for a human body consists in its being *the body united to a particular soul*: by ‚this, 'I always have the same body' will be a necessary truth. But *this* conception cannot be invoked in setting up the argument for the Real Distinction, since it presupposes that we understand already the identity of the immaterial soul, a consequence of the Real Distinction.

body can also think; conversely, the *I*, whose essence is to think, can never, even non-essentially, be extended. No property which essentially belongs to one thing can non-essentially belong to another. This follows at once in Descartes's system, because he so uses the notion of an essential attribute that all other properties of a thing with a given essential attribute must be *modes* of that attribute (*Princ.* i 53, 56). Matter or body being essentially extended, all other properties of matter are ways of being extended; similarly with the essential attribute of thought, which is the only other essential attribute – any other property of a thinking thing must be a mode of thought. So the conclusions that no extended thing can also think, and that no thinking thing can also be extended, follow immediately – but so immediately as to cast doubt on the premisses.

Finally in this chapter we must consider Descartes's claim that he, the thinking thing, is a *substance*. Attributes and their modes do not exist by themselves; they have to belong to substances. Descartes indeed takes the Real Distinction to distinguish two different substances (*Princ.* i 60), and regards the thinking thing whose essential attribute is thought as being one substance, a conclusion which is one of the most characteristic expressions of his dualism. The terminology of substance is not just an archaism in Descartes's system; the peculiar way in which he uses it embodies some of his most basic beliefs.

He explains *substance* in the *Principles* as follows:

By substance we can understand nothing else but a thing which so exists that it needs nothing else in order to exist. And in fact, as a substance which needs absolutely nothing else, only one can be so understood, namely God. All other things we perceive can exist only with the help of God's concurrence. So the term *substance* does not apply to God and to all other things 'univocally', as they say in the schools; that is to say, no meaning of that term can be distinctly understood which is common to God and his creatures. (i 51)

But corporeal substance, and created mind or thinking substance, can be understood under this common concept, that they are things which need only the concurrence of God in order to exist ... (i 52).

The idea that a substance can exist by itself without the help of any other substance is made central to the explanation of the Real Distinction in the *Reply* to Arnauld (*IV Rep.*: VII 226, HR2 101). Thus any created substance can in principle exist without dependence on any other created substance. While this is an important part of the notion of substance, it of course cannot serve by itself as a definition or explication of the notion, since it would be uninformatively circular. To get beyond this, we need to be introduced to the whole system of ideas substance–attribute–mode; and here the thought is that there is an asymmetry in the relations between substance and attribute, and again between attribute and mode. Attributes depend on substance:

... when we perceive that any attribute is present, we conclude that some existing thing or substance to which it can be attributed must be present also (*Princ.* i 52)

(Compare here also the formal exposition of Descartes's system which he attached to the *II Rep.*, def. V: VII 161, HR2 53.) But there is a problem in making the required asymmetry clear. If attributes cannot exist without substances, it is equally true that a substance cannot exist without an attribute, and this point is made by Descartes himself, who emphasizes that the distinction between substance and attribute is only a 'distinction of reason', and that we should not suppose that we can form any idea of substance divested of attributes (*Princ.* i 62–3; with reference to corporeal substance, ii 9). A similar point comes up with attribute and mode. A mode presupposes its attribute, but equally an attribute which is really present implies the presence of a mode – a thing cannot be extended without being extended in one way rather than another.

In the case of attributes and modes, the appropriate asymmetry seems to be this: to specify a given mode is to specify implicitly the particular attribute of which it is a mode – to be square is to be *extended* squarely; whereas to specify a given attribute is to imply only a range or disjunction of modes (in the case of extension, at least, an infinitely large one), and not as yet any particular mode. Can this account be extended to the relations of substance and attribute? If we cast it in terms of *particular* substances, the asymmetry seems to hold the wrong way round. One can specify clearly a given attribute, say that of thought, without specifying any particular thinking substance; this is what someone would do who said merely that *there was some thinking thing*. But it is not possible, as Descartes insists, to specify a particular substance without specifying its attribute; I could not possibly know what thing I was talking or thinking about, unless I knew either that it was a thinking thing or that it was an extended thing. In search of an asymmetry, we have to retreat, it seems, from the level of identifying or specifying particular substances, to that of the notion of substance in general. Perhaps the best that can be said here is that we have the very general notion of 'the subject of certain acts', as he puts it in the *Third Replies* (VII 176, HR2 64), and this notion is common to, and less specific than, the ideas of a thing that performs acts of thought, or, again, of a thing that performs physical acts; so we can infer validly from 'thought is exemplified' to 'something thinks', but from 'something acts' (i.e., there is some substance or other) we cannot determinately infer either 'something is extended' or 'something is thinking'. This not very satisfactory account of the matter has the weakness of not revealing at all any difference between the idea of substance as applied to God, and as applied to created things, a difference which we have already found Descartes emphasizing. That difference, however, has to do with the *causal* dependence of substances on one another, which, although it is an important aspect of the concept of substance, cannot be used to characterize the relations which hold in the series substance–accident–mode, since there is no room for the idea of a causal dependence of attribute on substance, or of mode on attribute.

The matter of the identification of a *particular* substance is a different question, and one that runs deep into Descartes's thought. Here there is a vitally important difference between the two attributes of thought and extension, a difference which Descartes's terminology sometimes serves to conceal. There seems to be a parallel between them so long as we confine ourselves to the level of universals or general terms. We can draw up a table of terms or concepts roughly as follows:

(I) SUBSTANCE: Thing which acts in the way specified as ...
(II) ATTRIBUTE: Thinking   Extended
(III) MODE: Doubting, willing, etc.   Square, revolving, etc.

This set of distinctions at the level of concepts is what Descartes appears to have in mind in, for instance, the *Third Replies*; and *Princ.* i 63–4 might seem equally to remain at this level. But Descartes explained to Arnauld (29 July 1648: V 221, K 235) that he did not just mean this, and that indeed the passage in the *Principles* was designed to make this clear:

... By *thought*, then, I do not understand some universal which includes all the modes of thought, but a particular nature which receives all these modes, just as extension is a nature which receives all shapes.

I take it that in this passage Descartes is not denying that there *is* a general concept of thought, but is rather saying what has to be in the world if there is anything that that concept applies to. His view seems to be that what has to exist is a thing of a certain kind or nature which, in 'receiving' the various modes, is the seat of a certain class of *events* – acts of understanding, volitions and so forth. Some of these events, moreover, are expressions of, or, again, causes of, more permanent modifications – the dispositions or states of the mind. Regarded as concretely realized, two different mental events, each of the same type, can be considered as two different modes – they are in a recognizable sense two different modifications of the concretely realized attribute of thought. Viewed in this way, what appear at level III on the mental side are, among other things, particular mental events. What corresponds to this at level III on the material side, similarly viewed, are various distinct modifications of extension or space: for instance, two distinct cubes. But here we see a basic asymmetry between the mental and the material sides. In the non-relativistic physical space which Descartes of course has in mind, every spatial object bears some determinate spatial relation to every other spatial object. All of them, and the spaces between them, can thus be regarded as modifications of the concretely realized extension of *one* extended thing or substance – physical space itself; whereas on the mental side, the events at level III have mental relations to one another only if they are modifications of one mind, and there are irreducibly many distinct minds. Plurality genuinely occurs on the mental side at level I; while on the material side, for Descartes, everyday references to a plurality of material substances really relate to level III, and are a way of speaking of what, more basically regarded, are modes of what, at level I, is just one extended substance, the whole physical universe.

Some such asymmetry between mind and matter is implicit in the mere spatial continuity of non-relativistic space, as contrasted with the lack of any analogous mental continuity between minds. But the asymmetry is much emphasized, and the view that there is, strictly speaking, only one extended thing is more deeply embedded in Descartes's system, by the peculiar view that he takes of matter, which strongly assimilates it to physical space. As we shall see in greater detail in Chapters 8 and 9, Descartes denies the possibility of a vacuum and regards the material universe as an infinite homogeneous fluid, in which different 'material objects' are distinguished from one another only by differential motions in the fluid (*Princ.* ii 23). The identity and separation of particular material objects can thus be seen as in a certain measure conventional relative to what is really there (cf. the letter to Mesland quoted earlier (IV 164–5, K 156–7); the discussion is illuminating, though one should bear in mind that the recipient was a Jesuit and the subject is transubstantiation).

The identity and separateness of minds, however, is in no way conventional and is objectively there, at level I. But how is it given to us? What conception can we form of this irreducible plurality of purely thinking things? When one puts together the isolation of an existent *I* through the *cogito*; the assumption that it must have some essential property; the conclusion that

that property is thought; and the argument that leads to the Real Distinction: one idea can be seen as central to Descartes's conception, an idea that we saw reason for doubting in the last chapter – that reflection on the first-personal point of view, the stand-point of consciousness, is *in itself* enough to provide the basis for the coherent individuation of items which can be basically characterized from the third-personal, objective, point of view.

Chapter 5

GOD

At the start of the *Third Meditation*, Descartes sums up the little that he so far knows: that he is a conscious being, that is

a being that doubts, asserts, denies, knows a few things, is ignorant of many, is willing or unwilling, and that has imagination and sense; for, as I remarked before, even if the things that I sense and imagine are perhaps nothing at all apart from me, I am nevertheless certain that these modes of thought [or consciousness] that I call sensation and imagination certainly exist in me, just as modes of thought. (VII 34, HR1 157)

In order to extend his knowledge further, he says, he will now look further into himself; and it is, of course, essential that it should be into himself he should look, that anything else that he can discover should be unravelled from the mental existence of which alone he is, at this stage, certain.[1]

The natural step for him to take next, he decides, is to classify his various types of thought, and to ask which of them are capable of being true or false. First, he observes that in his mind there are certain ideas, as when he thinks of 'a man, a chimera, the sky, an angel, or God'. These ideas he compares to 'pictures of objects', but this comparison is not to be taken literally – it is not at all Descartes's view that ideas are necessarily pictorial images. His formal definition of an 'idea', given in the *Second Replies*, is entirely general. Indeed, as he there points out (*II Rep.*, def. II: VII 160, HR2 52), in a certain sense in his view images are not ideas at all. That particular doctrine, however, is not of immediate relevance; what matters is, first, that ideas are at least not necessarily images, and second, that an idea by itself does not contain either truth or falsehood. To have an idea in one's mind is just to think of something, and just to think of

1. The account in the next pages is drawn largely from the *Third Meditation*, and I shall not give continual page-references to it. References will be given to passages from other writings.

something does not involve any claim that can be either true or false. Descartes does later in the *Third Meditation* say that there is a certain sense in which ideas can be said to be 'materially false', when 'they represent what is nothing as though it were something': we have an idea of *cold*, for example, which represents it as a positive quality of objects, when it may in fact be merely a privation of heat. However, this is no real qualification of the doctrine that ideas are not intrinsically true or false, since for the mind to be involved in any actual false-hood on the strength of one of these ideas it must do more than merely have the idea – it must move on to an assertion or judgement that things are in fact as this idea represents them.[2]

Every thought or state of consciousness, for Descartes, in-volves an idea. But some states of mind are evidently more than merely having an idea, or thinking of something – some further attitude or action of the mind is added. Thus in willing, fearing, approving and denying, more is involved than the mere object of thought: something is done towards this object. Of the thoughts that involve such attitudes in addition to an idea, 'some are called volitions or affections, and others judgements'. Now volitions and affections cannot be true or false, though they can be morally good or bad, or (differently) misguided or baseless. These last terms are not Descartes's; I use them to stand for the possibility, which he correctly recognizes, that a fear, for instance, may lack a real object – it may be a fear of something that does not in fact exist. Descartes says that not even in this latter sort of case can an affection or volition be regarded as false. In this, his view is no doubt sensible, but it must be said that the reason he gives for it is an extremely poor one: 'although I may desire evil things, or even things that never existed, it is none the less true that I desire them'. This does not prove that desires for the non-existent are not false, but only that they are not non-existent. The argument that Descartes offers here could just as well be used to show that beliefs or judgements could not be false, either, since if I believe what is

2. Descartes's theory of judgement in fact demands a conception of 'ideas' rather broader than the one presented here, but this does not affect the principle of the argument. See below, p. 182.

not the case, it is none the less true that I believe it. Descartes, of course, does not draw this mistaken conclusion: it is precisely judgements, when to an idea I 'add' affirmation or denial, that he recognizes as possibly being true or false. The principal occasion of falsehood is when I affirm that an idea which I have corresponds to something outside itself, that is to say, when I judge that something really exists 'conformable' to some idea that I have. Some such judgements, of course, he hopes will eventually turn out to be true; at the moment, he is in no position to know which, if any, may do so.

Descartes now turns to consider the possible sorts of *origin* that these ideas in his mind may have; and he distinguishes three possibilities. An idea might be *innate*, and have existed in his mind for as long as his mind has existed (however long that may be: of this he has at present no conception). Or it might be *adventitious*, and have arisen in his mind from some external agency. Or, lastly, it might be *fictitious*, the product of the mind's own invention, as he naturally tends to suppose ideas of the chimera and other such monsters may be, formed by the putting together of other ideas. Descartes seems to regard this division as exhaustive of the possibilities. He is careful to make the point, however, that he is not at this stage in a position to assign any particular ideas to one class rather than another, nor to assert that none of the classes is empty; it may turn out that all his ideas are adventitious, or all innate, or all fictitious (though if being fictitious essentially involves being put together from other ideas, not all can be fictitious). There is no certain sign by which an idea can straight off be assigned to one class rather than another. In particular, it is no certain sign that an idea is adventitious that it comes into consciousness involuntarily; for, as Descartes puts it, there may exist some faculty in his mind, as yet unknown to him, which gives rise to such ideas without his desiring them. Hence, although the involuntariness of those ideas which he calls *sensations* or *senseperceptions* naturally tends to make him believe that they are caused in him by objects outside himself, this tendency must be resisted, for this belief does not stand up to the rigorous tests of clearness and distinctness. It is merely a natural tendency, not an illumination of the natural light. His reservations on this score are increased when he reflects that he has certain ideas which he is tempted to regard as adventitious, but which, even if in fact they are so, cannot all *resemble* or be really conformable to their external cause. Thus he has, he says, two ideas of the sun, one of which, occurring in the mode of sensation, represents the sun as a small object, while the other, occurring in the mode of intellectual reflection from astronomical considerations, represents it as very large. Perhaps neither of these represents any object existing independently of him; what is certain is that both cannot represent it as it really is.

This three-fold classification of ideas in terms of their origins represents only very imperfectly what, from other passages, appear to have been Descartes's views; and those views are anyway far from clear[3]. Descartes gives the impression in the *Third Meditation* that he regards the three classes as not only exhaustive but exclusive – that is to say, no idea could belong to more than one of them. Elsewhere (*Notes against a Programme:* VIII–2 358, HR1 443; to Mersenne, 22 July 1641: III 418, K 108) he holds that *all* ideas 'which do not involve affirmation or negation' are innate. Among these, it seems, some are also adventitious, in the sense that they are 'triggered off' by external bodily causes, but their content, and hence their occurrence, can never adequately be accounted for entirely in terms of that causation: the innate potentialities of the mind make an essential contribution. The point emerges most strikingly in the case of sensations of pain, heat, colour, etc., which are, in the terms of the *Third Meditation*, paradigm examples of the adventitious; yet it is precisely with respect to these, in those other passages, that Descartes emphasizes the innate component, on the ground that with them it is all the more obvious that they do not resemble their corporeal causes, and hence that the mind itself determines their nature.

With regard to ideas of purely intellectual content, we do not have quite this reason for saying that they are innate; but they are innate in the yet more basic sense – which is what Descartes

3. For detailed discussion of several aspects not touched on here, see Kenny, *Descartes*, Chapter 5.

has in mind in the classification of the *Third Meditation* – that while development, practice and experience may be needed for human beings to be able to think with them, they do not really depend on corporeal causes at all, and they could play a role in abstract thought for a creature who did not have a body and needed no external stimulus to elicit these ideas in its mind. When Descartes says, as he eventually will, that the ideas, for instance, of the self and of God are innate in this most basic sense, he does not mean that the foetus in the womb thinks about them or even with them. He does believe that the foetus has experiences (as he has to, if the foetus has a soul, since the soul 'thinks always', but he supposes these experiences to be of a sensory kind, reactions to the intrauterine environment (to 'Hyperaspistes', August 1641: III 424, K 111). In saying that the abstract ideas are innate, he refers rather just to certain capacities that the mind possesses to come to use these ideas, and sometimes he sets the specification of such a capacity very low, comparing it to a disposition for being generous; or for contracting a particular disease, which can be found in certain families (*Notes against a Programme*: VIII–2 358, HR1 443). An appeal to this kind of capacity seems clearly too insubstantial for a theory which claims the *actual possession* of the ideas.

While this is so, and for other reasons too, the analogy is not strong enough for what Descartes wants, it is not true that the innateness claim even in the weakest form that Descartes gave it is merely vacuous. It is sometimes said, for instance, to be compatible in this form even with the claim that the ideas are entirely derived from experience, since it comes to no more than saying that the child must have the innate capacity to learn, i.e. to be affected by the environment. But this is wrong. For one thing, Descartes believed that these basically innate ideas could be developed without any experience at all, if only by a disembodied mind; but more importantly, even if experience is required to develop them, the innateness claim still does not reduce to triviality. For it at least entails that the child has a differential capacity to learn some things rather than others and that the product of learning – the thoughts that the child then commands – is not adequately or completely or determinately accounted for by the occasioning cause, the environmental factor in learning. This notion, that there is more to the mental product than could be accounted for in terms of environmental causation, is common to all Descartes's appeals to innateness: both with regard to the 'basically' innate ideas, and also as we saw just now, with regard to the ideas of sensation which are 'adventitiously' elicited.

However exactly an idea, and in particular an innate idea, is to be regarded, it is certain that for Descartes the possession of an idea is something that needs a cause; even an innate idea requires a cause. It is the question of the causation of his ideas that Descartes now pursues. And here he makes a sudden jump forward, receiving a deliverance from the 'natural light' at once more substantial and less plausible than many propositions about which he has felt qualms at earlier stages of his reflection:

Now it is manifest by the natural light that there must be at least as much reality in the efficient and total cause as in its effect. For where, pray, could the effect get its reality if not from the cause? And how could the cause supply the reality to the effect, unless it possessed it itself? From this it follows, not only that something cannot proceed from nothing, but also that what is more perfect – that is, contains more reality in itself – cannot proceed from what is less perfect.

This is a piece of scholastic metaphysics, and it is one of the most striking indications of the historical gap that exists between Descartes's thought and our own, despite the modern reality of much else that he writes, that he can unblinkingly accept this unintuitive and barely comprehensible principle as self-evident in the light of reason. The doctrine of degrees of reality or being is a part of the medieval intellectual order which more than any other succumbed to the seventeenth-century movement of ideas to which Descartes himself powerfully contributed. There were others, contemporary with Descartes, but not the product of a Jesuit training, who had less sympathy with such doctrines. Thomas Hobbes briskly wrote in his *Objections* to the *Meditations*:

Further I pray Des Cartes to investigate the meaning of *more reality*. Does reality admit of more or less? Or, if he thinks that one thing can be more a thing than another, let him see how this can be

explained to our intelligence with the clearness called for in demonstration, and such as he has himself employed on other occasions.
(*III Obj.* 9: VII 185, HR2 71)

Descartes sees no difficulty:

I have likewise explained how reality admits of more or less: viz.
in the way in which substance is more a thing than a mode is; and if
there are real qualities or incomplete substances, they are things to a
greater extent than modes are, but less than complete substances.
Finally, if there is an infinite and independent substance, it is more a
thing than a substance that is finite and dependent. Now all this is
quite self-evident . . . (*III Rep.*: ibid.)

The most important point about the notion of degrees of
reality as Descartes uses it in the *Third Meditation* is that (as
emerges already from this quotation) he applies it in two different, and complementary, ways. On the one hand, it determines
an ordering of the metaphysical categories of substance, accident and mode. They are ordered by degrees of reality because
modes are 'dependent' on accidents, and accidents 'dependent'
on substances, in that sense of 'dependence' which we found it
not easy to explain when these categories were introduced in the
last chapter (see pp. 124 ff.).

This is the first way in which the notion is used: an ordering
of categories. The other is an ordering *within* a given category,
in particular, in the category of substance. Here the only doctrine that matters for Descartes's purposes is that an infinite and
independent substance (namely God) is of higher reality than
any created substance; since the latter depend (in some causal
sense of 'dependence') for their existence on the former, but not
conversely, the sense of this is not difficult to grasp. In fact, it is
a slight misrepresentation of Descartes to say, as I have said,
that this is an ordering in one category, since this would imply
that 'substance' was used unambiguously of the things so
ordered; but strictly speaking, as we have seen, Descartes holds
that 'substance', though used unambiguously of all created substances, is used in a different sense of God. But since all he
means by this is that the first sort are created, and God is not, it
comes to very much the same thing.

There are traces of a more elaborate doctrine of the ordering

of substances in Descartes, by which even different created substances can have different degrees of reality. There is the reference, for instance, in the reply to Hobbes just quoted, to
'incomplete substances'; and Descartes does elsewhere (*IV
Rep.:* VII 222, HR2 99) give an example of an incomplete
substance, namely a hand, which is a substance, because a perfectly good material thing, but an incomplete one, because one
can understand its nature only by reference to a larger and
more complex structure of which it is properly part. In rather
the same strain, he regards a complex machine as of a higher
reality or perfection than some simpler object (as we shall see
below, p. 139. But these are basically unassimilated relics in
Descartes's metaphysics of views to which his own are in reality
fundamentally opposed. They belong to an Aristotelian concept
of substance which relates to a purposive or functional idea of
explanation; a hand is less 'complete' than a man because man
is a biological species, each member of which has hands which
serve a certain role in the life of that type of animal or being. But
Descartes's notions of explanation are utterly different from this.
Not only has he little use for this sort of idea in the mechanistic
picture of the universe that he will ultimately offer, but indeed he
gets into difficulties about there being any plurality of separate
physical substances at all, let alone 'incomplete' ones – as we
glimpsed in the last chapter and will see further in Chapter 9.

Even before one gets so far into the Descartes's system, there
are important ways in which the scholastic notions are put to
very different uses by Descartes and by his predecessors. In
speaking of the causal principle I spoke of a scholastic doctrine;
in discussing more generally Descartes's idea of substance and
attribute, I spoke of scholastic terminology. The distinction has
some importance. The causal principle is certainly a piece of
traditional doctrine. More generally, however, Descartes is
adapting scholastic terms to his own uses: it was significant that,
earlier, I had to explain his notion of attribute in terms of
thought and extension, that is to say, in terms of Descartes's
own revolutionary dualism. As always in the history of thought,
new doctrines have to appear to some extent in old clothes.
With Descartes, it is not always easy to tell whether it is just the

clothes or what they cover that is old, but in the causal principle that he suddenly introduces, we certainly have one traditional item in his novel structure.

To return, now, to the line of Descartes's argument: he proceeds to consider the degree of reality of *ideas*. Regarded in themselves, just as ideas, he can see, he says, 'no difference or inequality' among them; they are all on the same level, as being certain 'modes of thought' (we may notice here already how much metaphysical theory is creeping into Descartes's supposedly presuppositionless enquiry). However, this is not all that is to be said about the reality of ideas. For ideas are ideas *of* various sorts of things – they have objects; and the question also arises of the degree of reality that belongs to the object of any particular idea. This is not to be understood as meaning that any idea must be an idea of something that really exists in the world, or that in discussing the degrees of reality of the object of a given idea, we have to be discussing the reality of something which actually exists. As we have already seen, many ideas are ideas of things that do not exist at all. Nevertheless, such things can have a degree of reality, a degree of perfection that applies to that sort of thing regarded in the abstract. Descartes now advances a particular application of the causal principle which we have already quoted. Not only must the cause of any thing have as much reality as the thing caused, but, further, in the case of things (such as ideas) that have objects, the degree of reality required by their cause corresponds to the degree of reality of their object.

This principle is not as unintelligible as this abstract formulation has no doubt made it seem. We may take the example of pictures (to which Descartes has already compared ideas). All pictures, as such, would no doubt be said to have the same degree of reality (or, at least, all pictures which are themselves physical objects, such as paintings). But pictures are pictures of various things, and represent things, real or imaginary. What a picture represents, whether real or imaginary, may be called its object. The objects may, on some scale of perfection or reality, obviously have different degrees of reality. Thus if some elaborate machine is graded as of higher perfection or reality than a pile of sticks, a picture of the first will have more reality than a picture of the second will. (Cf. to Regius, June 1642: III 566, K 133–4.) Suppose that we are confronted with these two pictures, which are recovered, say, in some archaeological research. We shall now wish to ask questions about the origin of these pictures. At one level of questioning, the answers we shall be looking for will be the same for both pictures: we shall just be concerned with the ability of the past society to produce any pictures of anything – the provenance of the materials, and so forth. But at another level of questioning, the picture of the machine will raise questions that the picture of the sticks will scarcely raise. It will obviously suggest a level of development and sophistication not suggested by the second picture. We shall suppose either that the society had such machines, which the artist had copied; or else that the artist was of a developed imaginative talent which allowed him to conceive of such machines. In either case, there would be some content to saying that the origins of the first picture lay in some more complex state of life and imagination than was demanded for the explanation of the second picture. We must say, 'than was *demanded* for the explanation of the second picture', for of course it is not ruled out that the cause of the second picture was as complex as that of the first: it is just that it does not have to be so.

This is, of course, a very schematized example, and omits all sorts of important considerations, such as that a picture of sticks can in fact be a more sophisticated product because of its style of representation than the picture of a machine. But it is perhaps enough to make Descartes's thought clear. He in fact uses (not in the *Meditations*) the example of a machine to illustrate his point about ideas; if a man has an idea of a very complex machine, he says, then we can ask 'did he somewhere see such a machine made by someone else? Or is it that he has made such a careful study of mechanics, or is so clever, that he could invent it on his own account, although he has never seen it anywhere?' (*Princ.* i 17). This thought is the basis of the principle that the cause of an idea must contain at least as much reality as the idea contains, not just *qua* idea, but *qua* the idea of a particular kind of object. Descartes in fact expresses this principle in a further piece of scholastic terminology, which is of no importance, and only needs to be mentioned because, by an accident of linguistic development, the terms he uses sound to the modern reader as though they expressed exactly the opposite of what Descartes means by them. He calls the reality that anything possesses intrinsically, its *formal* reality; and he calls the reality that an idea possesses in virtue of its object, its *objective* reality. Thus all ideas have the same degree of formal reality, but different degrees of objective reality – because their objects have, or would have, different degrees of (formal) reality. Lastly, in expressing the principle that the cause of anything must contain *at least* as much reality as the effect, he says that the reality of the effect must exist in the cause either *formally* or *eminently: formally*, if there is just as much reality in the cause as in the effect, and *eminently*, if there is more reality in the cause than in the effect, the cause being of some higher type than the effect (this will be so with works of art, the mind of the artist being of a higher type of reality than any of his products). Putting all these terms together, Descartes's principle about the causation of ideas comes out like this: the cause of any idea must contain either formally or eminently as much reality as the idea possesses both formally and objectively.

It is not really necessary to worry about this unattractive terminology unless one is going to be misled by it. There is one ambiguity, however, which should be noticed now, though its importance will emerge only later. Descartes says that the cause of an idea must have at least as much reality as the idea has not only formally, but objectively. What this minimally implies is that if there are two ideas I(a) and I(b), having as objects respectively *A* and *B*; and if *A* has (as a type of thing) more reality than *B*; then I(a) needs proportionately more reality in its cause than I(b) does. Descartes seems sometimes to say, further, that I(a) needs as much reality in its cause as *A* itself would possess formally. But he should not say this. To say it surely implies that to exist objectively, in an idea, is as real a way of existing as existing formally, in one's own right, and this is something which Descartes denies (*I Rep.:* VII 103–4, HR2

10–11) and has, as we shall see shortly, good reason to deny.

Having established this structure, Descartes turns to examine the objective reality of his various ideas, that is to say, to look at them from the point of view of the reality of their various objects; and to ask whether he can find a cause sufficient for their production. And since he himself is the only existent thing that he knows of, this comes to asking whether he himself can be the cause of his various ideas. It is worth remarking at this point that, in embarking on this enquiry, Descartes is in fact making two logically distinct assumptions: not only that the cause of any idea must have as much reality as the idea has objectively, but also, and more basically, that ideas must have causes at all. Descartes does not in fact think that there are two different principles at work here. He thinks that everything must have a cause, and he supposes that this is entailed by the causal principle already quoted (p. 135), which states that the cause must contain as much reality as the effect; from which 'it follows ... that something cannot proceed from nothing'. Descartes regarded it as self-evident that if the cause must have as much reality as the effect, then no real thing can proceed from 'something' that has no reality at all. This reasoning indeed did appear self-evident to very many thinkers for a very long time; it was Hume who detected that the argument is circular. For even granted that causes must have as much reality as effects, this will apply only to cases in which there are causes, and to argue from this that it is impossible for something to proceed from nothing, because what is nothing has no reality, is to assume that everything must proceed from something, and must have a cause; which is what was supposed to be proved (Hume, *Treatise* I. iii. 3). In the *Second Replies* (VII 135, HR2 34–5), Descartes says that the two principles are 'identical'; to show this, however, he treats their dependence the other way round, deriving the principle of adequate reality from the principle that nothing can come from nothing, on the ground that if an effect had more reality than its cause, then the surplus in the effect would have come from nothing.

Using these notions, Descartes proceeds to enquire into the causes of his various ideas. As for his ideas of physical objects, various animals and so on, he sees no evident reason why these should not proceed from himself; his own degree of reality as a thinking substance may well be adequate to produce such ideas. But now he makes the crucial reflection that there is another idea that he has, for which this can scarcely be so. This is the idea of a Being 'sovereign, eternal, infinite, unchangeable, omniscient, omnipotent, and universal creator of everything that is outside' himself: that is to say, the idea of God. Now the reality that attaches to the object of this idea, unlike the others, is the highest conceivable degree of reality, total perfection. Hence, by the supposed causal principle, it requires a cause proportionate in reality to the object of the idea itself. Now this cause certainly cannot be himself, for he is finite and imperfect: as is shown – and here Descartes makes the most ingenious and economical use of the little knowledge available to him – by the fact that he is in a state of doubt, and wishes to know more than he does know, whereas a perfect being must be free of all doubt and limitation, would know all that there was to know, and (consequently) would know that he knew it. Hence there must be a perfect Being independent of Descartes himself who is the cause of Descartes's idea of God, and this perfect Being is of course God himself. Hence God really exists.

One obvious objection to this argument Descartes immediately takes up. This is that he could, after all, have formed this idea of God from his own resources, by just thinking away the limitations that constitute his own imperfection; starting with his own finite properties, he could imagine them extended indefinitely towards perfection. Descartes's answer to this is that his idea of God is not that of a being merely negatively infinite, that is to say, a being such that we cannot conceive of limits to his excellence, but that of a being actually infinite, of whom we know that there are no limits to his excellence; or, as he elsewhere puts the distinction, God's excellence is not indefinitely, but infinitely, great (*Princ.* i 26 ff.; for a rather different explanation of these terms see *I Rep.:* VII 113, HR2 17). As he also puts it in the *Third Meditation*, he could not reach the idea of God by taking his own imperfect state of knowledge, for example, and imagining it constantly increased; for such increase would only go on and on, and not reach God's condition of complete knowledge.

A different objection that he faces later in the *Third Meditation* is that perhaps the various perfections attributed to God do exist severally in the universe, but nowhere joined in one substance. Perhaps Descartes has received the ideas of these attributes from their various sources, and himself joined them up to form the idea of a single Being, who does not in fact exist. His answer to this is that 'the unity, simplicity, or the inseparability of all God's attributes, is itself one of the chief perfections that I conceive him to have' (cf. also *II Obj.*: VII 124, HR2 26; *II Rep.*: VII 140, HR2 38).

These answers have to work very hard if they are to save Descartes from a basic objection. We have seen that Descartes does not have to say, in order to honour the adequate reality' principle, that the idea I(a) of *A* has to be caused by something that has as much reality as *A*. There is good reason why he should not say this. An idea, even when it is viewed from the point of view of its objective reality, is still an idea, and hence, in Descartes's metaphysical classification, is a mode, a mode of the attribute of thought. It must, therefore, by the ontological ordering, possess less reality than a substance, in particular than *A*, supposing *A* to be a substance. To bring about this mode (and it is after all the existence of the idea that is at issue) surely cannot demand quite as much reality or perfection as is required by, or possessed by, *A* itself. This very general point is of course reinforced in that case, the one under discussion, in which *A* is God. God, as the argument insists, has more reality or perfection than anything else whatever. Hence if Descartes's idea of God is not itself God (which would of course be absurd), it cannot, however regarded, possess as much reality as God, and hence cannot demand as much reality in its cause as God possesses. So the argument seems to fall short of positing God as cause of the idea.[4]

4. In some versions of the Ontological Argument, which Descartes offers in the *Fifth Meditation*, and which we shall consider later in this chapter, it is actually a premiss that it is less perfect to exist in idea than in actuality. It is perhaps not clear whether Descartes's version requires this premiss. See below, p. 157.

It seems then that Descartes cannot, and does not, rely just on a general principle to the effect that the cause of I(a) must possess as much reality as A. He relies, rather, on special features of the idea of God: that the infinity and perfection of God, represented in his idea, are of such a special character, so far in excess of any other possible cause, that the only thing adequate to produce an idea of *that* would be the thing itself, God. Any finite cause, the thought seems to be, would be adequate to produce only an idea which from the point of view of objective reality would be finite or at best negatively infinite.

The not very convincing answers about the character of the idea and what that implies thus have to do a lot of work. They have the disadvantage, as objectors to Descartes pointed out, that they presuppose an idea of God a great deal more determinate and articulated than Descartes's finite mind can be expected to have. It is obvious that at this point he is being pulled in opposite directions. On the one hand, he has to claim (as he does) that he has a perfectly 'clear and distinct' idea of God as an actually infinite being combining infinite perfections in a real unity; if he does not claim this, he will be open to the objections that he does not really conceive of God as actually infinite, and so forth, and may merely have put together a hazy notion of some being indefinitely great. On the other hand, both his religious faith and the exigencies of his argument require that he cannot really conceive of God's infinity, since this must be inaccessible to a mind which is, as the argument itself insists, finite. Descartes's course for steering between these two poles is, in effect, that he can clearly and distinctly conceive *that* God is actually infinite, but not how he is (cf. *I Rep.*: VII 113, HR2 17). But that this is an unsatisfactory line of defence can be seen if one reverts to Descartes's own helpful analogy of the man who had the idea of a very complex machine. From the fact that a man had this idea, it will be recalled, it could be inferred either that he had seen such a machine (or, we might add, had been told about it) or that he was clever enough to invent it. But clearly such inferences will hold only if the man has a quite determinate idea of the machine. If a man comes up and says that he has an idea of a marvellous machine which will feed the hungry by making proteins out of sand, I shall be impressed neither by his experience nor by his powers of invention if it turns out that that is all there is to the idea, and he has no conception, or only the haziest conception, of how such a machine might work.

The tension in this position, which has both to demand and to deny determinate understanding of God's nature, emerges already in an early letter in which Descartes compares God to an earthly monarch, and the eternal truths to his laws (to Mersenne, 15 April 1630: I 145, K 11):

We cannot understand the greatness of God, even though we know him. But the very fact that we recognize it to be incomprehensible makes us think all the more highly of it; just as a king has more majesty when he is less familiarly known to his subjects, provided that they do not then think that they have no king, and that they know him enough not to be able to doubt it.

Why does Descartes say that he is imperfect? I quoted as the ground for his saying that he was finite and imperfect the fact that he doubted. This is the ground that he offers, though not entirely directly, in the *Third Meditation*; and there is an explicit statement to this effect in the fourth part of the *Discourse*, where he also mentions, as indicating his imperfection, certain other states, such as sorrow, which are such that 'I myself should have liked to be rid of them' (V I 35, HR1 103). But to this an objector might say: how can you be certain that the fact that you would like to be rid of certain characteristics that you have means that they constitute imperfections in you? Might it not be an error on your part to want to be rid of these characteristics? To such an objection, Descartes would of course have a ready reply: if he is wrong in wishing to be rid of these characteristics, then it is still the case that he is imperfect; it will still be an imperfection (though a different one) to have these wishes which one is wrong in having. Such a reply would naturally, with Descartes, take the form of an appeal to an imperfection of knowledge: if he were perfect, he would know that states such as doubt, whatever his feelings about them, contributed to his perfection.

Now Descartes does not in fact argue in this way; rather, he makes a direct appeal to the paradigm of perfection contained in his idea of God, and the evident fact that he falls short of it. Indeed, he sometimes suggests that it is only because of his having the idea of God that he knows that he is imperfect. As he puts it in the *Third Meditation*:

How would it be possible for me to understand that I doubt and desire, that is to say, that something is lacking to me, and that I am not completely perfect, unless there were within me some idea of a being more perfect than myself, in comparison with which I could recognize the deficiencies of my nature?

This reasoning of Descartes might at first glance seem to be circular – that he is in some way founding the existence of God on the recognition of his own imperfection, and at the same time recognizing his own imperfection in the light of the existence of God. But this suspicion would be mistaken. For Descartes is not recognizing his own imperfection in the light of the existence of God, but only in the light of his *idea* of God, the existence of which (in his view) requires no proof. If, further, his reasoning which I have just quoted were intended as a proof that he had an idea of God, then indeed he would be guilty of circularity; but it is not so intended. His idea of God enables him to recognize his own imperfection, and that recognition, together with the other steps in the argument that we have already discussed, leads him from the mere idea of God to God's existence.

However, the argument does reveal very illuminatingly some of the large presuppositions which underlie Descartes's methods. If he is to say that by comparing his own state with his idea of God, he can recognize his own imperfection, this is to presuppose that a comparison of his own state and that attributed to God in his idea is to the point; in effect, that his own striving after knowledge is correctly to be seen as an aspiration to God's state of perfect knowledge, and an aspiration which is one in the right direction, as it were, and which represents the higher aspects of his nature. But why should he take this for granted? In part, it is because he has taken over, as I have already said, some remnants of a medieval view of a universal ordering of reality, each thing striving in its own way to a certain perfection under God; and it is perhaps only in the light of such a view that it would seem to make sense to speak of the degrees of perfection of different sorts of things at all. For *as what* is Descartes claiming himself to be imperfect? If as a man, then he has no proof that he is imperfect – for perhaps a perfect man is one whose experiences include doubt and sorrow. But if not as a man, then as what? Certainly not as God; it would be senseless to suppose that what Descartes had discovered himself to be was an imperfect God. His answer is just that he is an imperfect *being*; and this, if it means anything at all, imports the enormously elaborate and speculative notions of the general ordering of reality which we have already noticed.

Perhaps Descartes might say here that he needs no assumptions which are not already implicit in his Method. It is a Method for the acquisition of knowledge, and the very fact that he has devoted himself to it involves an aspiration to knowledge, which in the light of his idea of the perfect and infinite knowledge of God, he sees can never really achieve its aim. The very fact that he knows so little, and has to take such pains to sift out falsehood, reveals his limitation and imperfection, once he has the idea of a knowledge which does not involve such pains. One might say: his commitment to the Method gives him the goal, and his need of the Method reveals how distant the goal is. But this line of argument, if it is to express Descartes's thought, really only reveals the presuppositions in another way. For his conclusion is that he is in some objective sense imperfect, not merely that he is imperfectly adapted to a task which he happens to have set himself, namely the pursuit of knowledge; and this presupposes that the pursuit of knowledge is not just an arbitrary aim to which he has committed himself, but in his proper or highest purpose.

This, then, is the route by which Descartes claims, in the *Third Meditation,* to reach a demonstration of God's existence. 'To tell the truth,' he says

I see nothing in all that I have just said which by the light of nature is not manifest to anyone who desires to think attentively on the subject.

However, even in this *Meditation*, he does not let the matter rest there; for, he says, and with some justice,

when I relax my attention, and the gaze of the mind is obscured by the images of sensible objects, I do not easily recollect the reason why the idea that I possess of a being more perfect than I, must necessarily proceed from a being which is really more perfect . . .

and so he will continue his enquiry, and ask himself another question. The question is: could I, who have this idea of God, exist, if God did not exist?

From whom, then, he asks, does he derive his existence? If not from God, then, he suggests, either from himself; or from his parents; or from some other similar cause less than God. But it cannot be the case that he has created himself. For if he had, then he would have no doubts or wants or other imperfections:

I should have given myself every perfection of which I have an idea, and hence I should be God.

It could not be that, having created himself, he would have found it impossible to give himself these perfections; since it certainly requires more power or perfection to produce a substance from nothing than to provide any attributes whatsoever, so if he could have created himself as a substance, he could certainly have provided himself with the perfect attributes. Here Descartes relies on the other application of the principle concerning degrees of reality which I distinguished above, which provides an ordering, not of objects within one logical category, but of the logical categories themselves;[5] the argument shows, incidentally, that Descartes is already quite certainly committed to the conclusion that he is a (thinking) substance, from the considerations of the *cogito* alone.

Nor can the force of this argument be evaded, he claims, by supposing that he has existed from all eternity, and has never

5. We can note that the ordering of reality between the categories is very strong: the argument requires that it needs as much power or perfection to create even a finite substance as to create infinite attributes.

been created at all. For – and this is an important doctrine for Descartes – it takes as much power or perfection to *conserve* a substance in being from one instant to the next as it does to create it from nothing. Hence if he had existed from all eternity, and there were no God or other force external to himself to maintain him in being, he would be maintaining himself in being, continuously creating himself, as it were, from moment to moment; and this, once more, would require a degree of perfection which would have allowed him to provide himself with all perfections. This doctrine of the need of causal power to conserve a substance reveals, incidentally, how deeply for Descartes the existence of anything at all depends on the existence of God. What he says here with special reference to a thinking substance, namely himself, of course holds *a fortiori* for the physical world of matter, the existence of which he eventually comes to recognize once more; and we can see in this how very different Descartes's view is from the sorts of views that gained particular currency in the eighteenth century, by which God created the world from nothing and then left it to run on by the laws which he had implanted in it. Such a view, deism, gives matter, and any other created substance, a momentum of existence, as one might say: once made, it will continue in existence unless, by a further act of God's, it is annihilated. For Descartes, it is the other way round, and any created thing tends constantly to slip out of existence, being kept in being only by the continuous activity of God. In this view, as in the related description that Descartes gives of himself, as being 'half-way between being and nothingness' (*IV Med.*: VII 54, HR1 172), one gets a sense of the insecurity of contingent existence, which represents one of the most genuinely religious elements in Descartes's outlook.

Thus, Descartes argues, he could not have created himself. But neither could he have been created merely by his parents, or some other being less than God; or at least, if he were, the same question merely arises again. For any such lesser agency would have had to have the idea of God, the idea of unified perfection, in order to transmit it to him; and it follows from this that the lesser agency could not be self-created itself, since if it were, it would have given itself the perfections contained in that idea and would itself be God. Hence it must have been created by something else, and with that, the same argument starts again. So eventually the path must lead back to God as creator; so God must genuinely exist.

This last part of the argument Descartes distinguishes very carefully from a well-known argument for the existence of God which appeals merely to the necessity of a First Cause for a series of contingent beings, or at least he distinguishes it from the temporal version of that argument. He says that, at least at this stage of his reflection, he can see no evident contradiction in the idea of there having been an infinite temporal sequence of contingent beings, with no first member, and hence he can see no inescapable force in the First Cause argument. He bases his own argument on two other considerations; first, the necessity of conservation, and second, the presence of the idea of God, which requires a perfect creator to have implanted it. This latter feature also distinguishes his argument from that of the First Cause in respect of what is proved; the First Cause argument claims to prove only the existence of some Necessary Being, who is then assumed to be God (God being defined, further, as a *Perfect* Being), whereas Descartes's argument, he holds, proves directly the existence of a Perfect Being.

Descartes's appeal to conservation, and the necessity of the existence of a power sufficient to keep him in existence, indeed distinguishes the later part of his argument from that of the (temporal) First Cause. Indeed, it directly gives the conclusion that no antecedently existing cause, such as his parents, could possibly suffice to explain his present existence, since no antecedent cause could conserve him; and this is a conclusion which Descartes, a little later, explicitly draws. Thus we are left only with the possibility that some co-existent cause, not itself God, keeps him in being; and this is disposed of, Descartes thinks, by the consideration that such a cause would have to have the idea of God, with what follows from that.

It is in fact obvious that the line of reasoning that Descartes is now employing to demonstrate God's existence is entirely dependent on the arguments discussed earlier, which appealed directly to his possession of the idea of God. Descartes makes it perfectly plain that this is his intention. At one point in the *Third Meditation*, after the second argument, he says,

one must necessarily conclude that, from the fact that I exist and that the idea ... of God is in me, the existence of God is very evidently proved;

and later,

The whole force of the argument consists in this, that I could not exist with the nature I have, that is to say, having in me the idea of God, if God did not truly exist.

In one of his *Replies* to Objectors he puts it, further, by saying

I have undertaken the further enquiry – whether I could exist if God did not exist – not in order to adduce a proof distinct from the preceding one, but rather to give a more thoroughgoing explanation of it. (*I Rep.*: VII 106, HR2 12; cf. *II Rep.*: VII 135, HR2 35)

That Descartes is right in saying that the second line of argument offers no proof independent of the first emerges very obviously if one considers the argument for saying that he could not have created himself – that if he had, he would have made himself God. This depends directly on his having the idea of God – and not merely diverse ideas of various perfections – and also appeals to the causal principle used in the first argument. The relation between the two arguments can be put like this. The first directly argues that the creator of the idea of God must be God; the second seeks to show that the creator of one who has the idea of God must be God, by means of showing that it could not be anything else.

Although the second line of argument does, in these ways, depend on the first, they are not in fact identical. The second adds something not explicitly offered in the first, namely that God created Descartes himself. But this addition only illustrates, in an oblique way, how the second line of argument only uses the same premises as the first, for this addition is in fact unjustified, and the second argument fails to make its extra point. There is one further possibility that Descartes seems not to have considered: that some cause less than God might have created and might conserve Descartes, while God implanted the idea of God in him. He merely assumes that any lesser cause of himself must contain the idea of God. But why should this be so, and even if it is so, why should this prevent that lesser cause being truly the cause of his existence? Of course, such a possibility will once more lead to the existence of God; it will lead to it, however, in *exactly* the same way as in the first line of argument, and the extra feature, concerning God as the cause of Descartes's existence, will not have been established.

In fact, Descartes does not consider the idea that God might not have created him, since it is already written into the idea of God that he did. The idea of God was first introduced, it will be remembered, as the idea of a 'universal creator of all things that exist outside himself', and the obvious consequence of this is drawn a little later – before Descartes embarks on his proof – in a definition of God which describes him as

a substance infinite, eternal, unchangeable, independent, omniscient, omnipotent, and by whom myself and everything else that exists (if there is anything) was created and produced.

This being the definition of God, the content of Descartes's idea of God, it will immediately follow that if a substance exists conformable to this idea (as the first line of argument seeks to show), that substance will in fact be the creator of Descartes himself, and has left in him the idea of God as 'a mark of the workman on his work'. As this image suggests, Descartes believes that the idea of God was implanted in him at the time of his creation; in other words, in terms of the three-fold classification of ideas mentioned earlier (p. 132), that the idea of God is *innate*.

This, then, is Descartes's line of argument for the existence of God in the *Third Meditation*. It starts, as it must, merely from the contents of Descartes's own mind. By using his possession of the idea of God, his conviction of his own imperfection, and the scarcely luminous causal principle, which he claims is obvious to the natural light, he has made the first break out of the circle of his own existence as a thinking substance. This break is, of course, of crucial importance for the route back from the doubt; it is only *via* the existence of God that Descartes regains the external world. We shall later see how God helps Descartes to regain it.

First, however, we must consider another, and quite different, argument for the existence of God which Descartes advances later on, in the *Fifth Meditation*. This latter argument is not postponed to the *Fifth Meditation* because it rests on further considerations not available in the *Third*. On the contrary, it contrives to be even more economical of premises than the earlier argument. Like that one, it starts from the idea of God; but it starts from that idea regarded merely as an idea or mental content, and makes no appeal to the *possession* of the idea by Descartes as an imperfect being. It is a pure argument from God's essence. Descartes's reason for putting his other argument first was not that he regarded it as more economical, but that he thought that its validity was more obvious. Of his later argument, from pure essence, he writes:

I shall not deny that this argument is such that those who do not keep in mind all the considerations that go to prove it, will easily take it for a sophism; so originally I was in some doubt whether I should use it, fearing that those who did not grasp it might be given an opportunity of rejecting the rest. But since there are two ways only of proving the existence of God, one by means of the effects due to him, the other by his essence or nature, and as I gave the former explanation in the *Third Meditation* as well as I could, I thought that I should not afterwards omit the other proof. (*I Rep.*: VII 120, HR2 22)

This proof, which he fears may appear sophistical, is basically very short. He has the notion of the *essence* of various sorts of things – features of those things that are necessarily contained in the mere idea of them. Thus it is of the essence of a (Euclidian plane) triangle that its angles should add up to two right angles; it belongs to the essence of a mountain that it should be accompanied by a valley, as he rather misleadingly expresses the proposition that there cannot be an uphill without a downhill (to Gibieuf, 19 January 1642: III 476–7, K 124). In general, statements of essence tell us nothing about whether the thing in question really exists; knowing that it is essential to a mountain to have a valley, I know only that if there is any mountain, there is also a valley, not that any mountain or valley actually exists – it is only the connection between the two things that is necessary. But, Descartes argues, the idea of God is a special case For the idea of God is the idea of a being who possesses all perfections – his essence involves every perfection. But one perfection is existence itself, so the essence of God necessarily involves existence. Hence from the mere idea or essence of God, it follows necessarily that God actually exists (*V Med.*: VII 67, HR1 181; *Discourse* Part iv: VI 36, HR1 104). The reason why this simple argument may appear a sophism, Descartes says, is that in general we make a distinction between essence and existence, so that we do not see that in the unique case of God his essence involves his existence.

This argument is often called the *Ontological Argument* for the existence of God, this name being first given to a somewhat similar argument advanced by St Anselm in the eleventh century, which was rejected by St Thomas Aquinas, and which has, particularly in recent years, been the subject of a surprisingly large number of attempts at resuscitation, which it has unsurprisingly resisted.[6]

Descartes tried to distinguish his argument from the Anselmian version criticized by St Thomas (*I Rep.*: VII 115, HR2 19); though what distinction precisely he intended to draw between the two arguments is not entirely clear. Some critics have thought that Descartes's argument is cruder and more immediately open to objection than Anselm's. What is certainly true is that it is less fully spelled out, and any reconstruction has to add something to what Descartes explicitly says. It was Descartes's version that Kant famously criticized (*Critique of Pure Reason, Dialectic*, A592–602), and ever since that criticism the standard objection to it has been that it treats existence as a

---

6. For a useful collection of materials, see *The Ontological Argument*, ed. Alvin Plantinga (New York, 1965). Plantinga's *The Nature of Necessity* (Oxford, 1974) argues against some earlier formulations (including one of his own), and offers a version claimed to be valid: for some comment on this, see below p. 161.

property of individuals, wrongly supposing that such a proposition as 'the Abominable Snowman exists' attributes existence to the Abominable Snowman, as 'the Abominable Snowman is yellow' attributes a certain colour to it. When it is said, loosely, that existence is not a predicate, this is what is meant: the denial need not rule out the possibility that 'the Abominable Snowman exists' attributes some property to something – for instance, as Frege held, the property of *being satisfied* to the *concept* 'Abominable Snowman'.

It can justly be objected (as it is by Plantinga) that it is not often made clear exactly what the force of this objection is, nor whether it applies equally well to all formulations of the Ontological Argument, but Descartes's rather simple version of the argument might be thought to succumb immediately, if any does, to this objection. A version of the objection was indeed put, before Kant, by Gassendi in his *Objections* (*V Obj.*: VII 323, HR2 186), in the form of saying

something which does not exist has neither perfection nor imperfection; and what exists and has various perfections, does not have existence as one particular perfection among them – rather, existence is that by which both it and its perfections exist, and without which, we can neither say that it has perfections, nor that the perfections are had.

Descartes's reply to this (*V Rep.*: VII 383–4, HR2 228–9) is rapid and purely verbal.

However, perhaps Descartes did have an answer to the objection, if he had bothered to state it. Kenny[7] has argued for an interpretation by which Descartes can consistently treat existence as a predicate, by making a distinction (parallel to one made by Meinong) between what 'is given' and what 'exists'. A triangle *is given*, if we can make true statements about it merely in virtue of its nature; it is a further question, whether any triangle actually exists. 'A triangle has angles equal to two right angles' is a statement at this level: no triangle may exist,

7. *Descartes*, Chapter 7, which gives evidence for, and an elaboration of, this interpretation. See also his 'Descartes' Ontological Argument', in *Fact and Existence*, ed. J. Margolis (Oxford, 1968).

and yet that statement be true. 'God is perfect' is equally a statement at that level, but in this case, and this case alone, the nature
or essence of the thing that is 'given' itself includes existence, so
to understand what God is is to understand that he exists. By the
distinction between the level of things 'being given' – the level
of 'pure objects', as it is also called – and the level of actual
existence, the Gassendi type of objection to the Ontological
Argument can supposedly be met.

There is room for doubt whether Descartes really held the
Meinongian type of view which Kenny ascribes to him, but I
shall not pursue that question here. I shall consider only what
such a view, if Descartes did hold it, would do for his use of the
Ontological Argument. In reaching the Ontological Argument
from such a view, Descartes would, as Kenny emphasizes, have
to lean heavily on a distinction which he makes at more than
one place: that between (something which has) a 'true and immutable nature', and something which is just an arbitrary
fiction, such as a golden mountain or a winged horse (cf. *V
Med.*: VII 64, HR1 182; *I Rep.*: VII 117, HR2 20; *Princ.* i
15). For if there were 'pure objects' corresponding to such
fictional specifications, then we could just include existence in a
given specification, and by an ontological argument deduce the
actual existence of any arbitrarily ·specified object (it was an
objection related to this that the monk Gaunilo made to Anselm
at the beginning of this long controversy). So it is only where
there is a 'true and immutable nature' that we can make predi-
cations at the 'pure object' level at all; and it is only God's true
and immutable nature which includes existence. There seems to
be no rule for determining what has a true and immutable
nature, and Descartes indeed contradicts himself on the subject.[8] Moreover, the restriction of 'pure objects' in this way
renders the Meinongian apparatus less appealing than it might
have seemed at first, since some of its appeal might be thought
to lie in this, that it provides a general account of subject-predi-
cate statements whose truth does not presuppose actual existence of the subject, and these should include statements about
fictional entities.

8. See Kenny, *Descartes*, p. 154.

Leaving that, however, we must ask what it is about God's true and immutable nature that makes actual existence a consequence of it. Descartes's usual, and very short, answer to this is that the principal mark of God's nature is his perfection, and existence is one such perfection. But this needs more explanation. For if it is just the concept of a perfect thing, *qua* perfect, that entails existence, then we face once more the problem that an ontological argument might prove the existence of items of other sorts – *perfect* items of those sorts. Granted the requirement of true and immutable natures, these items could not be mere arbitrarily specified perfect items, but given that F is some true and immutable nature, why should not an ontological argument prove the existence of a perfect F? This difficulty still remains if we move nearer to Anselm's formulation than Descartes does in the *Meditations* and explain the idea that perfection entails existence by saying that it is better, grander, more perfect to exist actually (as Descartes would say, formally) than to exist merely as the object of an idea (as Descartes would say, objectively). This consideration, which we touched on earlier in connection with the causal argument, does not by itself help with the present difficulty. For if it is better to exist actually than merely in idea, then it is presumably better in general so to exist, and any perfect F – where F is once more a true and immutable nature – will once more, in order to express its perfection, have to exist actually.

This shows that God's existence does not just follow from its being the case that, for some true and immutable nature F, he is a perfect F. What God is, is a perfect being, and that means that he is more perfect than anything else at all, not just, for some range of Fs, perfect among Fs. But then we are still left with the question of what it is about that absolute perfection which entails existence, and we need an answer to that, if existence is to be genuinely part of that true and immutable nature, and not just externally attached to it. Here it is no good falling back simply on the superiority of actual existence over existence in idea, for that consideration in itself would apply equally well to perfect F's of restricted, less perfect, types. What we need is something peculiar to God's essence and existence;

and it is clear, so far as Descartes is concerned, that he had in mind a particular mode of existence attributed to God: necessary or eternal existence. In the Latin edition of the *Fifth Meditation* he wrote '. . . God, to whose essence alone existence pertains' (VII 69); the subsequent French translation reads '. . . God, in the idea of whom alone necessary or eternal existence is comprised, and who consequently exists' (IX–1 55). Further, in the *First Replies* (VII 118, HR2 21) he writes of 'necessary existence, which is alone in question here' (cf. also *Princ.* i 14).

In these passages, 'necessary existence' does not mean, or just mean, 'existence entailed by the concept of the thing'. It means uncreated and eternal existence, the existence enjoyed by a thing of which it makes no sense to say that it has come to be or passed away. There is no doubt that in traditional belief this is the kind of existence that God is supposed to enjoy (it is for this reason that 'God is dead' represented a special kind of paradox). In this sense, necessary existence is part of the concept of God. But while this can be granted, and God as a pure object (to revert to the Meinongian terminology) is a necessary existent, it would be a straightforward fallacy to infer from this that therefore, necessarily, he exists. The claim about God's nature gives us only that if there is a God, there is an uncreated, eternal, etc., being; it does not give us that there is one. Some fallacious revivals of the Ontological Argument have depended on an equivocation at this point, as Kenny has well shown (pp. 162 ff.); he also makes the point, by reference to the *Second Replies* (VII 151, HR2 46), that Descartes was aware of the relevant distinction, though there are passages, including the *Fifth Meditation* itself and *Principles* i 14–15, where it does look as though it were this fallacy that Descartes was relying on.

By 'necessary existence', then, Descartes cannot just mean, for the purposes of the Ontological Argument, 'existence entailed by the concept', nor can he just mean 'uncreated and eternal existence'. He has to mean, rather, 'existence entailed by the concept inasmuch as the concept involves uncreated and eternal existence', and granted that (as we have just seen) the entailment of actual existence is not immediate, we are still left with the problem of explaining how the entailment works. Kenny (pp. 159 ff.) has referred to a passage in the *First Replies* (VII 119, HR2 21), which Descartes interestingly asked Mersenne to correct before publication (III 329–30, K 95), having certain words suppressed for fear that the author would be attacked 'at a place where he judges himself to be weakest'; and Kenny has supplied from this an argument by which Descartes connects existence, necessary existence, and omnipotence (which is of course a feature of God's perfection). God is a being who exists 'by his own power', and this is paraphrased to the effect that he actually exists by virtue of his omnipotence. Since he is omnipotent, he can do anything he wants; he (like everything else, according to what is called a 'scholastic common-place') wants to exist; so he exists. It might be wondered, Kenny remarks, whether pure objects can have desires, but he counters this doubt with the reflection (p. 161) that 'satyrs (though no satyrs exist) have the libidinous appetites ascribed to them by classical authorities'. This example, it must be said, is unfortunate, since a satyr is just the kind of fiction from which Descartes distinguished things that have true and immutable natures, and hence is not a pure object at all on Kenny's reconstruction. But the more basic difficulty with this fanciful argument is not whether pure objects could have desires, but whether those desires could have an effect – at least, outside the realm of pure objects. The idea that if a pure object has power enough, its desire to exist can be effective, seems utterly mysterious. The gap between essence and existence, the idea and the actuality of God, is as wide as it ever was.

A related way in which Descartes took the idea that God existed 'by his own power' is to be found in his interpretation of the doctrine that God exists *per se*, or is the *cause of himself*. Descartes wishes to take this traditional formula in a very strong sense, which comes very close to saying that God is the *efficient cause* of himself, where 'efficient cause', in the Aristotelian terminology, stands for that type of cause with which we are most familiar, where one object, event or state of affairs is said to bring about another. He does not actually say this, settling rather for the formula that God's causation of himself is 'analogous' to efficient causation. I think, however, that he puts it like this only to avoid our being 'involved in a verbal dispute', as he says (*I Rep.*: VII 111, HR2 15), although under pressure from his able critic Arnauld, he retreats rather further in the *Fourth Replies* (VII 235 ff., HR2 107 ff.). The obvious objection to saying that God – or anything else – can be the efficient cause of its own existence is that an efficient cause is prior to its effect, and obviously nothing can be prior to itself. Descartes, however, does not think that priority in time is essential to the notion of an efficient cause:

on the contrary, a thing does not properly conform to the notion of cause except during the time that it produces its effect, and hence is not prior to it. (*I Rep.*: VII 108, HR2 14)

This ingenious point must, however, lead to difficulties. For if we add to it the further principles[9] that every physical state of affairs has an efficient cause, and further that the whole causal system is integrated, there not being entirely separate causal chains, we seem to reach the result that all physical events must be simultaneous (as Hume pointed out, *Treatise* I. iii. 2).

Descartes in fact denies that God's causal relation to himself consists in any 'transeunt action', as he puts it. What he wants to say is principally that when it is said that God exists *per se*, this is not to be taken in a purely negative sense, to the effect that God has no cause; God *is* the cause of himself, and this is in some way to be taken positively and literally. Descartes's insistence on some notion of efficient causation in this connection may support the idea that he hoped to derive God's actual existence from God's being essentially one whose activity is self-sustaining. It is rather as though God is one who would be capable of thinking himself into existence but, being eternal, was relieved of the need ever to do so. This is quite close to what Kenny puts in terms of the desires of the ideal object, and no more appealing.

The structure of pure objects which Kenny uses to explain Descartes's Ontological Argument can itself be criticized.

9. Descartes did not accept these principles without qualification: see below, pp. 275 ff.

Kenny himself mentions the lack of principles of individuation for such objects, and makes also the interesting point that the possession of properties by objects which do not actually exist contradicts the principle of the *cogito*. It can also be argued, though I shall not discuss it here, that the principle for establishing what properties pure objects have at least requires a revision of classical logic and may actually lead to contradiction.[10] Not every formulation of the Ontological Argument, however, requires a world of pure or, again, possible objects to which existence can then be added as a predicate. The version now offered by Plantinga does not.[11] It lies a long way from specifically Cartesian concerns and I shall not try to discuss it here; but the attempt raises a question of general principle which is important. In this latest version, the Ontological Argument is admitted not to be 'a successful piece of natural theology' (p. 219), because it does not draw only on propositions which any rational man would be. disposed to accept. Besides some complex machinery of modal logic, the argument requires a premiss to the effect that maximal greatness is possibly exemplified. This premiss entails, but is stronger than, a premiss which Leibniz found lacking in Descartes's argument, to the effect that the idea of a Perfect Being is consistent; it is stronger enough to be inconsistent with many other propositions which rational men might equally well accept. This acknowledged fact scales down the ambitions of the argument very considerably from those of either Anselm or Descartes.

This raises the question of whether any version of the Ontological Argument could possibly constitute a proof. A proof is not just a valid argument: it is a valid argument with regard to which there is no more reason to reject the conclusion than to accept the premisses – if this is not so, the argument will function not as a proof of its conclusion, but as a disproof of its premisses. This point seems to be strangely neglected by modern proponents of the Ontological Argument. Their conclusion is that there is a being omnipotent, omniscient, eternal,

10. I have argued this in a comment on Kenny's paper, referred to above (p. 155), in Margolis ed.: *Fact and Existence*, pp. 55–6.
11. In *The Nature of Necessity*, see above, p. 154, footnote.

benevolent, creator of Heaven and earth; a being who is indeed still, in Pascal's famous words, 'the God of the geometers' rather than 'the God of Abraham, Isaac and Jacob', but whose existence or non-existence, nonetheless, must surely make some immeasurable difference to men's concerns. The premises from which this conclusion is drawn include a set of considerations, increasingly complex and certainly disputable, of philosophical logic. It is utterly unreasonable to believe that such premises are more certain than the falsehood of the conclusion. Here there is an important difference between Descartes and modern advocates of the Ontological Argument. Descartes at least offered his argument to readers who shared with him a world of which the existence of God was a formative and virtually unquestioned feature; moreover he thought that the premises of the argument were exceedingly straightforward. Modern advocates have neither excuse.

Descartes's arguments for the existence of God fail, and that fact is exceedingly important for his system and for its legacy. The road that Descartes constructed back from the extreme point of the Doubt, and from the world merely of first-personal mental existence which he hoped to have established in the *cogito*, essentially goes over a religious bridge. Taking his concern to be the foundations of scientific knowledge, these are provided by God; taking it to be the foundations of the possibility of knowledge, these too, and in a more intimate sense, are to be found in God, as we shall see in Chapter 7. It is deeply expressive of Descartes's historical position that while he asks a new question, and his first certainties are found, in a new way, in subjective consciousness, the completion of the task essentially depends for him on traditional conceptions of God. The collapse of the religious bridge has meant that his most profound and most long-lasting influence has not been in the direction of the religious metaphysics which he himself accepted. Rather, philosophy after Descartes was driven to a search for alternative ways of getting back from the regions of scepticism and subjective idealism in which it was stranded when Cartesian enquiry lost the Cartesian road back.

Chapter 6

ERROR AND THE WILL

From this one fact, that the idea of God is found in me, or that I exist possessing this idea, I conclude so clearly that God exists, and that my existence depends entirely on him in every moment, that I am sure that nothing could be known by the human mind more evidently or more certainly. And it seems to me that I now see before me a road which will lead from the contemplation of the true God (in whom all the treasures of science and wisdom are hidden) to the knowledge of other things. (*IV Med.*: VII 53, HR1 172)

IT is a fundamental feature of Descartes's system that the knowledge of God's existence is more certain than the knowledge of anything else except that of one's own mind; and, further, that the advance of knowledge to the recognition of anything other than God and one's own mind must itself be founded on God, as we have already noticed at the end of the last chapter. In particular, God provides the route that leads back to the physical world. God provides in fact the foundation of all knowledge; there is even a way, which we shall investigate in the next chapter, in which he provides the foundation of the knowledge of the basic certainties themselves. He provides all this in virtue of his creative power and his infinite benevolence, which guarantee that he is 'no deceiver'. From this there follow two, closely connected, assurances. The first is that the malicious demon who was suggested as a universal cause of error does not exist, for God himself, of course, is no such being, nor would he permit his creatures to be constantly deceived by any such. Second, the faculty of judgement which Descartes finds in himself was certainly received from God who created him, and God cannot have provided him with a faculty which, when correctly employed, will lead to error. This second assurance is in fact the more basic one: the existence of a faculty of judgement which, correctly used, will not lead to error, is sufficient to dispose of the fear of a malicious demon who is a universal cause of error.

At this point, however, Descartes is moved to wonder whether he may not have proved too much. For if indeed the benevolence of God guarantees in this way that the faculty of judgement cannot be systematically prone to error, how does it come about that Descartes is *ever* mistaken? Yet it was precisely from the recognition that he had been very frequently mistaken that his process of doubt started. To this question there might seem to be a very simple answer: that Descartes is, as he recognized in the course of his proof of God's existence, imperfect, and this imperfection evidently includes the liability to error. But this answer, though correct so far as it goes, does not explain enough. For one thing, it fails to locate precisely the particular imperfection that is the source of error, and it is only by doing this that Descartes can hope to make allowance for it. Since he is committed to a method for the discovery of the truth and the elimination of error, he must hope that there is something that he can do to circumvent his imperfection, or at least to know where it cannot be circumvented. In the second place, the fact that he is imperfect in a way that can lead to error itself needs explanation. For if he has been created as a rational mind by a benevolent God, why should he be imperfect in this way? Evidently God could have created him so as not to fall into error at all. As Descartes puts it, 'error is not a pure negation [*the French translation adds*: that is to say, it is not a simple defect or want of some perfection that ought not to be mine], but it is . . . a lack of some knowledge which in some way ought to be in me' (*IV Med.*: VII 54–5, IX–1 43–4, HR1 173). In scholastic terms, Descartes regards error as a *privation*, as, for instance, blindness is: it is only of creatures that ought to be able to see that we naturally say, if they cannot see, that they are blind.

Descartes's view that error is a privation seems to contain an ambiguity. In one sense, what he says is certainly true. There is an important difference between being mistaken about a certain matter, and being completely ignorant of it. For a person to have made a mistake, he must have been concerned with the matter in the first place – it is only if a matter has come up for him that a man is in a position to make a mistake. His being completely ignorant of a matter, however, means (in the pure case) that the matter does not come up for him at all, and hence (again, in the pure case) that he is not in a position even to make a mistake about it.

Granted this distinction, we can see a modest sense in which a man's having made a mistake introduces such notions as failure and privation, whereas blank ignorance by itself does not. The mere notion of one's being mistaken already implies an area of concern relative to which the mistake is something to be regretted, explained, rectified and so forth; the mere notion of a man's being ignorant (in the radical sense being discussed) does not. (We may recall an earlier observation (p. 46) that the Pure Enquirer is committed to truth, not to omniscience.) In this sense, we can see a simple truth in Descartes's claim that error is not just a negation but a privation.

There is another sense of this claim, however, in which it is far more problematical. This is the sense in which it means that the general liability to make mistakes or fall into error is a privation, where this implies that this general liability is a falling away from a more perfect condition that might have been looked for. Even granted that Descartes thinks that he has proved that he is created by an omnipotent and benevolent God, why should this create any presumption that he should be free from the liability to error? This is a significant Cartesian presupposition – that what one would expect the human mind to be is a rational instrument effortlessly embodying the truth, and that it is failure to live up to this specification that demands explanation.

Descartes gives a good deal of attention to trying to give an explanation at this point, and since one cannot understand his eventual recovery of the physical world nor his vindication of knowledge except in terms of his theory of error, we must follow the order of exposition that he himself gives in the *Meditations*, and consider this question next. In fact this is not a mere interruption or incidental clearing-up in the advance of knowledge from the Doubt. The theory of error is itself an important part of what he wanted to know when he set out on his enquiry. The Method demands more than some pieces of knowledge – it requires also an account of where knowledge is to be found, and how error is to be avoided, if it can be.

Descartes's question was: why should I, created and sustained by a God who is no deceiver, ever be mistaken? This comes in effect to two questions, one about himself, and one about God. Why should I sometimes be mistaken? And why has God created me as a being who can sometimes be mistaken – i.e. why has he not made me perfect? The second of these questions Descartes will not try to answer: God's purposes are inscrutable, and it would be both impious and pointless for his finite mind to try to fathom them. In general, he goes on to say, it is improper to look for final causes – that is to say, explanations in terms of purposes – in philosophy or science: it always involves the impiety of trying to discover more than God has revealed (*IV Med.*: VII 55, HR1 173). At this point Descartes is looking forward, and with some ingenuity (and also, perhaps, some disingenuity) is using the claims of piety against the ecclesiastics who opposed the mechanistic outlook of the new science, and who stood for a traditional conception of physics as involving the study of final causes in nature. Indeed, Descartes's ingenuity goes beyond this device of controversy, for while he does abandon in this way the second question, about God, he also produces an explanation of error which implies (as we shall see) that in one important respect, at least, the question does not even arise.

The first question, about himself, he will try to answer, and to do this, he turns yet again to consider the powers of his own mind. Although there are many different sorts of operation of the mind, they fall into two important classes: those that are operations of the *understanding*, and those that are operations of the *will*. This distinction, employed fairly informally in the *Fourth Meditation*, Descartes in fact regarded as fundamental and exhaustive (cf. *Princ.* i 32 ff.). What concerns us here is Descartes's application of this distinction to the problem of error. His first question in this connection is: where in these faculties of his mind can he find limitation? Certainly in the understanding. This is the faculty by which he 'apprehends ideas', and he can clearly conceive that there are very many ideas which he cannot apprehend, and that there are very many matters of which his understanding is too limited to allow him to form a conception. Thus he knows that God, whose understanding is infinite, must comprehend and have ideas of very many things quite unknown to Descartes. Similarly with the other faculties related to the understanding:

If in the same way I examine the memory, the imagination, or some other faculty, I do not find any which I do not recognize to be small and circumscribed in myself, while in God it is immense. (*IV Med.*: VII 57, HR1 174–5)[1]

While there are these limitations on the understanding, they do not in themselves lead to error. As we saw above (p. 131), the mere consideration of ideas, which is the business of the understanding, cannot by itself contain either truth or falsehood. (That Descartes applies this point also to memory shows, incidentally, that he must be thinking of memory here not as a faculty in virtue of which one claims the truth of such and such statements about the past, but merely as a faculty which offers up certain ideas for judgement.) Thus the limitations on the understanding, while they certainly exist, do not by themselves explain the liability to error – they only explain ignorance. In order to be involved in either correctness or error, we have to move beyond the mere having of ideas to judgement or assertion, and judgement, on Descartes's view, involves the will.

Now the will, according to Descartes, differs from the understanding in that it has no limitations:

It is free-will alone or liberty of choice which I find to be so great in me that I can conceive the idea of nothing greater: indeed, it is this that makes me understand that in some manner I bear the image and similitude of God. For although the power of will is incomparably greater in God than in me, both by reason of the knowledge and the power which, conjoined with it, render it stronger and more efficacious, and by reason of its object, inasmuch as in God it extends to a great many things; it nevertheless does not seem to me

1. In the passage of the *Principles* already referred to, Descartes makes it clear that he regards memory and imagination as different modes of the operation of the understanding; in the *Fourth Meditation* he is less specific.

greater if I consider it formally and precisely in itself. For it consists only in our being able to choose a thing or not choose it (that is, to affirm or deny, to pursue or shun it); or rather it consists only in the fact that in affirming or denying, pursuing or shunning, the things put before us by the understanding, we feel that we are not determined by any outside force. (*IV Med*.: VII 57, HR1 175)

Or, as Descartes explains the infinity or limitlessness of the will in the *Principles*:

The will may in a certain way be said to be infinite, because we perceive nothing which may be the object of some other will, even of that immense will which is in God, to which our will cannot also extend . . . (*Princ.* i 35)

The operations of the will by no means imply indifference, or hesitating between two contrary choices: the situation of indifference is merely the 'lowest grade of liberty'. The more clearly I lean to one side, whether in deciding what to do, or in asserting and denying – the more clearly, that is to say, that I recognize the reasons of 'the good and the true' that bear on the issue – the more freely do I choose.

We now have the situation that the understanding is indeed limited, but by itself cannot be responsible for error. In order to make any judgement, and hence to commit any error, the will must be involved – but the will has no limits. So what is limited produces no error, and what can produce error is not limited. So how is the liability to error connected with my limitations? The answer is of course that error arises from the relations between the will and the understanding. My understanding being limited, there are many matters that occur to me of which I have a confused and inadequate idea, but my will being limitless, it is only too easy for me to jump to a conclusion and make some hasty assertion which involves me in error. It is because the will 'ranges more widely than the understanding' that error arises. 'It is in the incorrect use of free will', as Descartes characteristically if not very clearly puts it, 'that that privation is to be found, which constitutes the nature of error' (*IV Med.*: VII 60, HR1 177).

It follows from this account that the avoidance of error is in my own power.

If I abstain from giving my judgement, when I do not perceive clearly and distinctly enough what is true, it is plain that I act rightly and am not deceived. But if I either affirm or deny (in such a case), I no longer rightly use my free will. If I turn in the direction of what is false, obviously I am deceived; while if I embrace the opposite, I happen on the truth, but only by luck, and I shall not be free from blame; for it is evident by the natural light that the perception of the understanding should always precede the determination of the will. (*IV Med.*: V I I 59–60, H R1 176)

'Obviously I am deceived' says the Latin; but the French words, *je me trompe*, literally 'I deceive myself', more exactly bring out Descartes's explanation of how, though God created me and God is no deceiver, I may yet fall into error. Two different difficulties are removed. On the one hand, to avoid error is in one's own power, and thus the way is clear again for the Method – it is up to me whether I pursue my enquiries with enough self-discipline to avoid hasty affirmation. On the other hand, we see that there can be no reproach to God. Indeed, he has given me a limited understanding, but that is entirely appropriate to a created being, and moreover, as we have seen, does not by itself involve the liability to error. He has given me a will which is perfect of its kind, indeed infinite, like God's own. To make use of this combination of faculties appropriately is up to me. Thus, though Descartes said he did not intend to enquire into the inscrutable purposes of God, there is nevertheless a sense in which God is justified after all.

The situation with error, then, is exactly the same as that with moral wrong-doing – the operation of the will is the same, whether one is concerned with reasons of 'the true' or of 'the good'. Descartes's account of the possibility of intellectual error in the face of God is straightforwardly an application of traditional Christian doctrine about man's relation to God in moral matters: God has provided us, as a special gift, with a free will that can be misused. One might well wonder whether the two cases are so similar, or were even regarded by Descartes as so similar, as this account of the will implies. For instance, 'the misuse of the free will' which leads to moral wrong would seem very often at least to consist in following some morally reprehensible desire, and it is unclear what parallel there is to this in the case of intellectual error (except perhaps in very special cases of, for example, a man's vanity being involved in holding some belief in the face of the evidence – and such cases raise enough difficulties of their own). Yet I think that Descartes did suppose that there was a parallel to this situation, the situation (in effect) of temptation. We shall see later that in Descartes's view there are certain factors involved in the mind's close association with a body which dispose the will to assent to propositions which are false. There is a difference between the temptations to moral, and to intellectual, error for Descartes: the first, as we have just remarked, characteristically take the form of contrary desires, the latter – as we shall see – the form of sensations (*misleading* sensations). But desires and sensations, though certainly different, have for Descartes enough in common in that they are both states of the mind which are grounded in the conditions of the body: it is the fundamental Cartesian contrast of the rational mind and the body that provides the unity between intellectual and moral temptation.

I shall now consider some difficulties that arise in Descartes's account of error. Very basically, his account of the will involves obscurity. There must be something wrong with his speaking, as he constantly does, of our 'using' and 'misusing' our will. For certain faculties, to speak of their being used or misused makes some sense: thus a gifted copywriter in an advertising agency might be said to be misusing his imagination, or a malicious wit his intelligence. But, if one is to speak of the will at all, these uses and misuses of other faculties must themselves be a matter of the will, and to say that a man misuses *his will* could only be to imply either that his will misuses itself, or that he has another will which is applied to the use of the first one. This sort of difficulty, however, is perhaps not the most profitable to pursue. Some of the difficulties are too small, being verbal obstacles which more careful formulation would remove. Others are, in a sense, too large, reaching back into the whole foundation of Descartes's theory of mind. At this point there are just two difficulties that I shall pursue: one concerns the doctrine that the will is infinite, the other, the connection between will and belief.

What does it mean to say that the will is infinite or limitless? Here we have first to notice that 'willing', for Descartes, does not entail 'desiring', if this latter implies some emotional content. Desiring is at most one of the modes of the will (*Princ.* i 32), and it is made clear in the *Passions of the Soul* that the desire that involves feeling is particularly connected with one's possession of a body, whereas willing as such is not. The most general notion connected with willing seems to be something like *choosing* or *deciding*: see the passage from the *Fourth Meditation* (VII 57, HR1 175) which was quoted above (p. 168). That the will is limitless, then, seems to mean that I can always *choose* anything – anything I can think of I can choose to be the case, without any 'felt obstacle'. But surely this is straightforwardly false? There is at once a difficulty about the sorts of things one can be said to choose. It might be thought that it was a mark of choice, as distinguished from wishing and so forth, that it relates only to things that are actions: I might like it to have been the case that such-and-such a horse won the last race, but I cannot choose that it should have done so. The connection with action is certainly basic. However, Descartes does not only use 'will' in such a way that, on any occasion when I will or do some willing, there is some action, X-ing, such that I choose to *X*: the case of assenting is, as we shall see, itself a counter-example to this.

But actions are the central case, and in discussing at this preliminary stage the view that the will is infinite, it will be simpler to consider just the application of that view to the case of actions. In that application, the view says: I can conceive of no action, which I cannot choose to do. But is this true? For what of things that I know or believe are impossible for me? Here Descartes will say that I may not be able to do the action, but I can always choose to do it: the inability comes in in the step from choice to performance. But this seems a misdescription of the notion of choice, for if a man knows that a certain action is completely impossible for him, then it does not seem that there is anything he can do which will count as his choosing to do it. Nor does it extend the field much to include the notion of his choosing *to try* to do it, of his 'setting himself to do it', in a

phrase that some philosophers have used. For if a man knows
that a certain action is impossible for him, he will very often be
equally at a loss as to what would count as trying to do it. How
should I try to arrive on the moon two minutes from now? (In
some cases, there *is* something that counts as trying to do what
one knows is impossible, but this is characteristically where the
impossibility consists in the degree of some obstacle: pushing an
immovably heavy weight might count as trying to move it, because pushing a less heavy weight is trying to move that. But for
very many cases there is no such extrapolation available.)

Here Descartes might say that his view stands despite these
points: we are still not confronted with a specific limitation *on
the will*, in the sense – to use his phrase – that there is any 'felt
obstacle' to the choosing itself. Even if we grant that there is in
a sense an obstacle to my choosing to do what I know is impossible, this obstacle is just a logical shadow of my consciousness
of the impossibility of the feat itself. If I cannot remember
something, I should perhaps improve my memory; if (in the
sense now under discussion) I cannot choose something, this
does not demand an improvement in my powers of choosing,
but an improvement in my powers to do whatever the feat is. So
the impossibility or limitation still lies elsewhere, not in the
power of choice. A similar point will arise if we consider a
different sort of case in which it might be said that a man could
not choose a certain course of action: the situation in which he
is incapable of thinking of it. Now this is quite different from
the last, and was disguised by the formula we have been discussing: 'I can conceive of no action, which I cannot choose to
do' – compare Descartes's own formulation (*Princ.* i 35),
already quoted, 'we perceive nothing which may be the object
of some other will . . . to which our will cannot also extend'. For
this is to presuppose that the man has conceived of the course of
action, but perhaps he might be limited precisely in his power to
think of alternative courses of action. This is indeed an important sort of limitation to which one is subject. But Descartes's
answer to this possibility is quite clear: the limitation is this time
in the power of the understanding, a limitation which he gladly
concedes. If we say of Alexander the Great, for instance, that he

could not have chosen to abandon his expedition to the East and devote the funds to the relief of the poor, because he was the sort of man, living at such a time, that the thought could not even have occurred to him: then we make a remark about the limitations on his understanding or powers of imagination, not on his powers of choice. The limitation is still elsewhere.

But if these cases are disposed of like this, will there not be still another sort of limitation which is, by contrast, quite evidently a limitation on the power of choice? What of a man who has conceived of various courses of action, knows that they are all possible for him, and just cannot decide between them? He, surely, 'cannot choose' in a straightforward sense – he can do the actions, and the thing he cannot do is, precisely, to choose between them. He experiences a 'felt obstacle' to the act of choosing itself. It is not entirely clear what Descartes would say about cases of this kind. He might say that, in some cases at least, the situation really is that the man's reasons for choosing this or that are extremely evenly balanced, and hence that it is not surprising, nor any defect in his will as such, that he cannot make the choice. Or, again, in some cases, he might say that the man can strictly speaking make the choice, but cannot produce the slightest effect thereby even within his own body: this is the situation that Descartes supposes to arise when the will is in conflict with the bodily passions, because the inertial force of the 'animal spirits' which are moving in the body prevent the soul operating upon it (see *Passions of the Soul* i 45 ff.; for a fuller discussion of the interventions of the soul, see Chapter 10).

However, it is not very profitable to pursue the answers that could be given, in Descartes's terms, to such difficulties, because, in his terms, there seems to be something wrong with the question from the start. We have been considering that a man can or cannot choose, or, in Descartes's word, will. But in fact there is yet a more basic difficulty, of how Descartes can apply the words 'can' and 'cannot' to *willing* at all. For him, the question whether a man can do a certain thing seemed to come to this: whether, if he sets himself to do it, he does it. And this again, for Descartes, comes to the question, whether the man's

willing the action has an effect. Hence it can scarcely make
sense, on this account, to ask whether a man *can will* this or
that, since this could only come to asking whether his willing to
will it had an effect, and no sense seems to have been given to
this question. It might be objected here that this difficulty only
arises because we are construing the 'can' in 'he can will this or
that' in an empirical sense, as referring to some possible feat;
whereas, it may be said, this 'can' should be taken only in a
logical sense, the question that concerns us being rather whether
it makes sense to say of a man that he wills or does not will this
or that. On this view, Descartes's doctrine of the limitlessness of
the will means 'there is no action of which it does not make
sense to say that a man wills it'. But this cannot be a correct
interpretation. For – certainly on Descartes's views, at least –
there is no idea or proposition of which it does not *make sense*
to suppose that a man understands it, either, so on this interpretation, the understanding would emerge as being limitless as
well, which is contrary to Descartes's expressed doctrine.

I think we are forced to conclude that Descartes's view of the
will as limitless is not fully intelligible. Its very formulation
seems to depend on notions to which no clear sense has been
given. In so far as his line of thought can be followed, I think
that what emerges is that the view is fundamentally vacuous:
that its defence depends on the strategy of allocating every limitation to which a man may be subject to something other than
his will. That the view is vacuous emerges also if one considers
the *freedom* of the will. That we are 'possessed of a free will'
Descartes regards as self-evident (*Princ.* i 39). Now this does
not mean that we have a will, of which we see self-evidently
that it is free (as it might not have been). To have a free will is
just to have a will: 'it is the greatest perfection in man to be able
to act by its means (sc. the will), *that is freely* . . .' (*Princ.* i 37) –
thus Descartes sidesteps what Locke (*Essay* II. 21. 14) was
later to describe as an 'unreasonable because unintelligible
question, viz. whether man's will be free or no'. Man's freedom
consists in his possession of a will. But one might hope that
man's freedom would consist in his ability to *do* certain things.
From the account of the will we have been pursuing, it will

follow that by the mere possession of a free will, man is not given the ability to do anything at all, except will. It no doubt will be true that he can do other things, but this will not be because he has a will, but because his willing sometimes has an effect. That the freedom of the will, on Descartes's account, gives us so little follows, I suggest, from the fact that his account of the powers of the will is ultimately vacuous. It starts out by looking as though it made vast claims for the power of the will, but it turns out that this vastness is an illusion created by a terminology.

While the doctrine is in this general way vacuous, there are two other respects in which it is not. First of all, it is not vacuous in the sense that it is an idle and detachable part of Descartes's system. On the contrary, it is intimately connected with his views on the nature of action and the relations between mind and body.[2] Second, it is not vacuous when applied to the particular question from which this discussion set out, namely the theory of error. This brings us to the second question that I shall pursue, the connection between belief and will – Descartes's account of assent.

When Descartes says that the will is limitless with respect to assent, he is saying more than when he claims that the will is limitless with respect to actions in general. This is because assenting is not just one action among others that I may will to perform, and then either succeed or fail. Assenting is itself a mode of willing, and when I assent, I do not succeed in doing something that I have willed to do, I just will something; and what I will is not itself another action, which is why, as was said earlier, 'willing' for Descartes is not always 'choosing to *do*'. Since assenting is just willing, it can be subject to no more limitations than the will in general. It is a pure mental act without even the sorts of limitations that may exist for other mental operations, such as those of the understanding. The power of assent is as limitless as the will, because it just is the will in one of its manifestations. What, then, does this doctrine mean? For the reasons already mentioned, we have to be careful of saying that it means that I *can* always assent to anything – for there is no clear sense in which 'can' and 'cannot' may be applied to the

2. For more on the will in this connection, see p. 287 ff.

will, and hence to assent. It seems rather to mean that with assenting, the question of one's abilities just does not arise. One assents or not, at will.

Now what is meant by 'assent'? There is one sense of 'assent' in which one might say that one may just assent at will: that sense in which assenting is just signifying, by some conventional means, agreement with something, as when one says 'yes' or 'I agree' to some proposition which has been asserted by someone. But this is not of course what Descartes has in mind. First of all, it is not strictly true that no question of one's abilities can arise in such a case. I may just be unable to say 'yes' or to make the sign of agreement, either because I am in some way aphasic or paralysed, or (less strongly, but more interestingly) because I cannot bring myself to do so. More basic than this, however, is the point that this is an intra-personal sense of 'assent', and that in this sense assent can be *insincere*: I may say 'I agree' when I do not really accept what the man is saying at all. Descartes is not in the least concerned with sincere or insincere overt performances of assent. He is concerned with the question of whether I accept some proposition myself – in that sense of 'accept' in which the man who insincerely says 'I agree' does not accept the proposition. Assenting is what is done by one who thenceforth really believes the matter in question.

But if this is what assent is, it is far from clear how assenting is even dependent on the will, let alone a mode of it. An objector is bound to say at once (as Hobbes did; *III Obj.* 13: VII 191–2, HR2 75–6): are there not a very large number of things that one just cannot believe, and others that one cannot help believing? And even if there is certainly an activity (philosophically puzzling enough in itself) of making oneself believe things that one would like to believe, it is surely no accident that it involves a complex process of forgetting and self-deception, in the account of which the unconscious mind will often be invoked. The wife who wishes to believe, in the face of overwhelming evidence, that her husband is faithful to her should, it might appear from Descartes's account, have an easier time than she does – she should just assent to the proposition that he is.

The relations of belief and the will constitute a large and very interesting subject. It involves not only the nature of self-deception, but also the ethics of belief, a subject which raises such issues as the content of saying that someone 'ought' or 'ought not' to believe a given thing on given evidence. Another important question which presents itself is this: if we agree with Hume against Descartes that belief is basically a passive phenomenon, and not a matter of choice or of the will, we must recognize, and explain, a point which Hume failed to recognize, that it is not a contingent fact that this is so – one's incapacity to believe or disbelieve at will is not a contingent limitation, as one's incapacity to blush at will is.

I shall not try to pursue these general issues here.[3] Descartes's formulations seem to raise such questions in the most radical possible way, since they do strongly encourage the picture of someone who had no evidence whether *p* was true deciding at will to believe that *p* – or, as we should rather say if we are to understand the role of the will in believing, *deciding that p*. (This formula helps to bring out Descartes's point that assenting is just willing, not choosing to do or bring about something else. *Deciding that* is related to *believing that* as *deciding to* is related to *intending to*, and assenting to a proposition in the Cartesian sense is no more deciding to believe than deciding to act is deciding to intend to act.) Again, Descartes's formulations invite us to think, as in the case of the tortured wife, that someone could just decide on a belief in the teeth of what they recognized as reasons against it. In the sphere of decisions to act, these kinds of possibilities are available for the will. We can arbitrarily decide to act in a certain way, in a situation of indifference; and we can, equally, decide to do a certain thing in the teeth of reasons 'bearing on the good' (though some philosophers from Socrates on have found this difficult to understand). If belief followed on assent, and assent were just a mode of the will, parallel possibilities would seem to follow for belief.

Descartes does not accept these consequences, because he actually uses the notion of assent under two substantial restric-

3. I have discussed some of them, very much in outline, in 'Deciding to Believe', in *Problems of the Self* (Cambridge, 1973).

tions. That these are necessary does suggest that he should not have regarded assent quite so simply as a mode of the will. However, they do serve to make his account in practice altogether more acceptable than it seems from its mere general formulation. The restrictions are, first, that the will is not invoked against what the thinker regards, and continues to regard, as overwhelming reasons for a certain belief, and, second, that its most important use lies in its being invoked negatively, that is to say, in connection with the suspension of belief.

The first point frees Descartes from claiming that someone could just decide to believe something against which he had what he regarded as overwhelming evidence, or even as very strong evidence, there being no considerations of any sort on the other hand. This removes the difficulty of the tortured wife, who was in this situation. It is clearly absurd to speak of someone's just deciding to believe something in such a case (as opposed to their deceiving themselves). This is connected with the fact that there is a logical link between 'A regards p as overwhelming evidence for q', 'A believes p', and 'A believes q'. The link is not simple (various qualifications are needed about A's not having forgotten about p, etc.), but a link exists. It is not a contingent fact that when people have what they regard as overwhelming evidence for a certain proposition, they usually believe that proposition – it is part of what it is for them to have what they regard as overwhelming evidence for it.

The second point is that the most useful application of the idea of will for Descartes is negative. This notion of withholding assent is what is fundamental to the Method of Doubt. Nor need this run into any conflict with the last point, when Descartes's Method is properly understood. Here again, it is not a question of withholding assent from a proposition for which, at the same time, one is aware of having absolutely overwhelming evidence. One does not, as it were, try to apply the will to sever the last link in the logical chain – one applies it to the whole chain. For what withholding one's assent in such a case will involve is *ceasing to regard the evidence as absolutely overwhelming*. This is just the point of the Method. Descartes's great idea in philosophy is certainly not that of an ascetic exercise of the will, to withhold assent from as many propositions as possible. It is meant to be a *critique* of knowledge, and as such involves the criticism of the reasons that we ordinarily take as overwhelming.

Of course, how far such 'withholding of the assent' can possibly or intelligibly be carried is another matter, which calls in question the Method of Doubt. But that there is such an activity is indisputable, and that there should be something like it is surely a precondition of there being any self-critical thought at all. Just to ask of some familiar pattern of thought, 'but does it follow?'; not to jump to conclusions; and so forth – all these are examples of the 'withholding of assent'.

While the withholding of assent is what is most important for his theory, Descartes's formulations are not confined to this negative operation of the will. He invokes positive operations of it as well. Some positive application of the idea can be given a sense just in terms of what has already been said. If a man accepts some ill-founded belief when he might, by due reflection, have withheld his assent, one can intelligibly speak of his having assented where he should not have done so, implying by that a kind of negative responsibility. It is his fault if he believes falsehoods which by due reflection he could have avoided. This rather weak application of the positive notion of assent perhaps presupposes another, stronger, application in which the notion of assent is not merely used retrospectively; this is the notion of one who, in the light of the evidence, consciously decides or makes up his mind what is the case. But granted that there is such assent – and I have already suggested that it is the idea of *deciding that p* that is needed here, not the idea of *deciding to believe that p* – it seems to be in place only in cases where the agent regards the evidence as less than overwhelming (or, in the retrospective and critical use, where he should have done so). If the evidence is overwhelming, and continues to seem so despite the maximum critical activity, there seems no room left for the notion of decision at all.

This point arises for Descartes with regard to the basic certainties of his system, in particular the *cogito*, the certainty which first turns back the Doubt. The experience that Descartes expresses in his account of its discovery is that of his mind encountering something that forces him to assent, and in fact he repeatedly says that if he clearly and distinctly perceives one of the basic truths – and that implies that the maximum of critical attention is being brought to bear on it – then it is *impossible* for him not to believe it.

... the nature of my mind is such that I would be unable not to assent to these things (which I clearly and distinctly perceive) so long as I clearly perceive them

he says in the *Fifth Meditation* (VII 65, HR1 180), and again 'I *cannot* not believe it to be true' (*V Med.*: VII 69, HR1 183): and similar terms of impossibility and incapability are used frequently elsewhere (*Reg.* iii: X 386, HR1 7–8; Regius, 24 May 1640: III 64, K 73–4; *VII Rep.*: VII 460, HR2 266; to Mesland, 2 May 1644: IV 116, K 149; *Princ.* i 43). The same idea of impossibility occurs also in an important passage from the *Second Replies,* which we shall be further concerned with in the next chapter, and which expresses Descartes's most clear and fundamental statement on what he took indubitability to be:

Among these [clear perceptions of the intellect] some are so evident and at the same time so simple that we can never think them without believing them to be true: as that I, while I think, exist; that things which have been done cannot be undone; and such things, about which it is clear that we have this (absolute or perfect) certainty. For we cannot doubt them, unless we think of them; but we cannot think of them without at the same time believing them to be true, as has just been laid down; therefore we can never doubt them without at the same time believing them to be true; that is, we can never doubt them. (*II Rep.*: VII 145–6, HR2 42)

In all these passages the basic image is of *irresistibility*. Sometimes, elsewhere, Descartes tries to combine this, uneasily, with some residual role for the will: so in the *Fourth Meditation*:

From a great light in the intellect there follows a great propensity in the will. (VII 58–9, HR1 176)

In at least one place he reaffirms the claims of the will to the extent of denying ultimate irresistibility. In a letter (IV 173, and cf. III 378, K 159)[4], he explains first that 'indifference' can mean two things. It may mean merely the situation in which one has no disposition to go in one direction rather than the other, and it is in this sense that he said in the *Fourth Meditation,* and repeats here, that indifference is the lowest grade of freedom. But 'indifference' can also mean the positive power of decision which is involved in any act of the will, and in this sense he says, it is involved even in cases where there are the very strongest reasons or evidences:

... so that when some entirely evident reason moves us in one direction, even if morally speaking we can scarcely be conveyed in the opposite direction, in an absolute sense nevertheless we can. For it is always open to us (*licet*) to hold back from pursuing some clearly recognized good, or from accepting some perspicuous truth, if we think it a good thing that the freedom of our will should be displayed like this.

This passage does seem strictly to contradict what Descartes says frequently elsewhere, and not in a direction which helps him, for he has more than one reason for needing to regard assent as ultimately, in the case of the basic certainties, irresistible. The Method is based on the idea of resisting whatever is resistible, of withholding assent as long as possible, and if everything were resistible, at least while the critical stance were adopted, nothing could ever be assented to except by abandoning the critical stance. Clearly Descartes does not suppose that this is so. But there is a further reason, implicit in Descartes's picture of assent itself, why he should take ultimate assent to be irresistible. We can see this if we ask what it is, on Descartes's view, that one gives one's assent *to*. In the original introduction of the notion of assent, beliefs or judgements (which can be true or false) were contrasted with the bare contents of the understanding, which were said to be *ideas*, and it looks as though

4. There is great uncertainty about both the date and the addressee of this letter, which exists in both French and Latin. Editors have tentatively taken it to be to Mesland, 9 February 1645; but it is worth remarking that it was to Mesland in 1644 that he offered the other view, cf. the reference above. – Kenny's edition (p. 159) has a mistaken page reference to AT IV.

Descartes means that that to which I give my assent is an idea. This is supported by the fact that that to which I assent can be (or fail to be) 'clear and distinct', and it is certainly to ideas that he characteristically applies these terms. But if this is his meaning, his use of the term 'idea' must cover more than he has, in the *Meditations,* so far recognized. For ideas have been introduced as ideas of (possible or actual) *things,* as the idea of a triangle, of God, of a chimera, etc.; and it makes no sense to say that one can assent to a thing, or to the idea of a thing. I can assent only to something of the nature of a proposition: one believes, or refuses to believe, *that such-and-such is the case.* Thus, if Descartes is to say that what we assent to are ideas, he must include propositional ideas. He must allow that there is an idea *that the angles of a triangle add up to two right angles*: or – if he wishes to retain the notion that every idea is an idea *of* something – he must include, not just the idea of a triangle, but the idea of *a triangle's being a figure whose angles add up to two right angles.* Some modification on these lines is necessary to make the notion of belief as the product of assent to ideas, comprehensible at all. If he takes the course suggested, there will admittedly be some difficulty in his saying, as he does, that no idea is in itself true or false, for one would naturally say that the idea that the angles of a triangle add up to two right angles is indeed true. But this is no great difficulty, since what Descartes means here can readily be expressed by saying that one who merely considers or has in his mind an idea does not thereby commit himself to any assertion, true or false.

There is, however, a more serious difficulty. Descartes repeatedly says that what one should do at the basic level of forcing back the Doubt is give one's assent to all and only those ideas that one clearly and distinctly understands. But what is it clearly and distinctly to understand a propositional idea? This might mean, minimally, that one sees exactly what is involved in the proposition, understands all its terms, etc. But this cannot be what Descartes wants, since one can in this sense clearly understand a self-contradictory proposition – if one did not, one would not perceive that it was self-contradictory. And self-contradictory propositions are not ones that one should assent to.

Nor will it be enough to say that one clearly understands a proposition if one not only sees what is involved in it, but also sees that it is consistent; for there are many consistent propositions (as Descartes would agree) which are false, and to which again one should not give one's assent. Hence it looks as though it can be good advice that one should assent to all and only the propositions which one clearly understands, only if the notion of 'clearly understanding a proposition' is itself taken to imply that one sees the proposition to be true. Clearly and distinctly to understand the proposition about the angles of a triangle, for example, is to see that it is necessarily true. But once this step has been taken – and I find it very difficult to see how Descartes can avoid taking it or another only verbally different from it – the theory of assent is in difficulty. For if in this sense I clearly understand a proposition – that is to say, I can see it is true – there is nothing else I have to do in order to believe it: I already believe it. The will has nothing to do which the understanding has not already done. (Cf. *IV Med.:* VII 59, HR1 176, quoted above, p. 169.)

The ambiguities of Descartes's language about assent to the basic certainties, which we noticed just now, can thus be seen to be not accidental, nor due to mere looseness of expression. There is a structural ambiguity which underlies them: the theory of assent itself requires a step which cancels out the notion of assent. Yet the fact that the theory of assent founders in this way on the basic certainties is not really a disaster for Descartes. An attempt to hold on to it in that connection could only involve him in yet further difficulties. With respect to propositions other than the basic certainties, moreover, the theory need not encounter the difficulties which have just been discussed. As we shall see later, there are certain cases in which it *is* enough that the 'clear and distinct understanding' of a proposition should be the understanding that it is *consistent,* and this of course does not involve the elimination of assent, since to see that a proposition is consistent is not already to see that it is true. The theory of assent will have a real part to play, together with the benevolence of God, in Descartes's vindication of knowledge, and his ultimate return to the material world.

Chapter 7

KNOWLEDGE IS POSSIBLE

In his progress back from the Doubt Descartes encounters and relies on a number of propositions which, at least at the time of encountering them, strike him with such overwhelming force of conviction that – in the phrase we have already encountered – he 'cannot but assent' to them. These are propositions which he is prepared at the time to say that he 'clearly and distinctly perceives to be true': for instance, in the *cogito,* that he is think-ing, and that it is impossible to think without existing; in the proofs of God, that he has an idea of God, and that a cause must have a reality adequate to its effect. In his eventual proof of the external world, he will rely on others. Among them is the crucial proposition that God is no deceiver. If the Doubt is genuinely defeated, and the possibility of the malicious demon finally banished, to be replaced by the assurance of a ben-evolent God, so that ordinary methods of enquiry, critically employed, are vindicated, then these various propositions must actually be true. Can Descartes claim that?

Certainly he regards such propositions as, at the time of their being considered, indubitable: the attentive mind inevitably assents to them, 'is unable not to assent' to them (*V Med.*: VII 65, HR1 180; for other passages in similar terms, see the refer-ences given above, p. 180). His fullest account of the nature of this indubitability is to be found in an important passage of the *Second Replies* which I have already quoted in the previous chapter (VII 146, HR2 42):

If there is any certainty . . . it must concern those things which are clearly perceived by the intellect. But of these some are so evident and at the same time so simple that we can never think of them without believing them to be true: as that I, while I think, exist; that things which have been done cannot be undone; and other such things, about which it is clear that we have this certainty. For we cannot doubt them unless we think of them, but we cannot think of them without at the same time believing them to be true ... hence we can never doubt them without at the same time believing them to be true; that is to say, we can never doubt them.

Descartes's reasoning here is very clear. Some propositions have the property that if someone thinks of such a proposition, he believes it: we may say that such a proposition is irresistible.[1] Descartes adds the acceptable principles, first, that if one doubts a given proposition, one thinks of it, and, second, that if one doubts it, one does not believe it (where this means of course that it is false that one believes it, not that one disbelieves it). Thus an irresistible proposition is indubitable, cannot be doubted: the sense of 'cannot' in this parallels the sense of 'must' by which, if one thinks of an irresistible proposition, one must believe it.

The sense in which one 'thinks of' a proposition, for these purposes, may be taken to be that one considers as carefully and reflectively as possible what is involved in its being true. In this sense, the 'eternal truths', the very simple logical propositions, are irresistible, since the most careful consideration of what they mean or involve makes one accept them. The proposition 'cogito' itself is irresistible, because thorough reflection on what it involves reveals that by that reflection itself one satisfies the conditions of its being true, and so one believes it. Someone might suggest that 'I have the idea of God' is, under this interpretation, irresistible, on the grounds that if I can adequately grasp what is involved in its being true that I have an idea of God (or, indeed, of anything else), then I must grasp what is involved in that idea – that is to say, I must actually have that idea. But I think that we should resist this argument, on the same grounds as we rejected in Chapter 3 (see above, pp. 87–8) the suggestion that 'I have the idea of God' might be self-verifying. It is not correct to say that fully grasping the truth conditions of 'I have the idea of X' must involve grasping the content of the idea of X. What is correct, and may mislead us here, is that *if it is true* that (in Descartes's sense) I have the idea of X, then if I reflectively and as carefully as

1. For the use of the term 'proposition' and other matters, see Appendix

possible consider the content of the proposition 'I have the idea of X', I will see that proposition to be true. In this respect, propositions of this kind resemble (as indeed they should do on Descartes's classification of them) statements of immediate experience, those first-personal psychological propositions which were recognized as certain under the general heading of the *cogito* (see p. 78 ff.). 'I am in pain', for instance, is not irresistible, in the sense defined, since the fact that I have 'thought of' the proposition that I am in pain, and carefully considered what is involved in its being true, does not necessarily make me believe that I am in pain. What is correct is that *if I am in pain,* and I carefully consider the proposition that I am in pain, I will see that it is true. This is a consequence of something stronger which we have already allowed, that 'I am in pain' is *eviden*t – that is to say, if it is true, I believe it.

One of the propositions which Descartes has needed in the journey to this point from the Doubt, the proposition that he has the idea of God, is not unqualifiedly irresistible, but the others that he needs are irresistible; and even if 'I have the idea of God' is not unqualifiedly irresistible, this only means that in principle someone *could* carefully consider it and yet not believe it – Descartes certainly does find that when he carefully considers it, he cannot but believe it, and that he has to assent also to the various consequences which he finds involved in the content of that idea. Thus, relative to Descartes's process of enquiry, this proposition, too, can be treated as though it were irresistible.[2]

It follows from this that the Doubt got as far as it did only by a measure of inattention. Descartes suspended in the Doubt, managed not to believe, a number of propositions which he now acknowledges to be irresistible; so he cannot have been, at the time of doubting them, properly thinking of them. Descartes accepts this (*VII Rep.*: VII 460, HR2 266; ibid. 546, HR2 231; to Clerselier. IX–1 204–5, HR2 126). This gives us another sense in which the Doubt is a 'fiction', besides the now

2. For the relations of irresistibility to some other epistemological concepts, and a formal account of what the Pure Enquirer knows, see Appendices 1 and 2.

familiar point that it is the procedure of a Pure Enquirer: it also has to proceed by not totally attending, in some cases, to what it is doubting. So a proposition can really be irresistible, and yet there be times at which I can doubt it, namely if I do not think clearly enough about it. All the more, the claim *that a given proposition is irresistible* can at some times be doubted, even if that proposition is in fact irresistible: I can achieve a sufficient degree of inattention from an irresistible proposition to believe falsely that if I did think carefully about it, I would not assent to it.

Irresistibility does not entail truth. That there are things which one cannot help believing when one thinks of them might be a matter of a psychological compulsion, one which the malicious demon would have been happy to implant. Now when I am actually thinking of a proposition which is irresistible, I cannot actually entertain this possibility, since then I believe the proposition, and to believe it is to believe that it is true. But when I am not, in that close way, thinking of the proposition, I can entertain that possibility. Descartes's situation is that the only reason he has for believing anything to be true is that it is either irresistible, or depends on something that is irresistible; so, when he is not actually thinking of anything irresistible, he can entertain the idea that nothing which he is disposed to believe is really true. So it looks as though there is room for another question: is what I clearly and distinctly perceive 'to be true' – that is to say, what I experience as irresistible – really true?

In the *Third Meditation* (VII 35, HR1 158) he says:

I am certain that I am a thing that thinks. Do I not then also know what is required for me to be certain of something? Obviously in this first knowledge (*cognitio*) there is nothing except the clear and distinct perception of the thing that I assert. This would indeed not be enough to make me certain of the truth of the matter, if it could ever happen that a thing which I perceived so clearly and distinctly could be false; and accordingly it seems to me that now I can establish as a general rule that everything which I perceive very clearly and distinctly is true.

There follows a page of very sensitive dialectic in which

Descartes balances against one another the conviction extracted from him by clear and distinct perceptions while he has them, and the 'very slight, so to speak metaphysical' possibility which still remains, that there is a deceiver who may make him err even in what seems most evident, a possibility which will be eliminated only by the demonstration of a benevolent and non-deceiving God. Commentators have been divided on the question whether the general rule 'whatever I clearly and distinctly perceive is true' itself needs, according to Descartes, or could receive, a justification.

A number of things which Descartes says suggest very strongly that he did think that it needed a justification, and that his reflections could provide it. Consider, for instance, this rather startling passage from the fourth part of the *Discourse*:

> That which I have just taken as a rule, that is to say, that the things we conceive very clearly and distinctly are all true, is sound (*assuré*) only because God is or exists, and because he is a Perfect Being, and because all that is in us issues from him ... If we did not know that all that is in us of reality and truth proceeds from a perfect and infinite being, however clear and distinct our ideas were, there would be nothing to assure us that they had the perfection of being true. (VI 38–9, HR1 105)

It looks as though reliance on our clear and distinct ideas does need a justification, and that this is provided by God. Similarly near the beginning of the *Third Meditation*:

> ... I must enquire whether there is a God, and, if there is, whether he can be a deceiver: for without knowledge on this matter, I do not seem to be able to be entirely certain about any other. (VII 36, HR1 159)

And at the end of the *Fifth Meditation*:

> And so I clearly recognize that the certainty and truth of all knowledge (*scientia*) depends uniquely on the knowledge (*cognitio*) of the true God: so much so, that before I knew him, I could not have a perfect knowledge of anything else. (VII 71, cf. 69; HR1 185, cf. 183)

Again, in a passage of the *Fourth Meditation,* though Descartes does not say that he has to justify clear and distinct perception by appeal to God, he nevertheless does so:

... so often as in making judgements I restrain my will, so that it extends only to those things that are clearly and distinctly represented to it by the understanding, I can never be deceived; for every clear and distinct perception is without doubt something, and hence cannot come from nothing, but must necessarily have God as its author – God who, being supremely perfect, cannot be the cause of any error; and consequently we must conclude that such a perception must be true. (VII 62, HR1 178)

The line of argument in these passages invites an obvious objection. Some of those who provided the *Objections* were not slow to realize this. As Arnauld mildly puts it in his comments (the *Fourth* set):

The only remaining scruple that I have is an uncertainty as to how a circular reasoning is to be avoided ... (VII 214, HR2 92)

Gassendi wrote:

... I note that a circular argument appears to have its beginning at this point, according to which you are certain that there must be a God and that he is not a deceiver on the ground that you have a clear and distinct idea of him, and you are certain that a clear and distinct idea must be true on the ground that you know that there is a God who cannot be a deceiver.[3]

Even the theologians who jointly provided the *Second* set of comments see the difficulty. They apply it to an earlier stage of Descartes's argument than Gassendi does, but the principle is the same, since, if God is the sole warrant for relying on clear and distinct perceptions, everything will be vitiated that relies on the truth of such perceptions without God's existence already having been established.

... it follows that you cannot clearly and distinctly know that you are a thinking thing, since according to you that knowledge depends

3. *Disquisitio metaphysica, seu dubitationes et instantiae: adversus Renati Cartesii metaphysicam, et responsa* (Amsterdam, 1644), Rebuttal to *Med. III*, Doubt I. i. English translation *The Selected Works of Pierre Gassendi*, ed. and trans. Craig Brush (New York, 1972), p. 204.

on the clear knowledge of the existence of God, the proof of which
you have not reached at that point where you draw the conclusion
that you have a clear knowledge of what you are. (VII 125,
HR2 26)

Descartes does not ignore these objections. To the theologians and to Arnauld he gives an answer which involves the
idea that it was only such knowledge as depends on memory
that he was referring to as needing reliance on God for its
certainty:

I announced in express terms that I referred only to the knowledge (*scientia*) of those conclusions, the memory of which can recur
when we are no longer attending to the reasons from which we
deduced them. (*II Rep.*: VII 140, HR2 38)

and he refers Arnauld to this reply:

There [sc. in *II Rep.*] I distinguished those matters that in actual
truth (*reipsa*) we clearly perceive from those we remember that
we formerly perceived. For first we are sure that God exists because
we are attending to the proofs that establish this fact; but afterwards
it is enough for us to remember that we have perceived something
clearly, in order to be sure that it is true; but this would not suffice,
unless we knew that God existed and did not deceive us. (VII 246,
HR2 115)

Replies in similar terms are given elsewhere. So to 'Hyperaspistes', August 1641 (III 434, K 119):

Certainly I have never denied that the Sceptics themselves, so
long as they clearly perceive some truth, spontaneously assent to it,
nor do they remain in that heresy of theirs, of doubting everything
except just in name, and possibly in intention and resolve. But I was
dealing only with those things that we remember having clearly
perceived earlier, not the things which we clearly perceive at the
present moment . . .

and he refers his correspondent to the passage from the *Second
Replies* which has just been quoted, and to the *Fifth Meditation*
(VII 69, HR1 183), which we shall come back to. Again, in
Principles i 13, *In what sense the knowledge of all other things
depends on the knowledge of God*:

... [the mind] persuades itself that these and similar things [that the angles of a triangle are equal to two right angles etc.] are true, so long as it attends to the premisses from which it deduced them. But because it cannot always attend to them, when afterwards it recollects that it does not yet know that it may not be of such a nature as to be deceived even in those things that seem most evident to it, it sees that it justly has doubts about such things, and cannot have any certain knowledge (*scientia*) until it has recognized its creator.

The same point seems to be made once more in the *Conversation with Burman* (V 178, C pp. 49–50).

What exactly is this answer? One way of taking it, which has been followed by some commentators,[4] is that what is in question is the reliability of memory, something which has been suspended in the Doubt, and which certainly needs God's vindication of beliefs which are not clear and distinct. The point will then be that clear and distinct perceptions need no further justification, and the 'general rule' is accepted by Descartes as correctly claiming their truth: so if we *do* know that at any time we clearly and distinctly perceived that *P*, then we can know that *P*. But often we only think we know, through memory, that we clearly and distinctly perceived something, and to validate that memory, God is needed. This will eliminate at least the circle that was first objected to (even though, as we shall see, it does not remove all difficulty), since we shall not have God validating the intuitions which proved his existence.

We may call the answer which this interpretation ascribes to Descartes, 'the memory answer'. Its basic materials, at least, accord well with some things that Descartes had said in an earlier work, in the third section of the *Regulae*. He distinguishes there between what he calls 'intuition' and 'deduction'. Intuition is the immediate grasp of some intellectual matter, where this covers both the grasping of the truth of some proposition, and the grasping of the validity of inferences: I can

4. Though not all his formulations are entirely unambiguous, this seems to be Gilson's view in his *Commentaire* on the *Discourse* (Paris, 1947): see especially p. 361. The view is firmly expressed by Willis Doney, 'The Cartesian Circle', *Journal of the History of Ideas* XVI (1955), 324–38; and in my own article on Descartes in *The Encyclopedia of Philosophy*, ed. Paul Edwards (London and New York, 1967), Vol. 2, p. 351.

'see' in intuition both that such-and-such is the case, and that one thing follows logically from another. Deduction consists of a chain of intuitions held together by memory: thus if I deduce *S* from *P via* the steps *Q* and *R*, the process is that, having intuited the truth of *P*, I intuit that *Q* follows from *P*, and then that *R* follows from *Q*, and that *S* follows from *R*, and this assures me that *S* follows from *P* and is true, because I remember that I intuited the truth of *P* and the validity of the successive steps, although I am not at the end point actually doing so. The fact that I do conduct an argument by deduction, in this sense, does not mean that I shall always have to – greater familiarity with it may enable me eventually to intuit the whole thing, in one act of the mind. The 'memory answer' will make direct use of this distinction, though Descartes does not stick to this terminology in his later works, often using 'deduction' to cover both[5]: the answer would come to saying that knowledge of God is necessary to enable me to rely on deductions, but not for reliance on intuitions. It presumably follows that everything up to and including the demonstration of God's existence can be done in intuition – where this should mean, eventually at least, that it can all be done in one intuition.

There are obvious difficulties, in fact, about the temporal aspect of 'intuitions'. Descartes says in *Regulae* iii (X 369–70, HR1 8) that it is deduction that first introduces the notion of succession in thought, and this suggests that an intuition has to happen in an instant. Here there seems to be a significant parallelism between the idea that God is needed to justify remembered intuitions, and the doctrine of the *Third Meditation* that God is needed to conserve anything in existence from one moment to the next (on this, see pp. 149–50). They look very much like epistemological and ontological versions of the same thought – without God's power, both knowledge and existence are confined to the instant. Descartes himself perhaps believed that time was atomic, consisting of what are called 'durationless instants'[6]; I shall not try to take further the ques-

5. For relations between the terminology of the *Regulae* and Descartes's later formulations, see Kenny, *Descartes*, pp. 175–6.
6. The phrase is used by Kemp Smith, who claims the view for Descartes

tion of Descartes's views on time, but it is worth remarking that the epistemological doctrine may have more need of temporal atoms than the ontological one. God's conserving power could consistently be regarded as operating as a continuous function, there being no period, however short, for which a created thing could stay in existence if God did not conserve it. But the analogue to this would be that an intuition was an actual intellectual event which took no time at all, and it is less clear how Descartes could use this notion. In fact, since Descartes's talk of intuitions evidently refers not to a mere theoretical postulate, but to the familiar experience of holding some set of considerations very clearly and concentratedly in one's attention, it is far from clear that a temporal atom would anyway be enough for it: what Descartes needs is rather a 'specious present' of the intellect, which is psychologically durationless, though in terms of clocks it may take time.

There is not much point in pressing these problems, since Descartes himself gives so little material to help us with them. There are two more central questions: whether the 'memory answer' is in fact Descartes's answer to the charge of circularity, and to what extent it would answer the charge, if it were his answer. H. G. Frankfurt has argued both that the answer would be inadequate, and that the 'memory answer' misrepresents Descartes's intentions,[7] and I shall at several points refer to his arguments.

That the 'memory answer' does not adequately represent what Descartes wants to say is suggested by his insistence, on

in *New Studies in the Philosophy of Descartes* (London, 1963), p. 202 ff.; I am not convinced that the texts he cites commit Descartes to the view. The same claim is made by G. J. Whitrow, *The Natural Philosophy of Time* (London and Edinburgh, 1961), pp. 155–6, in the course of an interesting historical account of temporal atomism.

7. In *Demons, Dreamers and Madmen: The Defense of Reason in Descartes's Meditations:* Indianapolis and New York, 1970. An earlier article, 'Memory and the Cartesian Circle', *Philosophical Review* LXXI (1962), 504–11, presents similar views. I do not accept Frankfurt's view of Descartes's general intentions and I reject some of his arguments (see below, pp. 197 ff.), but I am indebted to his discussion for convincing me that, in particular, Descartes did not intend the 'memory answer'.

several occasions, and at various points in his life, on suggesting that it is not just memories of clear and distinct perceptions but clear and distinct perceptions themselves that require validation by God. He often suggests this even in passages which have been taken to be evidence for the 'memory answer'. The quotations we have already seen from the *Third* and *Fifth Meditations*, to say nothing of that from the *Discourse*, suggest a position by which not merely that knowledge which depends on memory, but all our knowledge, depends on God. Other passages, too, though they may seem to point to the 'memory answer', on closer inspection turn out to point away from it – to considerations which may indeed involve memory, but which do not confine the question of God's validation to the faculty of memory itself. When in reply to the theologians he claimed that he had 'expressly said' that God's warrant applied only to conclusions which relied on memory, he evidently had in mind another passage of the *Fifth Meditation* (VII 69–70, HR1 183–4):

Although I am of such a nature that, so long as I perceive something very clearly and distinctly, I cannot not believe it to be true, yet because I am also of such a nature that I cannot keep the attention of my mind always directed to the same thing in order to perceive it clearly, and the memory of some judgement made earlier often comes back to me when I am no longer attending to the reasons on the strength of which I made the judgement; other reasons can be brought up which would easily cause me to change my opinion, if I were ignorant of God. Thus I should never have any true and certain knowledge (*scientia*) about anything, but only fleeting and changeable opinions.

Descartes then takes the example of his recognizing that the angles of a triangle are equal to two right angles, which he cannot doubt while he attends to the demonstration; but

as soon as I have ceased to direct my mind to it, however much I may recall having perceived it most clearly, it could easily happen that I should doubt whether it was true, if I did not know God.

So far, this might seem to be the position of the 'memory answer'. However, he immediately goes on to say some things which confuse the picture, and apparently bring us nearer once more to the more ambitious view which the critics attacked:

For I am able to persuade myself that I am so made by nature, that I may sometimes be deceived in things that I perceive most evidently, especially when I recall that I have often taken many things for true and certain, which later, influenced by other reasons, I have judged to be false. But after I have perceived in fact that God exists: because I have understood that everything else depends on him, and that he is not a deceiver, and I have gathered from that that all those things that I clearly and distinctly perceive are necessarily true – because of this, even if I am no longer attending to the reasons on account of which I judged this to be true, if I merely recall that I clearly and distinctly perceived it, no contrary reason can be brought up which would force me to doubt it, but I have true and certain knowledge (*scientia*) about it.

In this passage Descartes is involved with something more ambitious than the 'memory answer'. He raises the possibility that he may be deceived in things which he 'perceives most evidently', and what this means is that he can, before the discovery of God, persuade himself at a given time that things which at some other time he clearly and distinctly perceived were false. This goes outside the range of the 'memory answer', which admits only the possibility that he may falsely think, through deceptive memory, that he clearly and distinctly perceived something which he did not so perceive. It is important, however, that the passage does not admit, any more than any other passage of Descartes, the possibility that he should at a given time clearly and distinctly perceive something, and at that very same time admit the doubt that he may be mistaken. Again, he says that he has gathered from the considerations about God's nature that what 'he clearly and distinctly perceives is necessarily true', and this seems straightforwardly to report a step in his earlier reasonings, a step which, it might seem, was an essential one. But if it was an essential one, how does he avoid the circle?

Thus in the passage of the *Fifth Meditation* to which Descartes refers his critics, it seems not to be, after all, the 'memory answer' that is being given. Moreover, in that passage of the *Second Replies* in which, if anywhere, he is supposed to be giving the 'memory answer', he in fact offers a more ambitious view. The critics had also put their point by saying that it seemed to follow from Descartes's position that no atheist could be certain of anything, even of the simplest propositions of mathematics. Their reasoning— which they do not spell out — is presumably that if one cannot be sure that what one clearly and distinctly perceives is true unless one knows that God exists and is no deceiver, an atheist, who disbelieves in God, cannot be sure of the truth of anything that he perceives, however clearly and distinctly. This objection needs to be carefully expressed if it is to have weight, even if Descartes is taking the more ambitious position. For even from that position it will not follow that an atheist cannot feel certain in believing various propositions, nor yet that the propositions that he feels certain about cannot be true. All that can follow is that an atheist cannot ultimately have any right to feel certain about these propositions, since he disbelieves in God, knowledge of whom (on the more ambitious position) alone gives a man a right to believe that that which he feels subjectively certain about is really true. Descartes, in his reply to this point, does not directly take up the question of how the objection is to be interpreted, but says (VII 141, HR2 39):

That an atheist can clearly know that the three angles of a triangle are equal to two right angles, I do not deny; I merely say that this knowledge of his (*cognitionem*) is not true science (*scientia*), because no knowledge which can be rendered doubtful should, it seems, be called science. Since he is supposed to be an atheist, he cannot be certain that he is not deceived even in those things that seem most evident to him, as has been sufficiently shown; and although this doubt may never occur to him, nevertheless it can occur to him, if he examines the question, or it may be suggested by someone else, and he will never be safe from it, unless he first acknowledges God.

Here again we meet the idea that without the knowledge of God, one cannot be safe from doubt even about the things which are agreed to be clearly and distinctly perceived; once again, as in the *Fifth Meditation*, the point is made that the doubt and the clear perception cannot occur at once. Similar problems occur in the *Principles: Principles* i 30 seems to express a more ambitious view, and when one looks back from that to *Principles* i 13, which was quoted earlier as seemingly expressing the 'memory answer', one sees that that is not un-ambiguous itself.

It looks now as though the 'memory answer' is hardly any-where unambiguously presented, and there is good reason to think that it misrepresents Descartes. The search for a replace-ment will be encouraged, if, further, it is true that the 'memory answer' would not in any case meet the objection of circularity. Frankfurt[8] claims that for this answer to have any force, it would at the very least be necessary that when recollecting some previous demonstration, I should carry in my mind an actual intuition of the proof that God exists and is no deceiver, and there is no reason to suppose that Descartes regarded this feat as necessary, or, perhaps, even possible. But, if, as opposed to this, a mere recollection that God had been proved was enough, as Descartes seems to suggest, and indeed says in the passage quoted above from the *Fifth Meditation* (VII 70, HR1 184; see also to Regius, 24 May 1640: III 65, K 73–4), recollection will be being vindicated on the basis of a recollection, and we will be back with a very simple circle.

Frankfurt goes further, to suggest that Descartes is not con-cerned with the vindication of memory *at all*, and Kenny has also said[9] 'Descartes never seriously raises sceptical doubts about the reliability of memory'. If this means that memory has never been subject to the Doubt, this is false; in the *Second Meditation* (VII 24, HR1 149) Descartes says 'I am believing that nothing has ever existed of the things that my deceitful memory represents'. Moreover, at the end of the *Sixth Medi-tation* (VII 89, HR1 198), the use of memory is quite clearly represented as something recovered from the Doubt, at least in its application to empirical matters. But it is true that Descartes is far less explicit about the vindication of memory than one would expect him to be if the 'memory answer' were his answer.

8. op. cit., pp. 158 ff.
9. *Descartes*, p. 187.

A close reading of the texts already quoted does support Frankfurt's claim that 'Descartes's problem is not whether memory is reliable, but whether *what* is recollected – that something was deduced from principles that were evident – is sufficient to establish the truth of the conclusion in question. What he doubts is whether the remembered fact that *p* was proved at a certain time entitles him to be certain at a later time of *p*'s truth.'[10] Accepting this, the question arises of why *memory* is invoked in Descartes's answers at all. Frankfurt makes the point that granted the first-personal character of Descartes's enquiry, his own past is the one location for clear and distinct perceptions which are actual but not now present to him. In association with that, we can notice that there is a reason in Descartes's procedures why the possible unreliability of memory, under the Doubt, cannot be insisted upon: it would destroy the coherence of the *Meditations* themselves, many of whose statements refer to earlier reflections. We can represent this in terms of the model of Pure Enquiry – unless the Pure Enquirer tacitly makes some presumption about the memory of his own thoughts, there is no procedure of enquiry he can carry on at all.

There is another feature of Pure Enquiry which may help us to understand Descartes's aims in relation to the Circle: we shall come back to this shortly. We must first consider the conclusions which Frankfurt himself associates with the rejection of the 'memory answer'. He detaches Descartes's enquiry from any concern with truth, in the sense of correspondence to fact or independent reality, and claims that Descartes is concerned only with the consistency of what is achieved by rational procedures. Descartes's aim is said to be to 'show that the skeptic's attempt to overthrow reason fails. Descartes believes that he can accomplish this by making it clear that the most rigorous use of reason does not lead to a mistrust of reason, but, rather, to conclusions excluding all basis for such mistrust... Descartes' argument . . . is an attempt to show that there are no good reasons for believing that reason is unreliable . . .'[11] Thus

10. op. cit., p. 161.
11. op. cit., p. 175.

Frankfurt relativizes the Cartesian procedure to the sceptic's attack in a very radical manner: it is not the truth of what is clearly and distinctly perceived which Descartes requires, Frankfurt claims, but solely a consistent set of beliefs which cannot be undermined by the sceptic. The point is not that a non-deceiving God exists, but that reason leads to this conclusion.

This paradoxical interpretation of Descartes's intentions does not even, as Frankfurt admits,[12] free the system from circularity, since a validation of reason by reason is not obviously better than a validation of memory through memory. The price that has to be paid, moreover, is very high; to claim that Descartes was not concerned with truth flies in the face not only of the contents of his works, but of the title of one of them, as I pointed out earlier,[13] while the notion of truth itself is unquestioningly interpreted by Descartes in terms of the conformity of our ideas to reality. Frankfurt places some weight on a striking passage from the *Second Replies* (VII 144–5, HR2 41), which comes shortly before the account of indubitability which I quoted above (p. 184):

First of all, as soon as we think that we conceive some truth clearly, we are naturally inclined to believe it. And if this belief is so strong that we could not ever have any reason for doubting the thing that we believe in this way, there is nothing further to be looked for: we have on that matter all the certainty that can be reasonably wished. For what does it matter to us if someone pretends that this truth of which we are so strongly persuaded appears false to the eyes of God or the angels, and that therefore, absolutely speaking, it is false? Why should we worry about this absolute falsehood since we do not believe in it in the least, and have not even the slightest suspicion of it? For we are supposing a belief or persuasion so firm that it could not be removed; which is consequently in exactly the same situation as perfect certainty. (VII 144–5, HR2 41)

What this passage does is to present in a particularly emphatic and indeed rhetorical form the idea that for a person actually presented with a clear and distinct perception, no question can

12. op. cit., p. 177.
13. p. 35, note 2.

possibly arise of his being mistaken. It represents an expression of what goes with that state of mind, rather like those words which, in the *Third Meditation* (VII 36, HR1 158–9), Descartes says he spontaneously 'comes out with' when he is similarly convinced. There is no question here of any actual possibility, acknowledged by Descartes, that what we clearly and distinctly perceive could be 'absolutely false'. As Kenny points out,[14] it is not a matter of the proposition's appearing false to God or the angels, but of someone's 'pretending' this. Indeed, we could not possibly take seriously, in Descartes's system, the idea that something which was clearly and distinctly perceived by us to be true should appear false to God. What appears false to God, God being omniscient, is false, so this possibility would mean that God was, radically, a deceiver. The reference to 'absolute falsehood', in this sense, is not to be taken seriously.

We cannot understand Descartes if we break the connection between the search for certainty and the search for truth, or the connection between knowledge and the correspondence of ideas to reality. Let us go back to the Pure Enquirer, whose project, I argued in Chapter 2, is governed by both these connections. His aim was to maximize true belief. He recognized that if he had incorrigible beliefs, then to that extent he would be successful. This did not yet directly help him, since it did not tell him what to do to acquire such beliefs, but it did help him indirectly, by the way of eliminating those which were not incorrigible. This, with the psychological help of the fiction of the malicious demon, he has done, and then finds that he has encountered a number of propositions which are irresistible. These encounters, however, have not yet given the Pure Enquirer any knowledge (what Descartes, in more than one passage already quoted, calls *scientia*). There is even a sense, and an important one, in which they have not given him any beliefs. The perceptions of these propositions which have occurred so far, and in which they revealed their irresistibility, do not satisfy what is a virtually formal requirement on knowledge or (in a full sense) belief, that it should be an on-going dispositional state; it was a search for such knowledge that the Pure Enquirer

14. *Descartes*, p. 195.

was engaged in from the beginning (as we saw on p. 62). The clear and distinct perceptions (to use Descartes's terminology) which the Enquirer has had are all time-bound, in the sense that he may at one time clearly and distinctly perceive that P is true, but not at another. With the 'eternal truths', this will be because he is considering P at one time but not another. With the propositions that are, in our sense, evident, he may be convinced at t that P is true at t: but this does not in itself give him any on-going belief or knowledge about the state of affairs at t.[15]

Faced with the recognition that his clear and distinct perceptions are time-bound, there are just three things that the Enquirer might in principle do. One is to give up. But this would be quite unreasonable: he has not encountered any obstacle to his project, but merely been reminded of what was from the beginning one of its conditions. The second way would be to convert some selected clear and distinct perception directly into an on-going state by thinking about nothing but the irresistible proposition involved in it. But this violates the original condition that his project is enquiry: to freeze one's attention on a single certainty is to refuse to advance enquiry by using earlier knowledge. It is, in fact, very like the first course, of giving up, the Enquirer merely stopping one stage later than if he had nothing at all. The fact, moreover, that it would be arbitrary which irresistible certainty he clung to shows that this would be a policy which, absurdly, threw away resources he already possessed. (Perhaps there is one certainty which would recommend itself to the Christian Enquirer over all others as the object of such attention – the intuition of the properties of God. But the pure and continual contemplation of the idea of God is only one vocation, if indeed it is any terrestrial vocation at all: and the activity of Pure Enquiry is quite certainly a secular enterprise.) The third possibility, and the only one which could genuinely satisfy the original conditions of Pure Enquiry, is to admit some acceptance-rule for beliefs which are on-going

15. The sense of 'belief' which, for convenience, I have used in the definitions of 'evident', 'irresistible', etc. (see Appendix 1) is one which does allow beliefs to be time-bound.

and not time-bound as the clear and distinct perceptions are. This will in fact be the first acceptance-rule that the Enquirer will have adopted. We should not say that prior to this rule he has adopted the rule:

Accept at *t* what is clearly and distinctly perceived at *t* to be true.

This would not in any case be an acceptance-rule for beliefs in the on-going sense (it would generate only temporary states), and it would have no effect as an acceptance-rule, since there is no alternative to what it enjoins – what is clearly and distinctly perceived to be true is irresistibly accepted while it is so perceived.

What should the acceptance-rule be? The choice is governed by three conditions:

(i) It should generate on-going beliefs; this is what the rule is for.

(ii) It should involve the minimum possible risk of error; this is a consequence of the Enquirer's continuing conservative strategy.

(iii) It should be stable: the beliefs it generates should not be liable to being overthrown, and should be minimally liable to doubt, as enquiry proceeds. Actual conflict would indicate falsity; more generally, it is important that if Pure Enquiry can succeed, it should have a stable cumulative basis, not one that is constantly being recalled for consideration. As Descartes himself puts it, true knowledge (*scientia*), as opposed to mere persuasion, cannot be rendered doubtful (to Regius, 24 May 1640: III 64–5, K 73–4; *V Med.*: VII 70, HR1 184; *II Rep.*: VII 141, HR2 39). Condition (iii) has the consequence that any beliefs adopted under the rule should be consistent with the propositions which have been clearly and distinctly perceived to be true; for if they were not, one could unsettle these beliefs merely by attending to those propositions, which could be perceived to conflict with them. In fact, the beliefs adopted should include those propositions, for there are no other convictions which the Enquirer has to provide the material for on-going beliefs. Moreover, granted (ii), he should go as little beyond that material as he can. These considerations together mean that the conditions uniquely determine the adoption of the acceptance-rule:

(A) Accept as on-going beliefs just those propositions which are at any time clearly and distinctly perceived to be true.

The rule (A), together with Descartes's previous reflections, give him the injunction:

Accept: (1) God exists and is no deceiver.

(1) entails the important consequence

(2) What one clearly and distinctly perceives to be true is true

which has among its consequences

(3) (A) as an acceptance-rule for a truth-seeker is a sound rule.

Is there a circularity here? There will be a circularity in the sense complained of by Descartes's critics only if the sole basis Descartes can have for claiming to know (2) and (3) is his claim to know (1), and conversely. We have seen from several passages that Descartes does claim to base (2) and (3) on (1), and thinks he has reason to regard (A) as a truth-yielding rule only because he knows God's existence and benevolence. If we accept this, then it will have to be the case, if he is to avoid the circle, that he does not base (1) on (2) and (3). But perhaps this condition is satisfied. Cannot we say that Descartes does not have to have established (2) and (3) already in order to arrive at (1) – rather, he arrives at (1) merely by having intuited the reasons for it? This answer may seem still a good deal too close to circularity for comfort. Can the claim that he has intuited (1) – that is, very clearly and distinctly perceived it to be true – serve as a validation of (1), or as a support to a claim to know (1), unless (2) and (3) are true? – It cannot. Then can he properly claim to know (1) unless he can already claim to *know* (2) and (3)? If not, then certainly the circle has reappeared. But we do not have to agree that he cannot claim to know (1) unless he can claim *knowledge* of the general principles (2) and (3). Indeed, to insist that that must be so would seem to flow from some such demand as that the Enquirer can never deploy any consideration until he has validated that kind of consideration, and since he could do that only by deploying some consideration or other, this would make his project trivially hopeless from the start.

Descartes's ambitions for Pure Enquiry do not commit him to this absurdity. Rather, throughout his undertaking, he tries only to raise the test of possible doubt to the maximum which will actually make sense. In the present connection, his way of doing this involves making two distinctions. One is the now familiar distinction between occasions when he is actually intuiting the proofs of God, and occasions when he is not; the other is a distinction between particular doubts about particular intellectual perceptions, and systematic doubt about all intellectual perceptions. His use of these distinctions in answering the charge of circularity, and, relatedly, his attitude towards scepticism in these matters, can best be brought out if we take up a connection on which he insists between 'having true knowledge' and having a special kind of reason 'so strong that it cannot be knocked out by any stronger reason' as he puts it in the letter to Regius already referred to (III 65, K 74; and cf. the passages of *V Med.* and *II Rep.* also cited on p. 180).

If we take some irresistible proposition Q, Descartes says first that a person A has a reason of this kind for believing Q if he is actually fully considering Q. In fact, it is not entirely clear that A has a *reason* for believing Q which goes beyond his clear and distinct perception of Q: at any rate, there is nothing else more evident than Q from which A derives Q or on which he bases it. But the more important question is whether there is any reason that could be brought against A's conviction. This question divides into two. There is a psychological question, whether A in this state can be made doubtful of Q; the answer to this is 'no'. There is a logical or epistemological question, whether there are any good reasons which could count against it, even though A while intuiting could not appreciate them. These might be either particular or systematic reasons for doubt. The first are reasons *specially for doubting Q*: for instance, that it is inconsistent with some other proposition with an equally good claim to be true. But if this were so, then there would be some obscurity in A's perception, and A would not have done his best in clarifying his ideas. Whether Descartes can consistently admit that A might be in this position though A is convinced that he is clearly and distinctly perceiving, is a question we shall come back to shortly. The immediate point is that in the everyday sense in which there is sometimes a good reason of a particular kind for suspecting that A is confused with regard to something that he thinks is self-evident, in that sense it is often the case that there is no reason to suspect this. This parallels, for intellectual perception, a point made in Chapter 2 about sense perception. In the everyday sense in which there is a reason to doubt that some apparently bent sticks are bent, there is no reason to doubt this of others, and Descartes does not proceed by pretending otherwise: he does not try simply to generalize the particular everyday doubts. Similarly with intellectual perceptions, the question is not whether in each case some particular kind of everyday reason might be brought against A's conviction. The question is whether there might be brought against it the other, systematic, kind of doubt, the 'very slight, so to speak metaphysical possibility' that every such conviction might, after all, be delusory.

But in fact no good reason of this kind can be brought, Descartes claims, because God exists and is no deceiver. When A is not actually intuiting Q, he may be open to the consideration that systematic error is possible, and he may have no way of answering it. Descartes holds that here it makes a difference whether A believes in God or not (where belief in God is taken, of course, to include appropriate reflections on the systematic implications of God's being no deceiver). Descartes is consistent in claiming that, on his views, it makes a difference. Presented with the systematic doubt, the believer has a systematic answer, an answer which purports to explain in general the validity of the perceptions being questioned. The unbeliever has no systematic answer, has nothing to say to this point. The sceptic will object that while the believer has 'something to say', this in itself is not enough – what is needed is that what he has to say should express knowledge, and Descartes cannot claim this without falling back into a circle. Confronted with this sceptic, Descartes can only invite him to go through the proofs of God. If he understands them and is sincere, Descartes believes, the sceptic cannot but accept them:

> the Sceptics . . . have never perceived anything clearly; from the mere fact that they had perceived something clearly they would have ceased to doubt and to be Sceptics. (*VII Rep.*: VII 477, H R2 279)

If he accepts them, he will acknowledge that there is a general reason to be brought against systematic doubt. If he accepts them when intuiting them, and accepts that he did accept them when intuiting them, but simply refuses to accept them when, and because, he is not intuiting them, then it is appropriate to bring against him the consideration which we have already examined, that he is refusing a merely structural condition on having usable knowledge.

The argument can be put summarily like this. When one is actually intuiting a given proposition, no doubt can be entertained. So any doubt there can be must be entertained when one is not intuiting the proposition. If this is a particular doubt, then it must be dealt with by further intellectual inspection of this and other propositions. If it is the general and systematic doubt, then we have a general and systematic answer, the existence and benevolence of God. If either a particular or a systematic doubt is raised against that, then we can only turn to intuiting the proofs of it; Descartes believes that the sceptic must, if he intuits those proofs, accept them. If the sceptic then reverts to objecting merely because he is no longer intuiting, we can point out that the use of propositions one is not at that instant intuiting (the rule (A)) is a minimal structural condition on getting on at all, and that just as it would be unreasonable to spend all one's time rehearsing one intuition, so it would be unreasonable to spend all one's time rehearsing the proofs of the general answer to scepticism, an answer which we nevertheless possess.

Of course none of these procedures could convince a person who refused to reason at all that reason was valid. It is perhaps because Frankfurt ascribes this aim to Descartes that he complains of an ultimate circularity, and because he wants to trim Descartes's project to this aim that he represents it as so radically relativized to scepticism. In fact, it is not so much that Descartes's project is relativized to radical scepticism; rather, his approach to scepticism is relativized to his project, and in Descartes's view it is a measure of how successful his project is, that it enables him to answer such radical forms of scepticism. The project of Pure Enquiry uses scepticism, as we saw before (p. 62), pre-emptively, and its success (as Descartes supposes) generates answers to a large class of sceptics. The class is so large that it includes everyone who is prepared to acknowledge the result of a simple and maximally clear argument.

It is important that this is what the experience of confronting the arguments for God is supposed to be: it is nothing but clear reasoning, something which the sceptic, unless he is uninterestingly beyond the reach of rational discourse, cannot merely disown. It is not, then, as though the sceptic could complain to Descartes that concentration on irresistible propositions might be like sniffing some hallucinogenic gas, and Descartes's procedure like that of someone who, when a doubt was raised in the absence of the gas, proposed to dispel the doubt by inviting one back to the gas. Reasoning, unlike the gas, is something which the rational sceptic is involved in even when complaining of the gas, and he reasons to conclusions. He cannot merely dissociate himself from these conclusions, since he acknowledges them solely in the light of the reason he is using anyway.

Descartes's claim that he can, in terms of God, give a systematic and general answer to a systematic and general doubt does not imply that once we have it we shall commit no errors. Compatibly with there being such an answer, there is more than one way in which error is still possible. One, which we have encountered in Chapter 6, is of course that we may not take enough trouble, and may through precipitate judgement assent to something which is not clear and distinct. At this level, we can on any given occasion, by taking enough trouble, save ourselves from error. However, there is another kind of belief, in particular perceptual beliefs about the external world, with regard to which we are liable to occasional error however hard we try. If we are going to make perceptual judgements about the external world at all, there are errors which we will commit however conscientiously we clarify our ideas on the particular occasion. This is for reasons connected with our being bodily creatures: we shall examine them in greater detail in Chapter 8. In the case of these beliefs, God's guarantee operates only on the general level, guarding us against systematic error: granted we take enough care, then our ordinary procedures, even though they are inevitably liable to occasional error, are sound in principle.

This feature of the argument from God, that it provides only a general protection against systematic error, can be extended to the case of memory. In the case of the memory of perceptual matters, this is straightforward: such memory equally involves the body (cf. *Passions of the Soul* i 42), which works by regular laws and can thus in exceptional circumstances generate error. This consideration, however, may possibly not apply to the memory of intellectual matters, in particular of earlier clear and distinct perceptions. Descartes did claim that such memory, unlike the memory of sensations, involved no physical traces in the brain, but only a modification of the mental substance (to Mesland, 2 May 1644: IV 114–5, K 148–9). In another letter, however (to 'Hyperaspistes', August 1641: III 425, K 112), he takes a different line, saying that strictly speaking there is no recollection of intellectual matters at all, since we merely perceive them intellectually as well on the second occasion as on the first; though there can be genuine recollection of the *words* in which an argument is expressed, and that is a corporeal matter. That kind of recollection, at any rate, will be liable to occasional error. Even on the first account, by which there is non-corporeal intellectual memory, it is not obvious that there is no room for occasional error. No judgement about the past is itself a clear and distinct perception, and it might well be that the workings of the mental substance itself were such that occasional mistakes were possible, even for the conscientious thinker.[16]

16. Apart from this, it must be a mistake for Frankfurt to say (*Demons,*

It is even possible that occasional error should occur with regard to what one thinks one is clearly and distinctly perceiving. Descartes says:

there are very few who rightly distinguish between that which is truly perceived and that which is thought to be perceived, because few are used to clear and distinct perceptions. (*VII Rep.*: VII 511, HR2 307)

and this has caused concern to commentators[17] as undermining the reliance on clear and distinct perceptions. If we cannot tell those perceptions which really are clear and distinct from those that merely appear to be so, the rule 'all clear and distinct perceptions are true' will be only vacuously correct, and will not be epistemically effective. But what Descartes says here need not cause any real difficulty. It does have to be true for Descartes that with presumptively clear and distinct perceptions, unlike the corporeally mediated perceptual judgements, the most conscientious possible intellectual scrutiny must on each occasion yield truth. For this to be epistemically effective it has to be true, further, that the most conscientious possible intellectual scrutiny will reveal itself for what it is. But it is surely compatible with that, that even the practised conscientious intellectual perceiver should occasionally think that he has looked as hard as he can when he has not; and it is quite certainly compatible with it that people who are in no way accustomed to trying to get things clear and do not really know what it is to do so, should wrongly say that they have clear perceptions – and this last is all that Descartes is claiming in this passage.

If Descartes's system is to work, then of course it does have to be true that there is a totally irresistible demonstration of the existence of a benevolent God, which will inevitably convince anyone who in good faith has tried as hard to understand it as

Dreamers, and Madmen, p. 157) that those who ascribe the 'memory answer' to Descartes commit him to the absurd doctrine that memory is infallible, at least where what is recalled is a clear and distinct perception. All that they commit him to is that intellectual memory is generally correct, and in particular that it correctly recalls the proofs of God.

17. For instance Kenny, *Descartes,* p. 198 ff.

any conscientious thinker can try. This is necessary for Descartes's vindication of knowledge, and also sufficient, but it is also not true. The trouble with Descartes's system is not that it is circular; nor that there is an illegitimate relation between the proofs of God and the clear and distinct perceptions; nor that there is a special problem about the proofs of God when they are not intuited. I have argued that in these respects, it is structurally sound. The trouble is that the proofs of God are invalid and do not convince *even when they are supposedly being intuited.* But this fact, as I have already suggested at the end of Chapter 5, has very large consequences. Most simply, it leaves anyone who has got that far in Pure Enquiry with nowhere to go, since God was for Descartes the bridge from the world of himself and his ideas to anything outside that world; and the subsequent history of philosophy has found it hard to see what could replace that bridge, once the question has been put in those terms. Repeatedly, the philosopher who travels that far with Descartes has found that he has had to make do with what he has on the near side of the bridge, so that Descartes's own transcendental religious metaphysics has had a legacy which – when not merely hopeless solipsism – has consisted of phenomenalism and idealism, which Descartes would have regarded, rightly, as failing to offer knowledge of a real world.

In face of the collapse of Descartes's bridge, many have renounced the Cartesian search for certainty. It follows, I think, that they must renounce the conception of Pure Enquiry which motivated that search, though it may remain unclear exactly how much one can still do in that direction. One will not seek, by one grand design, to maximize the truth-ratio among one's beliefs, and perhaps will not even seek, systematically, at least, to increase it, but merely recognize that one is fallible and take what seem to be appropriate precautions against particular sorts of error in particular sorts of case. Some such modest strategy seems even more appropriate when we add a further reflection about Descartes's failure. Descartes took these hopeless arguments for the existence of God to be self-evidently valid, conditioned in this by historical and perhaps also by temperamental factors. We, who do not accept these arguments, cannot escape the reflection that we may seem to others, now or later, to be just as much in error in what seems to us just as self-evident. This reflection suggests that any method must be open to similar risks which rests so much weight on one supposed self-evident certainty, or indeed, perhaps, on any self-evident certainties.

A modest epistemic strategy, however, is not enough. There are consequences of Descartes's failure which come close to home even for those who renounce the search for certainty. According to Descartes, God guarantees that there is a world which exists independently of our thought, and that our judgements about it, if we are judicious enough in making them, will in general be reliable. In doing that, he also does something very fundamental: he validates a conception of what the world is objectively like, a conception which also includes ourselves as (Descartes supposes) comprehensibly related to that world. This is achieved through reflection on the Real Distinction and related ideas: it is a conception of ourselves as substantial immaterial things, in causal relations with a physical world conceived as extension (a notion I shall examine in greater detail in the next two chapters). We thus have, under God's dispensation, an objective conception of that reality within which we are included. One might say that what God has given us, according to Descartes, is an insight into the nature of the world as it seems to God, and the world as it seems to God must be the world as it really is. God is thus, on the Cartesian construction, deeply involved in our having what I called in Chapter 2 an 'absolute conception' of reality – a conception of reality as it is independently of our thought, and to which all representations of reality can be related. Such a conception would allow us, when we reflect on our representation of the world as being one among others, to go beyond merely assessing others, relativistically, from the standpoint of our own. I suggested that it was implicit in our idea of knowledge that such a conception should be possible, and that it should have a determinate content. The project of Pure Enquiry was supposed, in its most general philosophical significance, to answer the question whether knowledge is possible, by yielding, if successful, such an absolute conception. In Descartes's hands, it has done so, but in a way which essentially involves the appeal to God. If the arguments on that fail, as they do, then we have lost once more the absolute conception.

To give up the Cartesian search for certainty may seem a fairly easy option, but can we so easily give up the idea of an absolute conception of reality, if there is to be any knowledge at all? Even a thorough-going fallibilism does not make it easy to accept the reflection that one's entire conception of the world (including the place in it of one's fallibilist policies) may be, like any other such general representation of the world, a local idiosyncrasy, without there being any objective standpoint by reference to which such representations can be assessed.

If we take it (some, of course, would not) that Descartes's failure signals the failure of the systematic search for certainty, then three possibilities for these questions seem to be left. We might abandon the supposed connection between knowledge and the possibility of an absolute conception, and try to make clear a notion of knowledge which does without any such conception, and without even the idea that there might be one. Or we can preserve the connection, and deny the possibility of knowledge. Or we can preserve the connection, and seek to detach the idea of an absolute conception from considerations of certainty. To me, it is this third approach that seems correct, though it involves large difficulties; I shall come back to some of them in Chapter 10. First, however, we must see how Descartes, on the farther side of the religious bridge, and reassured that knowledge is possible, completes his picture of the world with an account of physical things.

Chapter 8

PHYSICAL OBJECTS

DESCARTES does not re-establish the existence of a physical world until he reaches the *Sixth*, and last, of his *Meditations*. His progress through the *Meditations*, however, is not so much like a straight line as like a spiral: a topic is taken up at an earlier stage of his reflections and then left, to be taken up again at a later stage. So it is with physical objects. Before he reaches the final point of arguing that they genuinely exist, Descartes has twice addressed himself to the questions of what they must be like if they do exist, and what must be the nature of his understanding of them. The first of these discussions is to be found quite early in his progress, in the *Second Meditation,* and the second – a very brief consideration of the 'essence of material things' – is at the beginning of the *Fifth Meditation.*

The passage of the *Second Meditation* (VII 30–33, HR1 154–6) contains a famous and baffling argument. The context of this argument is that Descartes has been considering the nature of the self, the existence of which he claims to have proved in the *cogito*; his conclusion being, as we have seen, that he is 'a thinking thing'. Although this self is the only thing which at this stage he is sure exists, and the only thing of whose nature he has any clear idea, he nevertheless is still tempted (he claims) by the common-sense thought that

corporeal things, whose images are framed by thought, which are tested by the senses, are much more distinctly known than that obscure part of me which does not come under the imagination. (VII 29, HR1 153)

To test this common-sense thought, he turns to consider what ideas he has of 'corporeal things', and it is the result of this consideration that we must now examine. Whatever the detailed interpretation of these results, their general upshot in the context of the *Second Meditation* is both clear and important: that the common-sense thought that physical objects are more clearly known than one's own mind is for Descartes false, and this conclusion he appears to regard as the main point of the argument about physical objects in this *Meditation,* as its title ('Of the Nature of the Human Mind; and that it is more easily known than the Body') itself reveals. One must bear in mind this centre of interest in considering the argument, which first of all I shall state in full, in good part in Descartes's own words.

Let us consider those things that are generally thought to be most clearly understood of all, namely the bodies which we touch and see; not indeed bodies in general – for such general perceptions are usually somewhat more confused – but one in particular. Let us take, for example, this piece of wax. It is very recently taken from the hive; it has not yet lost all the flavour of its honey; it retains some of the smell of the flowers from which it was culled; its colour, shape and size are obvious; it is hard and cold, it is easily handled, and if you strike it with your finger, it makes a sound; in fact, it seems to have everything that is necessary for a body to be known as distinctly as possible. But now, as I speak, it is brought near the fire: the last of its flavour is removed, the smell evaporates, the colour changes, its shape disappears, its size increases, it becomes liquid and hot, it can scarcely be handled, and now, if you strike it, it makes no sound. Does the same wax remain after all this? It must be admitted that it does; no one denies it, no one thinks otherwise. What then was it in the wax that was so distinctly understood? Certainly none of the things that I reached by the senses; for all the things that fell under taste or smell or sight or touch or hearing are now changed, but the wax remains.

Perhaps it was what I now think – that the wax itself was not the sweetness of honey, nor the fragrance of flowers, nor that whiteness, nor (that) shape, nor sound, but a body which a little earlier appeared to me as perceptible by these forms (*modis istis conspicuum*), and now by different ones. What then is it precisely that I am imagining? Let us consider, and, removing those things which do not belong to the wax, let us see what remains: obviously only something extended, flexible and changeable.

Descartes now goes on to consider whether this basic nature of the wax can in fact be grasped by his imagination, that is to say, whether he can adequately comprehend it in the form of images, and he concludes that he cannot, since he can conceive of an indefinitely large number of changes to which this extended and changeable body may be subject, but he cannot compass these in images.

I must concede, then, that I in no way *imagine* what this wax is, but perceive it with my understanding[1] alone; and I mean this particular piece of wax, for about wax in general it is even clearer. What then is this wax which is perceived only by the understanding? It is the very same that I see, and touch, and imagine, the same that I believed to exist from the beginning. But – and this is important – the perception of it is not sight, nor touch, nor imagination, and it never was, however it may have seemed at first; but an inspection of the mind alone, which can be either imperfect and confused, as it was at first, or clear and distinct, as it is now, inasmuch as I attend less or more closely to those things in which it consists.

Descartes next reflects that it is very easy to be tripped up by ordinary language in this connection:

For we say that we see the wax itself, if it is present, and not that we judge that it is present from its colour and shape; and I might conclude from this that I know the wax by the vision of the eyes, and not by the inspection of the mind alone; if it were not that I happened to glimpse from the window some men going by in the street, whom I should in ordinary usage say that I saw, just as much as the wax. But what in fact do I see except hats and coats, under which there could be automata? – Yet I judge that there are men there. Thus the thing that I thought I saw with my eyes I in fact comprehend merely by the faculty of judgement which is in my mind.

Lastly, Descartes draws from all this the conclusion that he knows his own mind better than he does physical objects. For all the perceptions and judgements that he makes concerning any such object will once again imply that he exists as a thinking thing; and even if the objects are not really there, he will have certainty that he has impressions as of their being there, is disposed to judge that they are there, and so forth. Moreover, the more he reflects on what the knowledge of physical objects would be like, the more he thereby comes to know about his own mind. Thus, he concludes, he can firmly reject the common-sense prejudice that physical objects are better known than the mind.

1. For this translation, see below, p. 223.

The argument about the wax involves five main steps: (i) the identity of the wax cannot consist in its sensible qualities, for all these may change, while the wax itself remains; (ii) the wax itself is merely something extended, flexible and changeable; (iii) the wax is 'perceived' not by the senses or imagination, but by the understanding, whose perception of it may be more or less clear and distinct; (iv) it is the same thing that I 'perceive' with the understanding and which I perceive with the senses; (v) what we ordinarily call seeing (and the same presumably applies to other forms of perception) is in fact judgement, or essentially involves judgement. I said just now that the argument of the wax was baffling. There are several possible interpretations of the argument.

Concentrating first on stages (i) and (ii), a possible interpretation might be that the argument is fundamentally a *metaphysical* argument which aims to show something about the essence or basic nature of physical objects, in this case about the essence of a piece of wax. On this showing, the argument rests squarely on the traditional connection between the ideas of identity and of essence: what is essential to a certain thing is that which is necessarily involved in its being what it is, and what is thus necessarily involved is what remains the same, however else the thing may change. We have already seen Descartes using such notions in his discussion of his own essence as a thinking thing, and remarked that it is because he holds that it is his essence to be a thinking thing that he concludes that the soul is always thinking (see above, p. 111). We shall see shortly that the notion of essence is complex in this connection. But if some connection of essence and identity is the main point of the present argument, its general upshot will presumably be that all the sensible qualities of the wax change, while the wax remains the same; but its essence is that which remains the same and does not change; therefore its essence does not consist in any sensible qualities – where this presumably means that a correct statement or specification of its essence will not mention any sensible qualities. What does remain constant is merely its being something extended, flexible and changeable. If we take this view of stages (i) and (ii), the rest of the argument, in particular stage (iii), will be an epistemological conclusion drawn from the first stages: since the essence does not consist in any sensible qualities, it cannot be the case that one grasps the essence by the senses. But to comprehend a certain thing, or in the intellectual sense 'perceive' it, is to grasp its essence: hence we do not comprehend physical things by the senses.

If this version correctly represents the argument, Descartes's reasoning emerges as patently invalid. For from the fact that a certain quality of a thing changes in certain circumstances, it by no means follows that no reference to that quality can figure in a statement of the thing's essence. For instance, the freezing or boiling point of a substance might figure in a statement of its essence. Similarly, it could be of the essence of wax, as wax, that it changed in colour, texture, etc. when heated: if a piece of material did not, one could be certain that it was not wax. If so, it would be false that there was no reference to colour and texture in the statement of its essence – on the contrary, there would be such a reference, only it would be a reference to a possibility of change in colour and texture. To suppose that a quality that changes cannot figure at all in a statement of a thing's essence is to confuse two quite different things. A statement of essence will indeed be a timeless and necessary statement, which cannot be falsified by changing circumstances, but it is quite a different thing, and a mistake, to suppose that such a statement itself cannot *refer* to changes in changing circumstances.

This point still holds even for sensible qualities which do not change in the way, for instance, that the colour of a litmus paper gives way to another colour, but which disappear, as the smell and flavour and characteristic sound of the wax are supposed to do in Descartes's example. Even these phenomena would not prove that there could be no reference to these qualities in a statement of the wax's essence – for it might be of its essence as wax that it had a smell in certain circumstances, and not in others. Since this is possible, one has to be wary of a rather more seductive application of the line of reasoning we are considering. It does look plausible to say that it cannot be of the essence of wax that it has a smell, for here is the wax after heating, which is still wax, and yet (we may suppose) has no smell. In one sense, this is correct: there are circumstances in which something can be wax and have no smell. But it still does not follow that the quality of smell has nothing to do with the essence of the wax, for there might be other circumstances in which it had to have a smell, if it were wax.

Related to these points is another difficulty that arises from the present interpretation. Suppose that we do waive the cases of smell, flavour, etc., which can actually be totally absent from the wax. Colour, however, seems to be in a different position: for while there are certain states of the wax in which it has no smell at all, there does not seem to be any state of the wax, at least as described in Descartes's example, in which it has no colour at all, and one might think (again, so far as the example goes) that it was always a property of the wax *to be coloured in some way or other*. It will not do to reply to this that it is insufficient because what Descartes is looking for (from whatever misguided conception) is some *determinate* quality that the wax permanently possesses. For his conclusion is that the property that the wax really possesses and which is essential to it is that of being *extended*, by which he means that it occupies space. What goes with being extended is that the thing has a certain shape and a certain volume – that it occupies an area in space determined, as one might say, in contour and in quantity. But it cannot be essential to the piece of wax that it have just one certain shape, for Descartes himself remarks that when heated it changes in shape. Hence all that can be essential to it is that it be extended *in some way or other*, and this is made clear by Descartes's saying that what is essential is that it is extended, *flexible* and *changeable*. So if a merely indeterminate extension, an extension which can be determined in various ways, will do for an essential property, why should indeterminate colour, the property of being coloured in various ways, be ruled out?

These criticisms have been made on the assumption that if the argument is concerned with essence, it is concerned with the essence of *wax*: that is to say, that the question at issue would be

(i) what makes wax, wax?

We must distinguish this from another question

(ii) what makes matter, matter?

which Descartes discusses at *Principles* ii 11, where he also goes through the sensible qualities and dismisses them, there on the ground that we can conceive of some body or other that lacks each of them. Even there, his argument, if we construe it as an attempted proof that the essence of material things lies just in extension and not in any sensible qualities, is invalid, since it would move from saying that for each sensible quality we can conceive of a material body without it, to saying that we can conceive of a material body with no sensible qualities at all. But such a procedure would at least be made more plausible by his considering the notion of a material body in general. (He indeed takes an example, that of a stone, but does not stick to it, making one of his points by reference to fire; and even with the stone, his reference to its being liquefied or powdered is not used as an example of its nevertheless remaining (a) stone, but of its remaining a *body*.) In the *Second Meditation* Descartes is emphatic that he is not discussing matter in general, but just the wax; and indeed, just this piece of wax.

This emphasis, on the particular piece, might suggest a third question:

(iii) what makes this lump of wax, this lump?

It might be suggested that this last question should be answered with the help of the answer to question (i): this would be so, if it were a *de re* necessary property of the lump, that it should be a lump *of wax*. But in fact, in his developed views, Descartes does not think that there is any particular thing which is necessarily wax; there is no particular thing which, if it ceased to be wax, would by that very fact cease to exist. The only essential attribute which any material thing has *de re* is that of being material, and it will be for scientific and not metaphysical reasons that a sample of a given stuff will be unable, if it is unable, to turn into a sample of another. Certainly no such conclusion could be reached just by inference from the changing sensible qualities of something which, it is insisted, is still wax, and this is all that Descartes considers in the argument of the *Second Meditation.* We are still lacking what exactly it is that that argument is supposed to contribute.

Question (iii) might suggest another, and slightly different, line. This would concentrate on the point at which Descartes says that the wax itself 'was not that sweetness, nor that fragrance, nor that whiteness, etc.'. These phrases might suggest that Descartes's interest is not so much in essential properties as against inessential, as in a *subject* to have any properties at all. This would be another traditional metaphysical concern, once more connected with identity. A thing's properties may change, while the thing endures, and this suggests the notion of an enduring subject – which may be termed a *substance* – which has at various times the various properties. If what Descartes is looking for is this substance, and the force of his argument is to uncover it, then he would not be disturbed by the point made against the last interpretation, that it might be an essential property of a thing to have one sensible quality at one time, and another at another. The question will still remain, *what* is it that has this essential property, and has the various sensible qualities?

If this is the start of the argument, then it will, once more, have a metaphysical beginning leading to an epistemological conclusion. Starting with the necessity of properties being supported by a substance, Descartes will then conclude that this substance can be known not by the senses but by the intellect. But how will this conclusion be drawn? In order to validate it, it looks as though Descartes will have to employ a premiss (similar to one used by the empiricist Berkeley) that *all that can be perceived by the senses are sensible qualities.* The argument will then run as follows. The wax endures though its sensible qualities change. In itself, it is the subject of those sensible qualities, the substance that supports the qualities as they change. This substance we can know about; but all we know by the senses is what we perceive by the senses and these are the sensible qualities, from which the substance is distinct; therefore we do not know about it by the senses.

This version is in some ways nearer to what Descartes wants, I think, than the first one. But it still raises considerable difficulties. First, it is not clear that Descartes would assent to the required premiss, that all that can be perceived by the senses are sensible qualities; for how is this to be reconciled with the further claim (stage (iv)) that it is the same thing that I perceive with the understanding and with the senses? If what I perceive with the understanding is the substance, and this is *ex hypothesi* different from the sensible qualities which I perceive with the senses, stage (iv) must surely be false. There is also a more particular difficulty. If Descartes's whole metaphysical interest here is in distinguishing substance from properties, and he is concerned with isolating the substance which has or supports the properties, how can he be satisfied with ending up, as he does, with a characterization of the wax which is itself entirely in terms of properties – the properties of being extended, flexible and changeable? Now it is Descartes's general doctrine that a substance is only 'by a distinction of reason' different from its essential attributes, and that one makes the nature of a substance known by listing its essential attributes (as we saw above, p. 125, in discussing the notion of substance). But this just shows that the search for the substance comes in effect to the search for the essential attributes, and this means that the second version of the present argument comes out in the end as insufficiently different from the first, since it is still essential attributes or properties that we are concerned with.[2] So we shall just be forced back on to asking what the arguments are for saying, on the evidence given by Descartes, that extension is the essential attribute of the wax, and we are faced again with all the difficulties encountered in considering the first version of his argument.

Both these versions, as we have seen, take it that the argument starts from metaphysical considerations, and ends in epi-

2. In reply to a criticism of Gassendi's that he had abstracted everything from the wax, Descartes writes (*V Rep.*: VII 360, HR2 213): 'I have never thought that in order to make a substance manifest one needs to do anything but discover its various attributes; so that the more we know of the attributes of a substance, the more perfectly we understand its nature'; and he then goes on indeed to refer to certain *sensible* attributes of the wax, such as it being white. This passage strongly suggests that to interpret the argument of the wax as a search for substance *as opposed to* attributes is mistaken.

stemological ones. This is, I think, their common mistake; the argument is properly seen as an *epistemological* argument which has – though they are not at this point explicitly drawn – metaphysical implications.[3] It is an argument not directly about the nature of physical things, but about our conception and knowledge of their nature. We know that the same wax is there after the changes, and this implies that we have a conception of the wax as something that endures through these changes. But how can we know this: whence have we got such a conception of the wax? Not from the senses, for 'everything that falls under the senses' has changed. We must have a conception of something that is first perceived as white, hard, etc., and afterwards perceived as of a different colour, soft etc. What is this conception? On reflection, Descartes discovers that he has the conception of the wax just as an extended, flexible and changeable thing: this, on the present interpretation, is an extra premiss of the argument, an immediate *donné* of consciousness, and *not* something derived from the previous considerations. Moreover, this conception is not a conception of the imagination, that is to say, a conception that is in his mind merely in the form of an image or set of images, for in having this conception, he understands that the extended thing is capable of an indefinite variety of changes, something that could not be represented by any set of images. It is a purely intellectual conception, something that he understands in pure thought, without the help of images.[4]

This latter part of the argument – that his conception of the extended thing is not dependent on the imagination – helps, I think, to shed light on the first part, about actual sense-perception. It is still not very clear exactly what the process of

3. I am indebted for this emphasis to the discussion by M. Gueroult, *Descartes selon l'ordre des raisons* (Paris, 1953), t. I, ch. 4.

4. A passage of *Notes against a Programme* (VIII-2 357–9, HR1 442–3) emphasizes that our conception of material things cannot be derived from experience but is innate, the product of our own faculty of thinking. It also helps to show that it does not just follow from this point that our conception of material things involves no sensory qualities: for our ideas of sensory qualities are also said to be innate. It thus supports the present interpretation, by which the conception of wax as pure extension is not something we arrive at by inference from reflection on the changes in sensory qualities, but is rather something we find we have.

argument is that justifies the step from 'everything that falls under the senses has changed' to 'the conception of the thing that has changed cannot have been derived from the senses'. But I think this can be understood if we see it, in its context of the *Second Meditation,* as an essentially simpler and less far-reaching line of thought than it was represented as being by the previous, metaphysical, versions. We started from the notion that we have a conception of the wax derived from the senses; what is it? That of the wax as hard, white, etc. – all the respects in which 'it seems to have everything that is necessary for a body to be known as distinctly as possible'. But then the wax changes in these respects, and yet we know that the wax remains: so the conception of it in terms of its original sensible qualities cannot have been adequate. Moreover, no other conception in the same terms could be adequate either, for all of them could only register a particular state, and this could not suffice to explain our conception of the wax as going through these various states. For – and this is where the point about the imagination comes in – on reflection we see that we have an idea of the wax as something capable of changing, not just in the way that it has just changed, but in indefinitely many other ways as well. Indeed, from the point that *being wax* is not a *de re* essential attribute, it follows (though Descartes does not here make the point) that it could change in such a way that it ceased to be wax altogether. This very general piece of understanding which is contained in our conception of the wax could neither be expressed in any possible set of images, nor merely derived from our sensory experience of the wax, which must necessarily have been limited.

Thus my conception of the wax is an intellectual conception, a conception of the understanding; this is what Descartes means when he says 'I perceive it with my understanding.'[5] 'Perception' here means the comprehension of a thing's nature, one's mental conception of the thing and of what it is. So when

5. The translation given above is of the original Latin text of the *Second Meditation,* but I have introduced the term 'understanding' from the French version. The Latin has *mente,* 'mind'. Descartes obviously came to see that this was misleading: to perceive something with one's senses is also to perceive it with one's mind.

Descartes says that 'perception of the wax is not sight, nor touch, nor imagination, and it never was ... but an inspection of the mind alone, which can be either imperfect or confused, as it was at first, or clear and distinct, as it is now', he does not mean (as he might easily be taken to mean) that there is *no such thing* as perception, in the ordinary sense, of the wax by sight or touch, but only confused perception of it by the intellect. What was confused was my conception of what the wax is, my thought about it as a physical object. This 'perception' of the wax – my mental grasp or comprehension of it – always was an intellectual notion, an idea used in thinking, and not just a sensory reaction to the world; it was originally confused because I muddled into it various sensory ideas or images which I wrongly supposed to be part of what the wax was. Now that I have recognized that I have a more adequate idea of the wax as purely an extended, flexible and changeable thing, my conception of its nature has become clear and distinct.

That I now have such a conception of course does not mean that I no longer perceive the wax by the senses. It may be that I do, and if I do, the thing that I perceive with the senses will be the very same thing as that of which I have this clear and distinct intellectual conception (stage (iv) of the argument). Yet I must not suppose that in perceiving it with the senses, I am more directly 'in contact' with it than when I think about it with the pure ideas of the understanding. If I say that I see that the wax is there, this can be misleading. For this can suggest that purely the sensory function of vision is involved. But this is wrong on two counts. To see that the wax is there is actually to *judge* that the wax is there, from certain sorts of evidence, and this is a function of the understanding. Moreover, if to see that the wax was there were a purely sensory business, the idea or conception of the wax involved in such a thought could only be a sensory idea, which we have already seen to be inadequate. Not only do I judge that the wax is there, but it is of a thing conformable to my clear and distinct idea of the wax that I judge that it is there.

In these last sentences, I have tried to give an interpretation of stage (v) of the argument, the stage which Descartes gives us with his example of seeing the men from the window. It may be objected to this interpretation that I have expressed it in terms of *seeing that* the wax is there, whereas of both the wax and the men, Descartes speaks merely of *seeing them,* and then says that what one is really doing in such a case is judging that they are present. This change might be thought to make Descartes's argument seem more plausible than it is, for it is more plausible to speak of *seeing that* as a function of judgement, than it is of merely seeing something. There are indeed several important differences between *seeing that* such-and-such is present, and merely seeing it; in particular, it is perfectly possible for someone to do the second without doing the first, as a man might be said to have seen, as a child, Lloyd George, but not to have seen that Lloyd George was present, since he had then no idea of who Lloyd George was. But this difference, and others related to it, are at this stage of no importance for Descartes's argument. For he is considering, by the whole structure of his argument, the case of first-person knowledge of what one sees, and in this special case, the difference just mentioned evaporates. For if I am in a position to say, to myself or others, 'I see Lloyd George', I am also in a position (barring trivial difficulties) to say 'I see that Lloyd George is present'.

While this is so, and hence within the framework of Descartes's discussion, it is possible to treat *seeing that* and mere *seeing* together, this limitation does mean that Descartes's conclusion cannot be generalized; he cannot conclude that all seeing involves judgement, but only that seeing when one knows what one sees involves judgement. In one way, Descartes might not have resisted this qualification, since he thought it proper to say of animals that, in a sense, they could see, though animals had no understanding or reason, and hence could make no judgements. However, on his view (see below, pp. 282–7), animals lacked even more than this capability, having no conscious experience of any kind. Thus for Descartes the 'seeing' which is an alternative to *seeing that* is a kind of 'seeing' which involves no sensation or consciousness, and if one were to insist that the state of a sheep whose behaviour is modified by light reflected from a wolf (*IV Rep.:* VII 230, HR2 104; cf. *IV Obj.:*

VII 205, HR2 85) does not merit the name of 'seeing', then it will be the case that for Descartes all seeing is *seeing that*. His reasons for this position lie mainly in a general view which links consciousness to reason, a view which we shall examine in Chapter 10. But on the present issue there may be another bad reason at work as well. In a letter to Plempius (3 October 1637: I 413, K 36), he says that animals do not see as we do, 'that is, being aware, or thinking, that we see'.[6] This involves a confusion, between having conscious experiences in seeing, and having the reflexive consciousness that one is seeing. The distinction which Descartes overlooks here – one which may be labelled as that between awareness *in* seeing and awareness *of* seeing – is a large one; it is also *not* the same as the one we have already encountered, between mere seeing and *seeing that*. To see Lloyd George is one thing, and to see that Lloyd George is present is another; to judge reflexively that one is seeing Lloyd George is yet another, which indeed involves judging that Lloyd George is present, but goes beyond that and involves a judgement not only about Lloyd George, but about oneself and one's seeing.

There is one further point to be mentioned about the example of the men seen from the window. In that example, it will be recalled, Descartes says that he does not really see the men; what he sees are hats and coats, and infers that there are men there. This might be taken to imply that there were some physical objects (in this case, hats and coats) that one did see in a way that did not involve inference. But this is not of course what Descartes supposes; he thinks that any conscious seeing of any physical object involves inference. The example of the hats and the men is an illustration of his point, not an exposition of it; and it is precisely introduced as such, as an example of how ordinary language may mislead one. Even in this case, Descartes is saying, one speaks of seeing the men, and this shows very clearly the looseness of ordinary speech. Descartes's

---

6. *hoc est sentiendo vel cogitando se videre.* Though it would not in any case make any difference to the present criticism, it is worth remarking that *sentiendo* also governs *se videre*: cf. four lines below, *dum sentimus nos videre.* Kenny's translation is perhaps slightly misleading on this point.

actual view is that we infer the presence of physical objects, not from other physical objects, but from our sensations, which are caused by the physical objects.

But this is yet to come. For the argument of the wax is in no way intended to prove the actual existence of physical objects. Descartes speaks in the course of it as though he were seeing an actual piece of wax, and knew he was, but this is only a vivid way of presenting a possibility – it is a thought-experiment. Nor (if my interpretation is correct) is the argument even intended to demonstrate what physical objects must be really like, if there are any. It does in fact lay all the essential foundations for that conclusion, but the conclusion itself is drawn only in the *Fifth Meditation*. What it does is to consider our conception or understanding of physical objects, and to try to show that the sensible images which we might readily take as giving us a clear idea of such things are in fact extremely confused. When we reflect, we find that even our idea of such objects is a pure idea of the understanding, and this serves the purpose, which is expressly that of the *Second Meditation,* of drawing the mind once more in upon itself, and revealing, as Descartes supposes, that it is in the mind's grasp of its own operations and conceptions that it advances in knowledge.

I have suggested in discussing the argument of the wax that Descartes's claim that his intellectual conception of the wax is merely that of something 'extended, flexible and changeable' was an immediate deliverance of the intellect for him, not something supposedly proved, and I said further that the reasonings of the *Second Meditation* laid all the foundations for his ultimate conception of the real nature of matter. They do this quite simply through the rule of the Method, 'whatever I clearly and distinctly conceive is true'. If it is just as an extended thing that matter is clearly and distinctly conceived, then this is what the nature of matter really consists in. This is the conclusion that is drawn, with only a little more elaboration, in the *Fifth Meditation*.

My principal task is to endeavour to emerge from the state of doubt into which I have fallen these last days, and to see whether any certainty can be had concerning material things. But before I enquire whether any such things exist outside me, I should consider the idea of them, insofar as they exist in my thought, and see which of them are distinct, and which confused.

I do distinctly conceive of[7] that quantity which philosophers commonly call continuous, or the extension in length, breadth and depth, of that quantity – or, rather, of a thing which possesses that quantity. Further, I can number various parts in it, and assign to those parts any variety of sizes, shapes, positions, and local motions, and to those motions any degree of duration. (V II 63, H R1 179)

Descartes then goes on to claim that these distinct ideas give him not only some general conception of matter, but also the conceptions of particular determinations of shape, size, etc. Thus he has a perfectly clear idea of a triangle, for instance, which is such that even if no such thing exists in the world 'outside him', he can comprehend its properties and essence. He makes again the now familiar point that his comprehension of the triangle is not a feat of the imagination, since he can understand an indefinite variety of changes in it, which go beyond the power of images. And this is all that at this point he says about the subject; the *Fifth Meditation* immediately changes course to provide the Ontological Proof of God's existence, which we have already considered in Chapter 5. As Descartes turns away from the subject, his readers are likely to be left standing in some surprise, for he promised an account of the essence of material things, but he seems to have given something that falls short of that, or is even completely different – an account of the intellectual conceptions that belong to pure plane and solid geometry or, more precisely, of such geometry which also includes the concept of motion – in technical terms, pure kinematics. The abstract conception of a triangle, the geometrical properties of which he understands, is surely not the conception of any *material object* at all. This feeling of surprise is justified, and, it must immediately be said, Descartes will add practically nothing later in his system to provide any reassurance

7. Descartes actually writes 'imaginor', 'I imagine'; and the French version (I X–1 50) offers 'j'imagine'. But it is quite clear that he does not mean this in his technical sense of 'imagine', in which this implies the having of images; on the contrary.

This abstract geometrical conception, latent in the notion of matter as extension, is Descartes's idea of matter.

One may be ultimately justified in the thought that Descartes's conception of matter has precisely left out something that makes matter material: Leibniz and Newton, in rather different ways, were to identify this element as *force*. But there is one aspect of his notion of extension which, if neglected, will make the conception seem even more inadequate than it is. This is the point that, for Descartes, any extended thing that completely occupies a given space excludes any other extended thing from occupying that space – matter keeps out other matter. This he regards, consistently with his general position, as a pure conceptual necessity; he is relying merely on the logical truth that two things cannot be in the same place at the same time. This logical truth is indeed insufficient to provide a foundation for the notion of matter in physics, since in physics we want, further, to be able to describe in quantitative terms the different sort of resistance that bodies can provide to the incursion of other bodies into a given space. We want a measure in particular of their inertia, and such a measure Descartes's physics is incapable of providing. While this is so, it is still important to bear in mind that Descartes's notion of extension does include this property of excluding other extended things from an occupied space. For granted his completely geometrical introduction of the notion, one might think that not even this much was implied. It is, after all, legitimate to think of two geometrical solids, occupying (in one sense) the same space, or parts of them doing so, as when one conceives of two polyhedra constructed on the same base. If Descartes's conception of a three-dimensional body were purely geometrical in the ultimate sense that even two such polyhedra counted as two separate three-dimensional objects, his conception of a material body would be even more inadequate than it is.

However, to fortify the notion of extension only with the consideration that one piece of it excludes another leads directly to another difficulty – or, at the very least, determines *a priori* to an embarrassing degree what Cartesian mechanics must be like (some further consequences will concern us in the next chapter). Matter as extension, and physical space, are identical (*Princ.* ii 11). It follows that any space consists of matter, so there can be no absolutely empty space, and the idea of a void or (absolute) vacuum is, for purely metaphysical reasons, incoherent. It is these conceptions that lie behind Descartes's uninviting argument (*Princ.* ii 18) – surprisingly reminiscent of the early Greek philosopher Parmenides – that there cannot be a void because, if there were a void between two things, then there would be nothing between them, which is to say that they would be next to one another.

This, at any rate, is the conception of what matter essentially is that Descartes has when, at last, he turns in the *Sixth Meditation* to answer the question whether any material things really exist in the world. The *Sixth* is the most complex of the *Meditations* in the various themes that it weaves together – as indeed one might expect, from its culminating position in Descartes's series of reflections. In it, Descartes tries not only to establish the existence of the material world. He also considers, very centrally, the special case of his own body, a portion of the material world to which, it seems, he (as a thinking thing) is very specially related, and he also brings forward the final expression of the 'Real Distinction' between mind and matter. In addition to these metaphysical themes, Descartes also crowns his endeavour in the theory of knowledge by uniting with all this his views of the origins of error, which we discussed in Chapter 6. I shall not attempt to follow all the strands of this philosophical counterpoint, as Gueroult has aptly called it;[8] some parts (such as the Real Distinction) have already been discussed, others (such as the relations of mind and body) are more profitably left to later. I shall concentrate on the argument for the existence of the material world, and the further developments in the theory of error. This will also involve a discussion of Descartes's reasons for thinking that some of the properties that we tend to ascribe to material objects really belong to them, while others do not.[9]

8. *Descartes selon l'ordre des raisons*, t. II p. 21.
9. The first part of the discussion follows the *Sixth Meditation:* I shall not give detailed page references to it.

Descartes approaches the existence of the material world by way of three, overlapping, sets of considerations. First, he considers yet again his faculty of imagination, and its difference from the pure intellect. The illustration that he gives of this is his comprehension of a geometrical figure, such as he has just been discussing in the last *Meditation*. In the case of some simple figure, such as a triangle or a pentagon, he might be tempted to think that his understanding of the properties of the figure was contained in his having an image of it. But then he considers the case of some more complex figure such as a chiliagon (a figure with a thousand sides). Here it is obvious that even if he can form some hazy image of such a figure, it will differ in no way from an image of a figure with one side more or one side less. Yet he can clearly understand intellectually the difference in properties of these various figures; it follows that this intellectual understanding can be neither derived from, nor adequately expressed in, images. This is another variant of the sort of point that Descartes has repeatedly made about the difference between the imagination and the intellect. Now, however, he asks a new question: if the imagination is both inferior to the power of the intellect, and unnecessary for understanding, why has he a faculty of imagination at all? To this he sees a possible answer – one explanation of this could be that he has a material body, and the having of images is something connected with such a body. He claims no conclusiveness for this consideration: it is just one possible explanation. Imagination, he claims, is in no way essential to his existence as a thinking thing, and he could get along, indeed get along better,[10] in the business of intellectual understanding, without it. Its existence suggests that this thinking thing may also have a body, to which, as he puts it, the 'mind is directed' in the having of images, while in pure intellection it is 'directed on itself'.

Next he considers this idea of his having a body. He reflects first that besides the images which he has just mentioned, there are many other sorts of mental phenomena which he was orig-

10. This, at least, seems to express Descartes's attitude in the *Meditations*. In the earlier work, the *Regulae*, he takes a more positive view of the usefulness of images to conceptual thought.

inally inclined, before the Doubt, to associate with his having a body. Some, such as pleasure, pain, and feelings of desire and aversion, seemed in some way to be felt 'in' the body; others, such as sensations of heat, colour, hardness and other tactile qualities, appeared to be mediated by the body, to be the modes of perception appropriate to his having bodily sense-organs in relation to the world of material objects. The body which, it seemed, went with these various experiences was certainly, if it existed, in a special relation to himself as a thinking and experiencing being:

I could not be separated from it as from other bodies; I experienced in it and on account of it all my appetites and affections, and finally I was touched by the feeling of pain and the titillation of pleasure in its parts, and not in the parts of other bodies that were separated from it.

Moreover, these various experiences seemed to be involuntary, not the product of the mind's own activity. All this contributed to the original natural belief that the thinking self was connected with a body, which was itself in relation to different physical objects. Now this original uncritical belief was rendered insecure in the Doubt, both by the very general doubts connected with dreaming and the malicious demon, and by more particular ones founded on particular sorts of illusions, which are possible (as Descartes here remarks) even with something as intimate to a person as pain – for are there not cases of people feeling pain 'in' a limb which has been amputated?

But now that Descartes knows of the existence of a benevolent God, who will not deceive him, perhaps he is in a position to recognize that while many of the ideas that he has of there being such a body and a world of physical objects are no doubt misguided, not all of them are. In particular he is in a position to reassess the significance of the fact that those experiences which appear to be experiences of objects in an 'external world', and which are distinguished by their vividness from the mere having of images, occur in his mind involuntarily. The causal principle which he regards as self-evident, and which he employed in his first demonstration of God's existence, assures him that these experiences must have a cause. This cause must contain either 'formally' or 'eminently'[11] enough reality to account for the existence of the experiences; that is to say, the experiences must either be caused in his mind by the sort of objects that they represent – physical objects existing independently of him – or by some 'higher' type of cause, such as God's own activity or the activity of some other mind less powerful than that of God. Both these possibilities are, in themselves, equally conceivable. But Descartes remarks that now, as at the beginning of his *Meditations,* he has a very strong natural tendency to believe that these experiences proceed from the first sort of cause, from physical objects which really exist. However hard he tries, he cannot banish the tendency to believe this. In particular, subjecting it to the most stringent intellectual criticism, he cannot discover in this belief any contradiction or absurdity. If therefore this belief were false – as it would be if the cause of these experiences lay, for instance, in the direct activity of God implanting such experiences in his mind – he would be in the situation that however hard he applied the methods of rational criticism, he still had a strong tendency to believe something false. But if this were the situation, Descartes argues, it would surely follow that God was a deceiver,[12] for God has created and conserves him as a rational mind capable of reaching the truth by a proper use of its faculties, and if the best possible use of these faculties left him with an inevitable tendency to error, God would be deceiving him. But God, who is benevolent, is no deceiver, so this cannot be the situation. Hence what he naturally tends to believe, viz. that these sensory experiences are caused by a physical world that really exists, must actually be true. Hence a physical world does, after all, really exist.

11. See p. 140.
12. Berkeley did think that our perceptual experiences came from God, without there being any material substances; so does Berkeley, on the Cartesian view, represent God as a deceiver? Not quite. Berkeley, unlike Descartes, thought that the notion of our experiences being caused by material substances was unintelligible. So this supposed alternative could according to him, be ruled out by *a priori* reflection. Thus Berkeley's procedure is in this respect not inconsistent with Descartes's requirements, though his conclusions are different.

This argument depends on an appeal to God's benevolence. It is important to see exactly how, and to what extent, Descartes makes this appeal. It should be noticed, first of all, that there is *one* conceivable cause of the 'sensory' experiences which Descartes should be able to eliminate without appeal to the idea that God is no deceiver. This is the possibility that these experiences actually proceed from Descartes's own mind, that he is thinking them up for himself. For if this were so, the experiences would not be involuntary, but voluntary, and as we have seen before, it is Descartes's view that the operation of the will, like all other mental operations, is always evident to the mind itself, so that he would necessarily know that they were voluntary. The mere fact that these experiences are felt to be involuntary – the fact that helps to distinguish them from other mental contents in the first place – is enough, for Descartes, to guarantee that they *are* involuntary, and hence to eliminate any explanation of them in terms of the activity of his own mind. Apart, then, from the true explanation that the experiences are caused by a physical world, we are left with only two other possibilities: that they proceed directly from God, or that they proceed from some other mental agency less than God, and it is these two possibilities that Descartes invokes the benevolence of God to rule out.

An important point about Descartes's appeal to the benevolence of God in connection with the material world is that he does *not* suppose – and he is extremely emphatic about this – that the fact that God is no deceiver will rule out all possibility of error. On the contrary, there are two quite different ways in which, despite God's benevolence, man may fall into error. First, he may do so by not using the Method to form clear and distinct conceptions; if his conceptions are obscure and confused, the appeal to God's guarantee will be of no avail. Second, even one who conducts his general thoughts clearly and distinctly may still be liable to certain *particular* errors in forming judgements about the material world; this liability lies in the nature of things, and is ineliminable. This matter, of particular errors, we shall come back to at the end of this chapter.

It is basic, then, to Descartes's view of God's guarantee, provided by God's nature as incapable of deceit, that it will operate only if man plays his own part, by forming clear and distinct conceptions. Here we see the relevance to Descartes's argument of what he has previously said about the connection of belief and will, particularly in that negative form that I suggested, in Chapter 6 (see p. 178), was the form in which Descartes essentially needed the doctrine for his system. If we are prepared to assert any proposition about the world that we feel disposed to assert, then we can scarcely expect God to save us from falling into error. God's guarantee will operate only if we do everything that is in our power first, by holding back from the assertion of confused propositions, and reducing all our conceptions to a clear and distinct form before making any judgement. If we do that, and still find ourselves strongly disposed to assert a proposition which we now understand clearly and distinctly, God's benevolence can finally be invoked.

Thus it is always important to form clear and distinct conceptions first, if error is to be avoided, but it is particularly important when one is dealing, as Descartes has been, with the highly general and philosophical issues of what the world is fundamentally like. When one examines what Descartes supposes to be the results of forming a clear and distinct conception of the physical world, one discovers how essential to him it is that one should perform that reflection before invoking God: for the conception that we can safely assent to is a long way from a naïve and unreflective conception of the world. The ultimate appeal to God does not just put back everything that was eliminated in the Doubt. The philosophical reflection has made a great difference to one's notion of what this physical world is like, the existence of which we can ultimately affirm. We have already seen how Descartes claims to have a clear and distinct conception of matter as extended substance, as the possible object of a pure geometry of motion. This conception was offered first, in the argument of the wax, as a conception which he found in his mind, and by using which he could comprehend the wax through its sensible changes. In the *Fifth Meditation,* described in somewhat greater detail, it advanced to being the essence of material things.

This might seem, at first glance, still to leave open the question of what sorts of other properties the physical world might have over and above this bare attribute of extension. Perhaps, for instance, it might really be coloured. But in fact, it emerges at the end of Descartes's enquiry that this is not so: the properties that matter has are just the properties contained in the fundamental attribute of extension. That this should be so can be seen when one recalls a feature of Descartes's notion of *essence*, which we have already encountered (see p. 124). To discover the essence of a substance is to discover its essential attribute, and any other property that a thing has must be some mode of its essential attribute. We cannot, according to Descartes, conceive of a physical thing's having any property which is not a way of being extended, of occupying space. Hence the only properties that physical things can really have are those of occupying space to such-and-such an extent (volume), with such-and-such boundaries (shape), and of moving: which last means that the boundaries may change, or the body may occupy different places at different times. These notions of change contain nothing except the notion of extension itself together with the notion of time, or more basically, for Descartes, the notion of *duration*, where this, he says, is merely 'that mode of a thing under which it is considered in so far as it continues to exist' (*Princ.* i 55, cf. 57).

But now it may be said: why should not colour be regarded as a mode of extension? If shape is a mode of extension, so that we can think, in effect, of a square as an object that is extended squarely or so as to constitute a square area, why should we not think of a green thing as something extended greenly, or so as to constitute a green area? The answer to this, in Descartes's terms, is that for him a mode of extension must be a quantitative mode – a way of being extended that can be understood in geometrical terms. But, besides this, he makes a more immediate appeal to reflection to establish that objects cannot really be coloured. He claims that if one really considers one's ideas carefully, one will see that the notion of ascribing to an object itself the colour that we perceive is downright unintelligible – as unintelligible as to ascribe to it as a real property the pain that it may cause us (*Princ.* i 68 ff.). What the world may well contain is variation in the properties of extension – differences in shape, texture, motion etc. – which correspond to the perceived differences of colour, but it cannot conceivably contain the differences in colour themselves. Indeed, God's guarantee can serve to assure us that in the world that causes in us perceptions of colour, for example, there will be 'corresponding, though not similar, variety', but it is only variety in the quantitative modes of extension that the world can really possess, and it is only a world so conceived that we can, relying on God's benevolence, assert to exist.

Thus it is that we have to get our philosophical conceptions of the physical world straight before we can turn to God's guarantee. It turns out that a clear conception here will contain a good deal less than originally one might have supposed. It will contain only modes of extension (including motion), and not colour, sensible heat, sound, tastes, smells, nor tactual properties in so far as these are understood in sensible terms; all these are only effects on our mind of the objectively existing differences in shape and motion. That is to say, to use the usual expressions that go with this view, the world itself has only *primary* qualities; some variations in these (e.g. differing physical characteristics of surfaces) are perceived by us as variations in *secondary* qualities (e.g. colour).

This distinction between primary and secondary qualities, which goes back to antiquity, is a commonplace of seventeenth-century scientific thought. Before we return to the question of God's benevolence and its relations to human error, we must consider how Descartes uses the distinction, and its merits. It may be worthwhile briefly to compare his treatment of this subject with a well-known account given by an empiricist philosopher, Locke.[13] Some of the same considerations are advanced both by Descartes and by Locke. Thus both seek to show that felt heat is no real property of objects, since it merges imperceptibly, by increase, into pain, which all would agree was not such a property; the force of this example is thought to go beyond the particular case, as illustrating how a quality which

13. Locke, *Essay on the Human Understanding*, II. 8. 8–26.

would ordinarily be regarded as being 'in the world' can by a very simple reflection be seen not to be. Both make the point that the primary qualities are perceptible by more than one sense (for Descartes, see *Princ.* iv 200). Descartes and Locke differ, however, in other respects. Thus Locke introduces the not very happy idea that we are more subject to illusion in respect of secondary qualities than we are with primary ones. No such claim is made by Descartes, and it is interesting that a majority of his examples of perceptual illusions are visual examples concerned with primary qualities, in particular with the apparent size and shape of distant objects (though see *Reg.* xii (X 423, HR1 44) for an example with secondary qualities, the world looking yellow to a man with jaundice).

More radically than this, there is an important difference between the qualities listed by the two philosophers as primary qualities, Locke including a quality which he terms *solidity,* of which no mention is made by Descartes. This difference is illustrative in more than one way of Descartes's position. Locke's account of 'solidity' makes it clear that he has in mind a certain sensible quality: it is what we experience if we take an object such as a football between our hands and then try to put our hands together (*Essay* II. 4. 1). Descartes recognizes that there are certain sensations that are produced by bodies resisting the motion of our hands when they come in contact with them, but argues that it might well be the case that whenever our hands approached a body, it retreated: in this case, we should never experience these sensations, and yet would have no reason to suppose that the bodies failed to be really material bodies. Hence this sensible quality can be no part of the essence of material bodies (*Princ.* ii 4). To this it may be replied that the body would still have the potentiality of producing these sensations in us, if by any chance we did come into contact with it, and that such a potentiality is all that Locke means by a quality in any case, so there is no real difference between them. But there is still a difference. For Locke, if we did not in fact have the sensations of resistance in encountering objects, we should have no concept of solidity at all, and an essential element of the 'materialness' of material bodies would be lacking from our thought. What takes the place of this in Descartes's views is the pure notion of the impossibility of two bodies being in the same place at the same time, and this notion has no need of being built on experience: it is an *a priori* concept of reason.

Thus there are certain differences between Descartes's and Locke's treatments of the subject, and of the two, Descartes's certainly goes deeper and is more clearly thought out. To take just one point, the notion of solidity we have just been discussing seems to be regarded by Locke as an absolute quality, not admitting of degrees: this is because he wants to apply it basically to Newtonian atoms, which for theoretical reasons had to be absolutely incompressible. But he willingly applies it to large-scale and compressible objects, such as footballs, and indeed it would seem that it was only from such objects that the idea of solidity he offers, in terms of sensations, could be derived at all. In Descartes's system the distinction between primary and secondary qualities is much better adjusted to the central role it plays, and it is very much clearer how it associates together, as it essentially does, two notions: the notion of the material world as it may be scientifically understood, and the notion of that world as it really is, as opposed to the ways in which it merely appears. As I have already suggested, Descartes's conception of physical science, and of the material world as understood by it, is inadequate, particularly because of his too drastic assimilation of the concepts of physics to those of pure mathematics. But this is not the point. If we substitute for those physical conceptions the best scientific conceptions we now have or can hope for, essentially similar questions remain about the distinction between primary and secondary qualities, though the list of primary qualities – the characteristics of the world which figure in physical theory – will be very different from any available in the seventeenth century. The questions will still concern the association of the two notions, of the world as it is scientifically understood and of the world as it really is. They are questions about the role of natural science in forming what in this study I have been calling the 'absolute conception' of reality.

However, there is a feature of Descartes's account of the

distinction which more seriously than any local peculiarities of Cartesian physics, raises difficulties. This is a feature which it indeed shares with Locke's account — that it is expressed in terms of a representational theory of perception. We are given a picture of the mind in direct contact only with its own experiences or ideas, 'outside' which there are objects, causing these experiences and imperfectly represented by them. Locke thought that our experiences in part resembled or were accurate copies of these objects, namely with respect to primary qualities. Descartes is more sophisticated on that score, holding that the relation of external physical motion and internal experience is complexly mediated, even if we look no further than the motions of the bodily sense-organs (*Princ.* iv 198; *Notes against a Programme*: VIII-2 359, HR1 443; *Dioptric*, sec. 4 and elsewhere). As we shall see in greater detail in Chapter 10, Descartes thinks that, strictly speaking, the purely mental ideas involved in perception do not *resemble* the world at all, and even with regard to the corporeal representations of the world in the brain, which he believes to occur as part of the perceptual process, he emphasizes that the important point is that they should be capable of conveying the required complexity of information about external things, not that they should resemble them (*Dioptric*: VI 113).

Any representational theory of perception is faced with the question of how we know, or what reason we have to believe, that anything exists at all outside experience. Descartes's answer to this, as we have seen, depends on God; without God, as we have also seen, it is not clear how the journey is to be effected. Locke's own attempt to make the journey by a more empiricist route was famously criticized by Berkeley, a criticism which has left a firmly established legacy of belief that the distinction between primary and secondary qualities is hopeless.

But Berkeley refuted the distinction only in terms of assumptions made by Locke, and indeed in terms of an assumption which Berkeley shared with him, namely that we are in direct contact only with a set of ideas. Moreover, consistent at least in this in his empiricism, Berkeley was an idealist, something that there is reason not to be. When we reject idealism, the questions of what elements, if any, of a representational theory of perception should be preserved, and of how the indispensable causal aspect of the concept of perception should be accommodated, are questions which, as before,[14] I shall not try to answer. The important point here is that a distinction of primary and secondary qualities can be detached from the representational theory of perception, and when it is formulated independently of that, it emerges as of very great significance.

It combines the notions of the material world as it is understood by natural science, and of that world as it really is. The idea of the world as it really is involves at least a contrast with that of the world *as it seems to us*: where that contrast implies, not that our conception of the world is totally unrelated to reality, but that it has features which are peculiar to us. By the same token, the world as it really is is contrasted with the world as it peculiarly seems to any observer – that is to say, as it seems to any observer in virtue of that observer's peculiarities. In using these notions, we are implying that there can be a conception of reality corrected for the special situation or other peculiarity of various observers, and that line of thought leads eventually to a conception of the world as it is independently of the peculiarities of any observers. That, surely, must be identical with a conception which, if we are not idealists, we need: a conception of the world as it is independently of all observers.

There is every reason to think that such a conception should leave out secondary qualities. The traditional arguments bring out the ways in which the secondary qualities depend on psychological factors, are a function not just of consciousness, but of the peculiarities of individuals or species. The point comes out well in this, that when we understand, or merely have some vague idea of, the kinds of processes that underlie the phenomena of colour (to take what everyone has always regarded as the best entrenched secondary quality, the one that we are most disposed to regard as 'in' things), we can easily understand why a thing should seem one colour to one person, another to another; or, again, why it should seem coloured to members of one species, monochrome to members of another.

14. See above, pp. 58–9.

In understanding, even sketchily, at a general and reflective level, why things appear variously coloured to various observers, we shall find that we have left behind any idea that, in some way which transcends those facts, they 'really' have one colour rather than another. In thinking of these explanations, we are in fact using a conception in which colour does not figure at all as a quality of the things.

Our ordinary language does not display these considerations about secondary qualities: in fact, it encourages us to deny them. We can draw distinctions between things seeming green and their really being green; and asked to describe, in an everyday context, a scene without observers (for instance, events occurring before there were any observers), we would unreflectingly use colour-words and other sensory terms. If there was grass in the world before there was consciousness, there was green grass. But these usages do not go very deep; or rather, we should say, we cannot assume that they go very deep. (If scientific enquiry turned out not to yield what the present line of thought requires it to yield, then perhaps our everyday distinctions will turn out to go as deep as anything goes. But we cannot assume that that will be so. Moreover, paradoxically, it would be an affront to other parts of our everyday thought if it did turn out to be so.) Our distinctions between what seems green and what is green are essentially based on agreement within the range of human experience, and human thought is not, in that limited sense at least, tied only to human experience: scientific and philosophical reflection can stand back from at least these peculiarities of our constitution. That thought was marvellously expressed already in the fifth century BC by Democritus, one of the first to introduce the distinction between primary and secondary qualities: 'colours, sweetness, bitterness, these exist by convention; in truth there are atoms and the void.'[15]

15. Diels-Kranz, *Die Fragmente der Vorsokratiker*, 6th edn, 68 B 125; he goes on to make the point that science cannot dispense with the senses altogether. Descartes rejected the philosophy of Democritus as no better than that of Aristotle and others (*Princ.* iv 202; and cf. the French version, IX-2 320, cited H R1 298), but this was because, particularly, it accepted atoms and the void, not because it drew the distinction.

So it is with our descriptions of the unobserved. We can say, and indeed say truly, that grass before there was consciousness was green: certainly '. . . was green' does not mean '. . . looked green to someone'. But equally '. . . was amusing' does not mean 'amused someone'; the term 'amusing', like 'green', is not (at least in that very simple way) relational. But it is, nevertheless, relative, relating to human tastes and interests. Descriptions which embody it, though they may not explicitly mention or include a distinctively human perspective, recognizably and diagnosibly come from that perspective. One can in describing an unobserved scene properly describe it as amusing, but if one's attention were specially directed to describing it as it was without observers, one would have good reason to leave that concept aside. It is much the same with 'green' or any other secondary quality term: they may not mention their human relativity, but they only too obviously display it to reflection.[16]

How exactly the truth-conditions of statements containing such terms are to be regarded is a hard and, I suspect, unsolved question. A familiar line is to treat '. . . is green' as in fact relational, though complexly and hypothetically so, equivalent roughly to '. . . is of such a nature as to look green to standard human observers in standard circumstances'. Under such an analysis, ascriptions of secondary qualities will in fact mention human relativities, and while, in a sense, objects really will have secondary qualities – since they really are of such a nature as to . . . etc. – nevertheless it will be clear both why and how secondary qualities should be laid aside in giving the conception of the world as it is without observers: 'of such a nature' can in principle be specified in terms of primary qualities, and the rest is irrelevant to characterizing the world without observers. However, this relational way of analysing secondary quality statements (which is Descartes's own way, as I understand him) may well not be correct. For one thing, it leaves us with the discouraging task of explaining ' . . . looks green' in some way which does not presuppose any prior understanding of '. . . is green'. How the relational pattern of analysis might possibly

16. I agree in this with David Wiggins, 'Truth, Invention, and the Meaning of Life', *Proceedings of the British Academy* LXII (1976).

be replaced is part of a larger question, how the partial views and local experiences are themselves to be related to the world as conceived in independence of them.

If we do think that we have reason to lay aside, with regard to the conception of an unobserved world, descriptions in terms of secondary qualities, what reason have we to think that we can do better with primary qualities, the properties of the world as characterized by natural science? Can we really distinguish between some concepts or propositions which figure in the conception of the world without observers, and others that do not? Are not all our concepts ours, including those of physics? Of course: but there is no suggestion that we should try to describe a world without ourselves using any concepts, or without using concepts which we, human beings, can understand. The suggestion is that there are possible descriptions of the world using concepts which are not peculiarly ours, and not peculiarly relative to our experience. Such a description would be that which would be arrived at, as C. S. Peirce put it, if scientific enquiry continued long enough; it is the content of that 'final opinion' which Peirce believed that enquiry would inevitably converge upon, a 'final opinion . . . independent not indeed of thought in general, but of all that is arbitrary and individual in thought'.[17] The representation of the world that would be so arrived at must, if it is to fill the role required by the traditional distinction between primary and secondary qualities, be more than some minimal picture which merely offers the most that a set of very different observers could arrive at, like some cosmic United Nations resolution. Its power to be more than this would lie in its being explanatory, and in the way in which it would be explanatory. The picture, that offered by natural science, would explain the phenomena: it would explain them, moreover, *even as they present themselves in other, more local, representations.* It is this consideration that gives the content to the idea, essen-

17. From *A Critical Review of Berkeley's Idealism*: in *Charles S. Peirce, Selected Writings* (*Values in a World of Chance*), ed. Philip P. Wiener (Dover, edition, New York, 1966), p. 82. Cf. also the passage from Peirce quoted by Wiggins, op. cit. Peirce's formulations of the idea tend to make the convergent progress of enquiry sound more simply cumulative, linear, and merely inevitable, than we have any reason, or need, to believe it could be.

tial to the traditional distinction, that the scientific picture presents the reality of which the secondary qualities, as perceived, are appearances.[18]

But this means that we need more than a conception of the world without observers; we need an equally impartial conception that includes not just the material world, as so far characterized, but its observers as well. The scientific representation of the material world can be the point of convergence of the Peircean enquirers precisely because it does not have among its concepts any which reflect merely a local interest, taste or sensory peculiarity. However, while these various particular modes of experience are not projected on to the description of the world in this representation, nevertheless the experiences themselves, the tastes and interests from which the investigators have abstracted, do actually exist, are something in the world. So the representation of the world without consciousness must be capable of being extended so as to have a place for consciousness within the world; moreover it must be extended in such a way as to relate the various points of view comprehensibly to each other and to the material world. This extended conception will then be that absolute conception of reality, the idea of which was introduced in Chapter 2 as something, putatively at least, presupposed by the possibility of knowledge.[19] The absolute conception should explain, or at least make it possible to explain, how the more local representations of the world can come about – it is this that would enable us to relate them to each other, and to the world as it is

18. This is the aspect which is precisely left out in Ryle's unfortunate analogy between the physicist and the accountant of a library, common-sense perception being analogous to the reading and appreciation of the books (*Dilemmas* (Cambridge, 1954), Chapter 5). The hardiest historical materialist would not claim that the accountant could explain the contents of the books from his figures.

19. It can now be seen that this presupposition does not mean that each thing we know must figure, at least as it stands, in the absolute conception of things: we can know that something is green. Rather, our knowledge as a whole must be rooted in that conception, and while some of our knowledge must represent the world as it (absolutely) is, other things we know must merely be comprehensibly related to that conception. This is already a very strong requirement.

independently of them. For instance, it should enable us to understand how certain things can seem green to us and not to others. Moreover, this conception of the world must make it possible to explain how it itself can exist. This conception is not something transcendental, but is an historical product of consciousness in the world, and it must at least yield a comprehension of men and of other rational creatures as capable of achieving that conception. It thus involves a theory of knowledge and of error: it serves to explain how members of these species might come to have or fail to have a true conception of themselves and of the world.

It is not less than this, I think – or not much less[20] – that is involved in the distinction between primary and secondary qualities, where that is interpreted in the traditional and the only interesting way, as claiming that it is primary and not secondary qualities that characterize the material world as it really is. I believe that these ideas are not incoherent, and have some faith that they are correct. But certainly they involve extensive intellectual commitments, not easy to fulfil. Those commitments can be seen, as one might expect, as arising from the collapse of the means that Descartes used to answer these questions. One requirement is to produce, or at least show the possibility of, the explanations which will link the material world as conceived under primary qualities with psychological phenomena such as the perception of secondary qualities, and, further, with cultural phenomena such as the local non-absolute conceptions of the world and indeed the absolute conception itself, including in that the possibility of physical science. Descartes gave an explanation of these things which, as we have seen, essentially involved God, validating our powers as rational beings to know the world of matter. Moreover, his explanations essentially involved his dualism. What share the world with matter, in his absolute conception of things, are immaterial substances; he saw such things as objectively existing in the world

20. Some very sketchy considerations in Chapter 10, about the nature of the psychological, will suggest that rather less will be available, but not so little as to be hopeless.

(I suggested in Chapter 3) because he wrongly thought that he could move from the mere fact of consciousness to an objective 'third-personal' view of the existence of a conscious thing. As a matter of fact, his view of the mind or soul as an immaterial substance does not make it particularly easy for him to relate mind and matter, and his difficulties in this respect are indeed notorious. If we reject his substantial dualism, the problem we shall have in trying to articulate the absolute conception is not merely: given psychological facts, how are they to be related to the physical? It is rather: what kind of thing is added to the physical picture of things when consciousness is added to it? What sort of facts, from an objective or absolute standpoint, can psychological facts be? We shall come back to these difficulties, and Descartes's, in Chapter 10.

Another commitment one will have in trying now to pursue these ideas is to detach the notion of the absolute conception, including the physicalist picture of the material world, from the demand for certainty, in particular for certainty in science. Descartes connected the search for the absolute conception directly with a search for certainty, and thought moreover that the combination of God's guarantee and his own clear and distinct perception of the nature of matter as extension revealed with certainty the basic nature of the physical world, and the concepts appropriate to describing and explaining it. We cannot admit any such certainty. The roughly Peircean conception I have sketched involves at most an ideal limit of certainty as the *end* of scientific enquiry, that 'fixation of belief' to which such enquiry tends. It in no way involves certainty as the point from which such enquiry must set out, nor as a point which we must suppose it to have already reached, nor need we think that our present physical conceptions are adequate or unshakeable. To suppose, on the other hand, that we have no conception at all of what an adequate physics might look like would hopelessly weaken these notions – even the conception of an absolute conception, so to speak, would look too pale if we accepted that. But we have no reason to accept it. On the contrary, theories which have the powers that our theories have (powers whose effects show up in non-scientific representations of the world, though only the scientific representation of the world explains[21] that fact) could not fail to represent in some way how the world really is.

Anyone who thinks that the whole idea of the convergence of scientific enquiry is an illusion, will of course think that the idea of the absolute conception, as discussed here, is baseless. Such a critic may think that scientific theories are a cultural product which it would be senseless to suppose could be freed from local relativities; he may suppose that even within the history of human science the notion of convergent scientific progress is a myth. Such an outlook has its own serious difficulties: it has to explain the success of our theories (their intercultural success), and it must more generally acquire from somewhere a stable conception of the world of nature, in relation to which it can understand cultural phenomena such as science and its own view of science. Against any such view can be set the realist outlook which sees science as essentially a means by which, in another phrase of Peirce's, 'our beliefs may be caused by nothing human, but by some external permanency – by something upon which our thinking has no effect'.[22] Exactly how, and exactly to what extent, it can be this is a central and continuing question for the philosophy of science. Certainly the

21. This is meant to suggest an objective asymmetry. It may be objected that there is no objective asymmetry, on the ground that the notion of *explanation* is itself relative to a picture of the world: thus a scientific picture of the world can unsurprisingly win in terms of a scientific conception of explanation. (Some of Wittgenstein's later writings, particularly *On Certainty*, seem to suggest such a view.) But it is quixotic to deny that a transcultural idea of explanation is associated with the idea of *that representation of an event which enables one reliably to produce it* – however the event may then be described. (Cf. on this, John Skorupski, *Symbol and Theory* (Cambridge, 1976), especially Chapter 4 and Appendix.) Relatedly, it must be a mistake to separate radically a theoretical from a 'merely technological' level of scientific explanation.

Even apart from this, there could be another asymmetry, lying in the capacity possessed by the scientific picture and merely lacked by others, to generate an explanation of its own and others' explanations. But this level of asymmetry is admittedly further removed from the scientific picture's physicalist base.

22. In *The Fixation of Belief*: op. cit., ed. Wiener, p. 107.

realist outlook does not demand the simple positivist 'fact-copying' picture of the scientific process, nor a simply linear conception of scientific progress, against which contemporary anti-realist views are often an exaggerated reaction.

With regard to Descartes, at any rate, it can be said that the commitment to realism, and to an absolute conception of the world which includes a conception of matter given by a realistic physical science, is fundamental to him. It can even be said, I think, that any view which loses touch with realism in these matters is more deeply opposed to the Cartesian outlook than any which retains the realist connection – even if that latter abandons, as it must, all the characteristic Cartesian beliefs in God, in dualism and in the search for certainty.

This discussion departed from considering what view of the world it was that could, on Descartes's argument, be under-written by God. We have seen that it is a view solely in terms of primary qualities. This is at the level of philosophical truth or error; such large-scale mistakes as that the world is in itself coloured must be removed first by reflection. But what now about particular mistakes, such as that of the man who falsely thinks that his foot has not been amputated, because he feels a pain 'in' it, or of one who takes a distant tower to be round rather than square? Here we have natural tendencies to believe things that are false; how is the benevolence of God related to these?

There is a problem here for Descartes. There are some perceptual mistakes, and mistakes based on sensation, which the most careful man would make, if he is going to make judgements about the physical world at all. So either God's guarantee is going to give us no particular beliefs about the material world at all, in which case we shall have made no substantial advance, and with respect to particular beliefs about the material world we shall still be in the Doubt; or, alternatively, if we allow God's guarantee to extend to particular beliefs which, after critical inspection, we naturally tend to hold, God's guarantee will allow us sometimes to be wrong.

Descartes's answer to this difficulty is to take the second horn of the dilemma. We must, first, as already has been said, use the critical intellect to rid ourselves of general misconceptions about matter. Having done this, we can trust our natural tendencies to form particular beliefs about the physical world, and sometimes we shall be mistaken. But this does not matter. For we have banished the fear of systematic illusion. We shall be in the perfectly familiar situation of sometimes being mistaken, but being able to recognize and correct our mistakes. Of course we should, on Descartes's view, take every possible step to reduce our liability to error, and in particular we must, by increasing natural knowledge, allow for the misleadingness of our perceptions. There will still be cases left over in which mistake occurs, but this is to be expected: we are bodily persons, with the disadvantages that that entails.

This is the epistemological upshot of God's guarantee. If we are ourselves careful, we need not fear systematic error, which is what mattered, and though particular error remains, that is our condition, and does not much matter. But a theological difficulty might seem to remain. If by trusting our natural tendencies to believe, we sometimes go wrong, how is God, who has implanted these tendencies, to be justified? Descartes's answer is once again an application to the field of knowledge and belief of a theological argument familiar in other contexts. God works through established and regular physical systems, and that he does this is itself part of his providence. It is of the nature of such systems that they can sometimes produce misleading results. In the case of the man with the amputated foot, for instance, the situation, as Descartes explains it, is that we have certain nerves leading to the foot, pressure on which causes the sensation of pain which is felt 'in' the foot. When the foot has been amputated, certain pressures on the end of this nerve in the stump must inevitably produce the same effects as were experienced as when the nerve reached down into the foot and was pressed there. Similar reasonings apply elsewhere. Much the same is true of misleading appetites, such as that of a patient with dropsy who wants to drink all the time, when this is not to his good. Here again Descartes speaks in terms of a natural tendency: as he puts it, 'nature teaches me that' I need a drink when I feel certain sensations of dryness in the throat, and so forth. These sensations can, in exceptional circumstances, be caused by some condition other than the need for drink: the mind will then wrongly conceive a desire for drink. But this is just the result of there being an established causal mechanism in the body.[23]

We may still ask why God should have chosen to create us in this way, so that on occasion, however conscientiously we reflect, we shall be misled. Here Descartes disclaims, as usual, any knowledge of God's purposes. We can only know that the actual state of affairs serves in some way his providence. Here one encounters an uncomfortable feeling: not just the one always occasioned by the retreat into what Spinoza called 'the asylum of ignorance', but a more immediate embarrassment with the earlier part of Descartes's argument. For if at this point God's purposes become so inscrutable, how can Descartes be so sure at the earlier stage that God could not have, for his own purposes and without being a deceiver, arranged it that we should have experiences as of an external world without there being an external world? It will not be enough for Descartes to say that in his earlier argument he was not appealing to God's purposes, but only to God's nature, of which Descartes can at least clearly understand enough to see that he is no deceiver. For it is only in the light of God's purposes, surely, that one could be certain that, in giving us a strong, but resistible, tendency to believe in an external world which was not there, he would be acting *as a deceiver*. There is a tacit appeal to God's purposes, and an appeal to the purposes of an admittedly inscrutable God is a weak foundation for our entire belief in the existence of an external world. If there is an answer to this, it no doubt lies once more in the distinction between systematic and particular beliefs. That we should be misled in particular matters about the external world is not a frustration of our fundamental nature as rational minds: to be mistaken in systematic and philosophical beliefs, would be. In such an answer one could sense the Platonic presupposition that it is as pure rational intelligences that men have their real worth and purpose, and that although we find ourselves with bodies, we must recognize

23. For further discussion of the theory of bodily sensations, see p. 285 ff.

that fact as a limitation. Such a presupposition is highly characteristic of Descartes's metaphysics. It is much less characteristic,
however, of his outlook on science, technology, medicine and
practical affairs.

Chapter 9

SCIENCE AND EXPERIMENT

THE physical universe for Descartes consists of one, infinitely extended, homogeneous, three-dimensional thing (*Princ.* ii 21–2: 'indefinite' is Descartes's own preferred word for the kind of negative infinity involved). It has, and can have, no gaps in it; it follows that there cannot be a plurality of worlds, and any extended thing there is, is some local part of the one extended thing. There are, further, no ultimate atoms, or parts of matter which are 'indivisible of their own nature' (*Princ.* ii 20) – matter, in Descartes's conception of it, has necessarily the geometrical property of being continuous. The truth in scientific atomism, according to Descartes, is merely that there are some small packets of the extended substance which travel around as a whole. This conception enables him to set up models of physical processes involving particles, but this means for him only matter moving, as it happens, in a particulate way, and does not involve items which are in any more fundamental way atoms.

These 'parts' of matter are in their turn distinguished from their environment only in terms of their local motion: in fact, all differential properties of matter, including properties of sorts of matter, are a question only of differential motion (*Princ.* ii 23). Such kinematic differences are invoked to explain, for instance, condensation and compression, phenomena which might seem to present a difficulty on the Cartesian account. By the fundamental requirement, mentioned in the last chapter, that matter necessarily excludes other matter, together with the absolute continuity of matter, it follows that matter in itself is absolutely incompressible. If it were compressible, then more of it could occupy the space previously occupied by less of it, without anything moving out of the way, and that is impossible. What are compressible are given sorts of matter, e.g. air: when a body of air is compressed, what happens is that matter of a different kind leaves the pores of the body of air, so that the body of air does come to occupy a smaller volume, but only by displacement of matter from its interstices. The air and this other sort of matter are differentiated, again, only by differences of motion. Since air can be compressed with equal ease in a container of arbitrary thickness, it follows that the subtlest form of matter can pass with equal ease through the walls of any container: this consequence (which belongs to the long and complex history of the idea of the ether) was to prove an embarrassment to Cartesian physics.

The impenetrability of matter and the non-existence of the void had another important consequence, that all physical motion must take the form of motion in a closed curve. Only in this way can other matter instantaneously take the place of matter which has been displaced. This consequence was drawn also by Aristotle,[1] though most other considerations which Aristotle had associated with his plenum or void-free universe, Descartes rejected in rejecting, as he self-consciously did, the principles of Aristotelian dynamics. The innumerable circular motions or (roughly) whirlpools in the continuous fluid of the universe are the *vortices* for which Cartesian physics is famous.

One feature of Aristotle's world-view which was most basically rejected by Descartes, as also by Galileo, was the notion of local laws of motion: the idea that the terrestrial environment, besides being in the middle of a moderately sized universe, was special in defining the natural motions of the elements, earth and water naturally moving towards the centre of the earth, air and fire away from it, while the heavens had a matter of their own (the 'quintessence') which had its own dispositions, in particular to move in circles. Descartes shared with Galileo the revolutionary insights that the heavens are of the same matter as the earth, that the universe is infinite and has no centre, and that there are only universal laws of motion, and – at the physical level at least – no local kinds of things with local habits. Descartes and Galileo both broke with Aristotle also in offering as a general law an inertial conception of motion – that, other things being equal, matter will continue in a state of rest or uniform motion. Descartes, however, moved further than Gal-

1. *Physics* IV. 6 (214ᵃ⁻ᵇ). Cf. *Physics* VIII. 8, 9.

ileo did towards the conception of uniform motion which was to prove fundamental to Newtonian mechanics, that expressed in the law of rectilinear inertia: a moving body acted upon by no force will move in a straight line (cf. *Princ.* ii 37, 39).

While Descartes has the credit of having formulated a version of this law (but one importantly different from the Newtonian law, since he lacked any adequate conception of force, or, consequently, of mass), it is an important feature of his physics that he was not in a position to make any real use of it. In the Cartesian universe, as we have seen, all bodies move in some closed curve, and moreover, it is a metaphysical necessity that they should so move. We cannot consider how a body would ideally move if it were not in an environment of other matter influencing its motion, since such a state of affairs, through the equation of matter and physical space, is absolutely unintelligible. So the hypothetical force of the law of rectilinear inertia remains necessarily uncashable. For Galileo, by contrast, the consideration of how a body would move under ideal conditions (for instance, a body falling in a vacuum, or a ball rolling on a horizontal surface under zero friction) was fundamental to his method of the analysis of motions, and could be coherently employed. It is his sophisticated use of such thought-experiments which, as much as anything else, makes Galileo's discussion of physical issues (for instance, in the book which precipitated his condemnation, *The Dialogues Concerning the Two Chief World Systems*) seem to the modern reader full of power and insight, whereas Descartes's seems antique, programmatic and unfruitful.

It is often said that Descartes's physical system is too abstract, and in one sense it is; but in another, it is not abstract enough – that is, it is not capable of the right kind of abstraction.[2] Having thought away *in general* everything but what he took to be the minimal basis of a mathematical physical system, he was left with no way in which he could think away the particular conditions of a particular physical transaction, and be left with anything coherent at all.

For all that, physics in the Cartesian pattern retained an

2. I owe this point to C. C. Gillispie.

influence for many years, even into the eighteenth century. The subsequent treatment of matters left unsatisfactory by Descartes is a question for the history of science: his radically incorrect laws of impact, for instance,[3] or his ambiguous dealings with the velocity of light. I shall not try to take up these matters, or other details of Descartes's physical system. There are issues, however, which are important for Descartes's theory of knowledge, and which we should consider: the status he attached to scientific knowledge, and the procedures, consequently, that he thought appropriate to physical enquiry. As we have already seen, the conceptual resources of his science, the question of what notions can appropriately be applied in physical theory, are very strongly determined by his metaphysics. The question arises whether, for him, the whole of physical theory was supposedly determined at the metaphysical level, and in principle, at least, discoverable by entirely *a priori* reasoning.

It has often been thought that there is some obscurity or ambiguity in Descartes's attitude to these questions. Those who know Descartes only from the *Discourse* may have felt some surprise when after what at least seem like very extensive claims for the power of human reason to know the world around us, he makes in the sixth section an appeal for funds to support experiments or guided observations, and moreover gives a justification of their necessity in terms of the very richness and fruitfulness of his explanatory principles, something which without further interpretation seems scarcely to make sense. If we look elsewhere in his writings, we can find what appear to be virtually direct contradictions on these issues. Consider for instance the following group of passages:

1.   (i) (*Mersenne has told Descartes that the mathematician Desargues is upset because Descartes proposes to give up geometry*)

But I have only decided to give up abstract geometry, that is to say, research into questions which serve only to exercise the mind; and I am doing this in order to have more time to cultivate another

3. See E. J. Dijksterhuis, tr. C. Dikshoorn, *The Mechanization of the World Picture* (Oxford, 1961), sections 206 ff.

sort of geometry, which takes as its questions the explanation of the phenomena of nature. If he cares to consider what I have written about salt, snow, the rainbow etc., he will recognize that all my physics are nothing but geometry. (To Mersenne, 27 July 1638: II 268)

(ii) (*Reacting to Gassendi's hostile comments on the* Meditations)

But I have something to console myself with, since he here connects my physics with pure mathematics, which I especially wish them to resemble. (To Clerselier, about Gassendi's *Instances*, in the French edn of the *Meditations*, 1646: IX-1 212–13, H R 2 131)

(iii) (*His readers should familiarize themselves with the elements of geometry*)

For I clearly state that I recognize no other matter of corporeal things, than that matter, which can be divided, shaped, and moved in all ways, which geometers call quantity, and which they take as the object of their demonstrations; and I consider nothing in it except those divisions, shapes and motions; and I admit nothing as true about those, except what can be deduced from those common notions whose truth we cannot doubt, by a deduction so evident that it can be taken for a mathematical demonstration. And since all the phenomena of nature can be explained in this way, as will emerge in what follows, I think that no other principles of physics should be admitted, nor any others wanted. (*Princ.* ii 64)

On the other hand, Descartes is capable of writing:

2. You ask whether I take what I have written about refraction for a demonstration; and I think that it is, at least to the extent that it is impossible to give a demonstration in this matter, without having first demonstrated the principles of physics from metaphysics (something that I hope to do one day, but which has not been done up to now), and to the extent that any other question of mechanics, or optics, or astronomy, or any other matter which is not purely geometry or arithmetic, has ever been demonstrated. But to demand of me geometrical demonstrations in a matter which depends on physics, is to want me to do the impossible. And if one called demonstrations only the proofs of geometers, one would have to say that Archimedes had never demonstrated anything in mechanics, nor Vitellion in optics, nor Ptolomy in astronomy, etc., and this is

not what is said. In such matters, one is satisfied if the authors, having presupposed certain things which are not manifestly contrary to experience, should have gone on consistently from there and not made any error of logic, even though their suppositions were not exactly true. (To Mersenne, 17 or 27 May 1638: II 141–2, K 55)

Can this apparent conflict be resolved? The first thing to notice is that the passage 1(i) and the passage 2 were written within two months of one another to the same correspondent, which should discourage the view that what we are basically faced with is a change over time in Descartes's views. In fact there were changes in Descartes's views on these and related matters during his lifetime, but they were not simple nor even in one direction, and they do not serve to resolve these problems. It is true that he became increasingly aware of the size of the task that lay before the new science, and lost some of his early optimism, particularly with regard to his favoured project of applying medical science, based on physics, to slow down aging. He told Huyghens in January 1638 that he hoped to live for more than a hundred years (I 507); in June 1639, when he was forty-three, he expressed, again to Huyghens, the hope of living another thirty years; seven years later he wrote to Chanut (15 June 1646: IV 441, K 196):

... so that instead of trying to find means to preserve life, I have found another way, much easier and more certain, which is not to fear death.

(The Abbé Picot, a devoted Cartesian, was not up in his master's later thoughts when, hearing of Descartes's death aged fifty-four, he for some time refused to believe it was possible.)

The growing sense of the size of the scientific and technological task was not, however, accompanied by any increasing emphasis on the need for empirical research or observation. In his early days, he lays some emphasis on the value of surveys of the field of enquiry in the manner of Francis Bacon: thus a 'history' of celestial appearances in Baconian style would be useful (10 May 1632: I 251, K 24). The 'enumerative surveys' of the *Regulae* do not exclusively apply to empirical surveys, as

Regulae xi makes clear; Descartes has in mind also surveys of possibilities or alternatives established *a priori*, and this is what is principally in question in the fourth of the rules of the Method listed in the second part of the *Discourse* (V I 19, HR1 92). But a place is allowed for the acquisition of pieces of empirical information, as when he would like to know whether all snail shells twist in the same direction, even in the Southern hemisphere (23 December 1630: I 196). Later, it is not that there is no interest in the results of empirical enquiry; there is indeed a reference in the *Principles* to the Baconian 'history' (see below, p. 263). It is rather that he lays greater emphasis, as we shall see, on the need for crucial experiments to decide between explanations.

The clue to reconciling these passages must be found, if at all, in understanding them, not just in Descartes's development. How much do the passages (1) commit him to? A central thought in them is one that we should already be prepared for: that the *subject-matter* of physics is, in a sense, the same as that of geometry. This is a point that Descartes makes also in the *Regulae*, and he draws from it a consequence almost exactly the same as that drawn in 1 (iii), the passage from the *Principles*:

So from all this we should conclude not indeed that only arithmetic and geometry are to be taught, but merely that those who are looking for the right road to truth should not concern themselves with any object (*objectum*), about which they cannot have a certainty equal to that of the demonstrations of arithmetic and geometry. (*Reg.* ii: X 366, HR1 5)

The characteristic of any such 'object', we learn from *Regulae* iv, is that it admits of 'order and measurement'. Towards the end of his life, in the *Conversation with Burman* (V 160, C p. 23), Descartes said that geometry and physics have the same *objectum*, and expressed the difference between them merely in terms of possibility and actuality:

The difference consists just in this, that physics considers its object not only as a true and real being, but as actually existing as such, while mathematics considers it merely as possible, and as something which does not actually exist in space, but could do so.

The real force of this identity of subject-matter is that it implies the conceptual equivalence of physics and geometry: there are no special physical concepts, and with regard to its language, study of nature is just, in the purest sense possible, applied mathematics. With regard to the difference that remains between the reference of the mathematical language as used in physics, and its reference in pure mathematics, the way that Descartes puts the mátter to Burman, in terms of a 'being' such as a triangle actually existing in space or not, fits well with the apparatus invoked in the Ontological Argument for God's existence, particularly in Kenny's reconstruction of that (see pp. 155 ff). Elsewhere, however, a slightly different emphasis is given, as in *Regulae* xiv (X 448–9, HR1 62), where the body actually extended in three dimensions is the reality, and line, surface etc., merely 'mental abstractions', a formulation telling against the almost Meinongian realism about possible objects expressed in the Burman passage. But whichever emphasis is taken, the same basic point emerges, that there is no conceptual difference between pure mathematics and physics, and there follows from that the important consequence that there can be no obstacle at this level to demonstrations being as clear and intelligible and compelling in the one case as in the other. In both cases arguments of an entirely geometrical character, open to the natural light, can be presented: from the point of view of the conceptual material involved, physics does admit of demonstrations every bit as clear as those of geometry, for they can involve no other material.

So in what sense does physics *not* admit of demonstrations in the same way as geometry? Here Descartes's concern is not with the conceptual material, but with the status of the *premisses* of the demonstrations, and the relation of those to reality. In the letter to Mersenne from which passage 2 was quoted above, it is important first of all to distinguish two different points. One is that he has not yet offered any derivation of physics from metaphysics; the second is that the premisses offered in mathematical physics cannot be expected to be 'exactly true'. I take this second point to be independent of the first: that is to say, even if physics had been derived from metaphysics, that second problem would still exist. The language of the letter makes it clear, I think, that it is not just because the derivation from metaphysics is missing that the second difficulty arises, and this interpretation is borne out by the state of affairs in the *Principles*. There, the metaphysical derivation has supposedly been effected, in that the conservation of motion and other basic laws have been 'deduced' from God's nature. The deduction indeed offers not much more than a general salute to God's immutability: we shall come back to this later (see below, p. 268). But even if the metaphysical derivation of the laws is granted, it is clear from the *Principles* that the laws, while they place constraints upon what can happen in the world, cannot in themselves determine exactly what mechanisms exist in the world, nor in themselves make it possible for us to know what mechanisms exist in the world.

This accords with much of what is said in the letter 2 to Mersenne. The physicist postulates a mechanism: its description must be, of course, in the perspicuous language of geometrical kinematics. The mere fact that it is postulated is not itself an objection. Moreover, it may not matter if what is postulated is not entirely correct, so long as it saves the phenomena, and it may not matter for the derivation of the phenomena what exactly the mechanism is, some very general property of it sufficing to make the required explanatory point.[4] Thus any one of several mechanisms which accord with the general constraints on the system might underly a given phenomenon; and this is why astronomers can derive true conclusions from false premises (*Dioptric*: VI 83), a point which Descartes was to put to heavy use in connection with his embarrassments in face of the Church, but which is by no means introduced by him merely for that reason.

So far, then, we have three sorts of constraints on the kinds of mechanism which the physicist can postulate. They must be couched in the concepts of kinematics: they thus admit of form-

---

4. Descartes's illustration of this point is unfortunate: that for the explanation of refraction, it makes no difference if light is propagated instantaneously – all that matters is that it follow the same laws as local motion. But his application of the laws of motion to explain refraction seems to require light to have a finite velocity.

ulation in terms of geometrical argument. Moreover, their operation must be within the terms of the laws of motion (themselves 'deduced' from the properties of God). They must explain the phenomena. But all of this still underdetermines the true model, since more than one model can, for any given phenomenon, satisfy these conditions. When Descartes says in the letter to Mersenne that it does not matter if the premisses are not entirely true, he is making a point there about what can reasonably be expected in the present state of the art, perhaps even in any foreseeable state of it. He does, of course, believe that there is a true mechanism underlying the phenomena; he is very remote from the operationalism which takes the criterion of physical truth to be merely the issue of what calculating device will most economically predict the phenomena. The question remains of what means he thinks we have of coming to know the true mechanism, and what certainty he thinks can be attained in such enquiry. It is here that we encounter Descartes's view (or at least the view of his maturity) about the role of experiment.

Descartes emphasizes, correctly, that experiments are no use unless one has some insight into the nature of the problem; as, early on, he said that one had to get some insight into the nature of light in order to discover the anaclastic (the configuration of a lens which will focus light to a point), which can be discovered neither by simple observation, nor by pure mathematical postulation (*Reg.* viii: X 393–4, HR1 23–4). More elaborate and refined experiment can be actually misleading unless one has the right idea in the first place. One should start with common observation and reflection: experiments are both more necessary, and safer, the further on one is (*Discourse* Part vi: VI 64, HR1 120). Harvey, in his enquiry into the circulation of the blood (which Descartes, sparing in his approval of other investigators, much admired), had been misled by a certain conjunction of observations; this was a case in which the same phenomenal effects could be produced by either of two causes, and what was needed was an experimental set-up in which a certain phenomenal effect would be produced if one of the causes were operating, and not if it were not (*Description of the*

Human Body: XI 242). This is the differential or crucial experiment, and this is what Descartes is referring to in the well-known passage of the *Discourse* (Part vi: VI 64–5, HR1 121):

But I must also confess that the power of nature is so ample and vast, and these principles are so simple and general, that I observe hardly any particular effect which I cannot see straight off could be deduced from the principles in several different ways; and my greatest difficulty in general is to find in which of these ways it depends on them. As to that, I do not know of any other way than once more to look for some experiments of such a nature that their outcome will not be the same if the effect is to be explained in one of these ways, as it would be if it were to be explained in the other.

It is important to see here that to 'deduce' an effect from the laws of nature does not mean to arrive at a statement of that effect from the laws of nature alone by purely logical reasoning (which is what the modern meaning of the word might lead one to expect). If that were the meaning, then alternative deductions would all be equally valid, and there would be nothing to choose between them except perhaps in terms of their length or elegance: any idea of invoking experiment to decide between them would be unintelligible. What Descartes means here by 'deducing' an effect is the process of postulating a mechanism for it within the constraints set by the concepts and laws of his physical theory, and the situation he refers to is that in which more than one such mechanism could produce all the phenomena so far observed. The aim of the experiment is to elicit further phenomena, differentially related to these possible mechanisms.

There is a clear statement of such alternatives at *Principles* iv 204, where Descartes appeals to the familiar image of the two clocks, equally accurate and externally indistinguishable, which nevertheless have different works. There is a rather less clear statement at *Principles* iii 4 ('Of phenomena or experiments, and what their use is for philosophy'):

Now we set before our eyes a brief account[5] of the principal phenomena of nature, the causes of which are to be investigated here; not so that we should use them as reasons in order to prove

5. 'historia': The Baconian term, cf. above, p. 258.

anything, since we want to deduce the basis (*rationes*) of the effects from the causes, not the basis of the causes from the effects; but solely so that we can turn our minds to considering some rather than others out of the countless effects which we judge can be produced from the same causes.

Descartes is not supposing here that different effects could be produced from exactly the same cause, determinately specified. When he says that countless effects can be produced from the same causes, he identifies the causes in a general and unspecific way – roughly, in terms of general schemata of explanation offered by his theory. In terms of causes and effects, the basic situation that Descartes has in mind in discussing experiments could be as well put by saying that what is the same apparent or phenomenal effect may be, in terms of its hidden mechanical structure, a different effect, and hence an element in a different causal structure. So it is that directed experiment, aimed at observations which could never come about by chance, will need to be conducted by able men with resources, if 'all the truths are to be deduced from these principles that can be deduced from them', and this could take several centuries, he writes to Picot, the translator into French of the *Principles* (IX–2 20, HR1 215); 'deduction' here has to be taken in the same way as in the passage of the *Discourse*.

Descartes thus agrees that any *given* phenomenon might be explained on his principles in more than one way, and experiment is needed to distinguish between different mechanisms. But is this more than the result of our ignorance, confronted with particular phenomena – or, at any rate, the result of the ignorance of any finite observer, confronted with only a subset of the phenomena of the universe? Is it the case that if enough phenomena are considered together, the possibilities decrease, until for the universe as a whole there is only one possible explanatory structure? Descartes sometimes claims that this is so. So in writing to Mersenne (28 October 1640: III 212, K 79):

I think that one can explain a given particular effect in different ways, all of which are possible; but I think that one can explain the possibility of things in general only in one way, which is the true way.

Similar points are made in a letter to Morin (13 July 1638: II 199, K 58); to an unknown correspondent (?June 1645: IV 224–5); and in *Principles* iii 42, which incidentally makes the point, essential equally to Descartes and to Galileo, that astronomical explanation and terrestrial mechanics have to be unified.

As larger ranges of phenomena are brought under unified mechanical explanation, our belief in the explanations should increase:

> As to the things that I have supposed at the beginning of the *Meteors*, I could not have demonstrated them *a priori*, except by giving the whole of my physics; but the observations which I have necessarily deduced from them, and which could not be deduced in the same way from any other principles, seem to me sufficiently to demonstrate them *a posteriori*. (To Vatier, 22 February 1638: I 563, K 48)[6]

This could be taken to imply that physics, when complete, might be 'demonstrated *a priori*'. (The 'things supposed at the beginning of the *Meteors*' mostly concern the various particulate structures of different sorts of substance: *Meteors, Discourse* 1, VI 231–9.) What might be meant by an *a priori* demonstration of all physics? The strongest sense of this, in Cartesian terms, would be this: that the whole of physics could be deduced by purely mathematical reasoning from first principles which are of such a character that anyone who clearly and distinctly understands them must assent to them. In this, strongest, sense there is more than one reason for asserting that Descartes did *not* believe that a complete physics would admit of totally *a priori* demonstration.

The claim that physics could be *a priori* in this strong sense is to be distinguished from the claim merely that it could be certain. Descartes is, after the return from the Doubt, prepared to admit as certain some propositions, such as the existence of the external world, which are not such that clear and distinct per-

6. For some (not entirely helpful) remarks on his use of 'demonstrate', 'prove' and 'explain' in scientific connections, see the letter to Morin of 13 July 1638 (II 197 ff., K 57–8); the explanation given there relates to the sixth part of the *Discourse*, VI 76, H R1 128–9.

ception of them extorts assent: in their case, as we have seen, clear and distinct perception that they are consistent, together with a strong disposition to believe them, together with the benevolence of God, justify assent to them.

Descartes does claim, and in his later work, that *certainty* can be claimed for a complete science, up to God's guarantee of our knowledge of an external world. In *Principles* iii 43 he says

If we use no principles except those that are most thoroughly evident, and if we deduce nothing from them except by mathematical reasoning, and if at the same time the consequences we deduce from them accurately cohere with all the phenomena of nature, we should seem to be offering an insult to God, if we suspected that the causes of things, discovered by us in this way, were false, as though God had created us so imperfect that we could be deceived although rightly using our reason.

At the very end of the *Principles* he first claims 'moral certainty' for his scientific principles, that is to say, certainty sufficient to ground action (iv 205) – not, in Descartes's book, a very strong claim. But he immediately (iv 206) goes on to claim more than this, that our certainty transcends moral certainty; and it is clear that he thinks that he can attach to the scientific system the degree of certainty that can be attached, under God's guarantee, to the belief that there is an external world at all. That is to say, the belief in the scientific system is – or at least ideally can be – as certain as the belief that there is anything at all for such a system to apply to.

This, however, could mean either one of two different things. It could mean (i) that the degree of certainty that God's guarantee offers is *equal* to that offered in the case of the belief in the external world: on this line, there might be propositions other than the belief in the external world which God had to guarantee to provide certainty for science, but which he did indeed guarantee. Alternatively, it might mean (ii) that it is just the proposition about the existence of the external world which is in question: once God has guaranteed that, he has provided the guarantee for science.

In discussing these alternatives, I shall speak of God's 'external' guarantee, meaning by that the guarantee that God supplies, according to Descartes, for propositions which we are strongly disposed to believe when we clearly and distinctly conceive them, but with which clear and distinct perception by itself reveals consistency, not truth. (We are not concerned here with any guarantee extended by God to self-evident propositions or purely *a priori* reasoning, the issue discussed in Chapter 7.) To illustrate the difference between the two views (i) and (ii), we can consider the total claim made by the Cartesian physicist as consisting of the conjunction of four parts: (a) a set of principles, laws of nature; (b) deductions drawn from these by mathematical reasoning; (c) a claim that (a) and (b) explain a set of phenomena, P; (d) a claim that P objectively exist in reality. The view (ii) allocates God's 'external' guarantee only to element (d); all of (a), (b) and (c), on this view, can be known purely *a priori*. The alternative view (i) finds the 'external' guarantee applicable elsewhere as well.

Let us start with the question of its application to (c). (c) is ambiguous. It might indeed mean that certain purely logical relations obtained between the laws and *P*, as that certain mechanisms, sufficient to generate *P*, are possible within the constraints of the laws. In this sense we may allow that (c) can be known *a priori*. But this does not yet serve to identify *the* explanation of *P*: we encounter the familiar point that there is more than one way in which *P* can come about, given the laws. When he has less than the full set of phenomena to work on, these alternatives are real alternatives for the scientist, as we have seen. As he takes larger sets of the phenomena, the alternatives, as we have also seen, narrow down. They narrow down, however, only granted certain principles of explanation, which use notions of simplicity, economy, etc. God could, even within the limits of our *a priori* understanding, bring about the phenomena in the world by a vast variety of arbitrary mechanisms, which we would never be able to unravel. In order to narrow down the explanations, we have to believe that he has not done this, but has made the world as we, using principles of simplicity, etc., and thinking as clearly as we can, will be disposed to understand that it is made. This is not a purely *a priori* matter, and requires another use of God's 'external' guarantee, as well as that applied to (d) – the guarantee, that is to say, that what after conscientious investigation, using the best methods available to us, we are compellingly but not demonstratively led to believe, must be true.

Although it is not altogether easy to extract an answer from the texts, I think that it is this last, more complex, account that best fits Descartes's views. If we adopt it, we shall have applications of God's 'external' guarantee to two beliefs: that the phenomena are really there, and that the explanation we are led to, granted (a) and (b), of those phenomena, in the light of canons of simplicity, etc., is the true explanation. This will give us two areas in which the complete physics will not be *a priori* in the strongest sense, identified above.

It leaves us with the claim that the element (a) of the physical theory, the laws of nature themselves, can be known purely *a priori*. But is even this much a correct account of Descartes's thought? Some of what he says strongly suggests that it is: so a passage of a letter to More (5 February 1649: V 275, K 243, quoted below, p. 273); *Principles* ii 64; and *Principles* iii 43. Yet not all these assertions are quite so strong or unambiguous as they first look. *Principles* ii 64 (quoted above, p. 257, in our first set of passages) is, in the way already discussed, basically about the 'object' of physics, and the mathematical conceptual apparatus of its demonstrations. *Principles* iii 43, which has also already been quoted, p. 266, refers to *principia*, principles, *evidentissimè perspecta*, literally 'most clearly seen through', *tresévidens* in the French version; the article as a whole, as we have seen, relates to the benevolence of God, and it seems permissible to read this expression as referring to that clear and distinct perception which reveals consistency rather than truth, or at least as including that.

There is room for a suggestion (it cannot be stronger than that) that Descartes did not regard his basic laws of nature, or all of them, either as intrinsically self-evident, or as derivable by entirely logical reasoning from self-evident metaphysical premises. He speaks of 'deducing' the laws of nature from considerations about God's nature, in particular his immutability, but here we must remember that weak sense of 'deduce' which we have already encountered in considering his remarks about experiments. Descartes gives only very general arguments in support of associating these particular laws with God's nature, and it could hardly escape anyone's notice that some alternative laws might be thought equally appropriate consequences of that nature. His thought may not be that the nature of God uniquely determines the laws of nature, or all of them, but rather (as with the 'deduction' of the alternative mechanisms for a given phenomenon) that God's nature sets constraints on what the laws of nature should be, requiring in particular that there should be a conservation law. The first two of his laws, that a body remain in the state in which it is, unless something changes it, and that a moving body, other things being equal, continue to move in a straight line, are perhaps regarded by him as being more closely linked to the immutability of God than his third law, the (seriously mistaken) fundamental law of impact, from which he derived other (and equally mistaken) more particular principles: a reading of *Principles* ii 36 to 53, in which these laws are offered, seems to bear this out. Thus while the properties of God should assure us, no doubt, that there are laws of nature, and set constraints on what they can be, and may even in a special case determine a law of nature uniquely, it may not be the case that all the principles or laws of nature that Descartes uses are believed by him to be determinately deducible by pure logical reasoning from the nature of God, nor, still less, to be intrinsically self-evident. What exactly all the laws are perhaps can be known with certainty only when we discover that a given set uniquely serve to explain, under the God-guaranteed criteria of explanation, the complete range of phenomena.

The claim that we know any feature of the external world requires God's 'external' guarantee. So, I have suggested, does the claim that a given total set of mechanisms constitutes *the* explanation, under canons of simplicity, etc., of the phenomena. Lastly, God's 'external' guarantee can perhaps be found involved even in the identification of some of the fundamental laws of motion. So if these accounts are correct, the Cartesian picture of physics is in several directions removed from any ideal of an *a priori* structure of purely deductive knowledge drawn from purely self-evident axioms. But even if the last two points were waived, it would still not follow that the body of scientific knowledge could be attained *a priori*, for a basic question remains about the mere contingency of the phenomena and what they are. The points just discussed concentrate attention on the certainty, or again *a priori* character, of scientific reasonings *granted the phenomena*; but we must consider also the status of the fact that these are the phenomena.

We are concerned here not with the question of there being any material world at all: that is an ultimate metaphysical contingency, for which no explanation can be found except the purposes of God – that is to say, for Descartes, no explanation can be found. Nor are we concerned with the question that if there is a material world, it consists of pure extension with parts in motion: that, for Descartes, is not a contingency, but a necessity, which can be known (as we saw in Chapter 8) *a priori*. The question concerns what the world happens to contain – that is to say, in Cartesian terms, what the distribution of motions in the world actually is.

The question of what motions the world contains is not of course exactly the same as the question mentioned just before, of what phenomena the world contains. For, as we have seen, a given phenomenon could express more than one kind of hidden motion or mechanical structure. But we can, for all that, treat the two questions as the same for the present purpose. For a given set of motions or mechanical structures will determine a definite set of phenomena; while a given total set of phenomena, at least, will determine a definite set of motions, once we are given both the laws of nature and the God-guaranteed criteria of scientific explanation. So we can put the question in the form: is it for Descartes a contingency, something not accessible to *a priori* reason, that the world contains the motions that it does contain? Let us assume– though we shall see later that we should not assume even this – that it is not for Descartes a contingency, assuming the laws of nature, that the world contains its present distribution of motions granted that it contained some earlier distribution of motions: that is to say, that the world is a deterministic system, its earlier states mechanically determining its later states. If we assume this, then the question turns to the earlier distribution of motions, and to the development of the universe into the state we now observe.

This is an issue on which Descartes had a good deal to say, which sheds some light on our present question. The light it sheds, however, is notably filtered, for this is an area in which, more than any other, his published remarks are coloured by fear of theological controversy. In *Principles* iii 45, he says that the model he offers of the development of the physical world, plants, animals etc., must actually be false, since it conflicts with Christian belief as founded on the book of Genesis, but that it will be worthwhile to consider the consequences of a developmental model of the visible universe, even though we know from divine revelation that it is not actually true. It is certain that this does not represent Descartes's actual belief.[7] The same concern is shown in the fifth part of the *Discourse* (V I 42 ff. HR1 107 ff.) where he refers to the treatise *Le Monde* which 'certain considerations' had prevented him from publishing – in fact, his hearing of the condemnation of Galileo. The developmental story which the treatise contained is equally presented as a myth, the history of a 'new world', different from the one that actually exists. But he had written to Mersenne at the time of the condemnation (April 1634: I 285, K 25; this letter offers interesting evidence for Descartes's attitude to the Church):

You doubtless know that Galileo was censured a little while ago by the Inquisitors of the Faith, and that his opinion about the movement of the earth was condemned as heretical. I must tell you that all the things I explained in my Treatise, among which was also this opinion about the movement of the earth, so depend one on

7. In the *Conversation with Burman* (V 168–9, C pp. 36–7) Descartes refers to a project of reconciling his account with Genesis – or, one might rather say, reconciling Genesis with his account – by giving a metaphorical interpretation of the Genesis story. He says that the matter should be left for theologians. See Cottingham's note on the passage, though his statement 'Descartes had long hoped to provide a detailed reconciliation ...' gives an impression of greater seriousness and zeal than is warranted; particularly if one accepts the engaging anecdote about what Descartes said to Mlle de Schurmann, quoted in A T's note I V 700–701.

another, that it is enough to know that one of them is false, to recognize that all the considerations I use lack force ...

So far as the movement of the earth was concerned, he tried to cover himself in the *Principles* in two ways, saying both that his account was to be taken as a supposition which could be false, and also that on his account the earth could be said not to move (*Princ.* iii 19; 'That I deny the movement of the earth more carefully than Copernicus and more truthfully than Tycho'); though the sense in which the earth did not move was merely that it did not move relative to the vortex which constituted its orbit round the sun, and this is a sense in which, as he himself pointed out (*Princ.* iii 27), no other planet moves either, so that it would surely be a very relaxed Inquisitor who could take this as an adequate expression of orthodoxy.

The denials of the developmental theory are to be seen then as tactical rather than genuine. The theory seems to admit genuine ultimate contingency about the distribution of motion in the universe:

... but how big these parts of matter are, how quickly they move, and what curves they describe, we cannot determine by reason alone; because those things could have been arranged by God in countless different ways, and only experience can teach what way he chose rather than another. So we are free to assume anything we like about those, so long as its consequences agree with experience. (*Princ.* iii 46)

Since the behaviour of the kinds of substances we find in the world is equally the product of their primary qualities, it is also true that God could have created different kinds of substances (*Discourse* Part vi: VI 64, HR1 121). We can thus think of various worlds that God might have created; but it does seem to be Descartes's view that the laws of nature are invariant between all possible worlds (*Discourse* Part v: VI 43, HR1 108).

In this, Leibniz was to disagree with Descartes, conceiving of the laws of nature as themselves among the things that differ in different possible worlds. The relations between their positions, however, is not straightforward. The tendency of the present interpretation is perhaps to bring Descartes's position rather closer to Leibniz's than is generally allowed, and the question is worth a brief consideration. The disagreement between them will be clear if we suppose Descartes to have thought of the laws of nature as anything like logically necessary: for Leibniz, 'truth of reason', unlike 'truths of fact', were invariant between possible worlds, and he took the laws of nature to be 'truths of fact'. There is, as has been said, evidence to support this view of Descartes's intention, for instance a passage from a letter to More (5 February 1649: V 275, K 243), contrasting, it seems, the laws of nature with matters of fact:

... I find no reasons in physics satisfactory, except those which have that kind of necessity that one calls logical, or based on non-contradiction; granted only that one excepts those things which can only be known by experience, such as that there is just one sun around this earth, or just one Moon, and such things.

I have suggested, however, that we are not forced to take this view; it may be that Descartes did not take such a strong position, but thought that in order to identify at least some of the laws of nature, one had to make an appeal to God's benevolence, with regard to the canons of scientific explanation. That, if it is Descartes's thought, is an epistemological thought: what it says is that if we are naturally, after critical enquiry, disposed to believe that some set of laws are the true laws of nature, then it would be an offence to God's benevolence if they were not the true laws. This does not rest on the thought, central to Leibniz's outlook, that God's benevolence will determine, quite apart from what we are disposed to believe, whether he should create the world governed by that set of laws. According to Leibniz, God in his benevolence created the best of all possible worlds, and one determinant of whether a given possible world is the best is what its laws are. Descartes is little interested in such questions, which belong to the inscrutable purposes of God. For him, God's benevolence expresses itself in the concern for our intellectual and other welfare, and that requires only that the true laws should match our conscientiously acquired hypotheses, not that intrinsically they should be of a certain character.

However, there is for all that a strong parallelism between the position we are now ascribing to Descartes and the Leibnizian position. Those canons of scientific explanation – simplicity, economy etc. – which are used by the rational enquirer and which, on the present account, are guaranteed by God's benevolence, are just the same criteria that Leibniz appeals to in considering what laws would be displayed by the best of all possible worlds, that is to say, the world which the benevolent God will choose to make actual. Moreover, Descartes does not regard the rational enquirer's use of these canons as just a peculiarity which he happens to have, which God's benevolence has brought into harmony with other features of the universe: he thinks of it as, objectively, a kind of perfection. This sets up a connection between the epistemological and the ontological thoughts, and there emerges at the end a kind of isomorphism between the Leibnizian considerations and those used, on the present account, by Descartes, despite the differences between them.

Descartes's developmental model of the universe as given in the *Traité du Monde* and reported in the *Discourse* (Part v: VI 42, HR1 107) started with a state of total disorder. In the *Principles* (iii 47) he prefers to start from a more ordered condition, approximating more closely to the observed distribution of the fixed stars; but he emphasizes that he could equally have derived the observed state of the universe, using his scientific principles, from the disordered state or indeed from virtually any initial condition whatsoever – from almost any state one could get, by his principles, to the observed state by some route or other. This extraordinary claim Descartes seems to regard as expressing a strength of his system, but we should surely rather see it as revealing its weakness. For while there may be some set of initial states which could each develop into the given observed state of the universe, there must surely be on any purely mechanistic view of the matter an indefinitely large set of initial states which are such that no later state they will reach in accordance with the laws of nature is equivalent to the present observed state. Under deterministic conditions, Descartes's strongly convergent assumption seems entirely gratuitous.

It does not look as though Descartes made clear to himself the strong implications of this claim, and this would accord with a more general tendency of his not to think of his mechanistic system in such strongly determinist or, again, predictive terms as seemed natural in later developments of classical mechanics. For him, it is basically enough if one can think of types of mechanism which can underlie or generate the phenomena. As we have already seen in considering his talk of the necessity of the arguments in physics, he seems more concerned with the logical character of their mathematical expression than in the degree to which some state of the universe, so characterized, determines its successors. It is the semantics of ultimate scientific description, how processes are to be characterized in terms of the mechanistic philosophy, which absorb him, rather than any overall picture of the universe as a closed mechanical system.

Indeed, he is committed by other features of his philosophy to denying any absolute physical determinism. For he holds that souls, thinking substances, are items in the world to which the laws of nature do not apply: the laws of nature apply to the world of extension, and souls are not extended. One power of the soul is to will, and it is certainly Descartes's view that willing can be effective in the world of extension, that is to say, that physical changes occur which would not have occurred if it had not been for the mental action of a soul. He thought that such interventions were compatible at any rate with his law of the conservation of motion, which was indifferent to the direction of a motion (how the will is supposed to intervene is something we shall consider in more detail in the next chapter). He seems to have thought indeed that such interventions were compatible with *all* natural laws. If that is so, it will not merely be that there are exceptions to physical determinism in those cases where the will actually intervenes. Something stronger follows. Since the physically undetermined will can bring it about that a particular physical state of affairs Ej rather than any other state of affairs should obtain at time t, and can do this without violating any law of nature, it follows that the state of affairs obtaining just before t, together with the laws of nature, cannot determine either that *Ej* or that some state of affairs other than *Ej* obtain at *t*. So the laws of nature and the earlier state of affairs underdetermine what is to come next, that is to say, the system is not deterministic.

Despite the prestige that it acquired (Newton himself was impressed by it in his earlier years, and constructed some of his *Principia* precisely to refute the Cartesian model), Descartes's physics was not able to yield powerful and strongly constrained hypotheses. Again, despite his emphasis on method, and the heuristic emphasis of much of his work, the system is basically too indeterminate to be of much heuristic value. In the *Regulae* (see particularly *Reg.* v) Descartes emphasized the basis of his method as the reduction of the complex and the obscure to the simple. This, so far as physics was concerned, had two aspects in particular. One was the analysis of complex motions into simple motions, but this was not an idea that in the end he was able to put to such fruitful use as Galileo, for the reason we have already touched on, that his system is incapable of the right kind of abstraction. The other aspect was the reduction of the phenomenal to the mechanical, the essentially obscure ideas of the senses to the perspicuous ideas of kinematics. But this general idea tells one little about how to achieve any particular reduction or explanation. It was the *very idea* of mechanism that gripped Descartes, and there remains something essentially programmatic about his scientific system. *Ce roman de la physique*, Christiaan Huyghens brilliantly called it, and some of the difficulties of interpretation stem from the features of it which must make us regard it more as an emblem of a successful mechanistic system, a place-holder for what such a science might turn out to be like, rather than a fully determinate physical theory.

It was a successful physical theory that Descartes wanted – though we must remember that the criteria of such success were formed themselves by an historical process to which Descartes's was one of the contributions. He wanted this because his interest was as much, in fact more, in science as it was in metaphysics. But he needed it also for his metaphysics. For his metaphysical purposes, the aspect which mattered most was that of the fundamental vocabulary or conceptual system of physics, rather than success in explaining particular phenomena. But the two aspects cannot be separated,[8] since it is only in terms which include the success of determinate explanations that one can judge the conceptual structure of a physical theory, and assess its claim to tell us what the world is really like.

The foundations of Descartes's science are to be found in his metaphysics, both with regard to God's vindication of systematic enquiry, and also in virtue of the supposed metaphysical insights into the nature of matter. In this latter respect, he certainly carried metaphysical reflection into territory which would now be recognized as essentially belonging to physical science itself. In Descartes's assumption that the basic vocabulary of physics, its materials for conceptualizing the material world, could be established *a priori*, independently of what particular explanations might turn out to be correct, we do find a point at which his science can be rightly said to be too controlled by metaphysics. What Descartes does not claim, however – and if earlier arguments are right, is further from claiming than has often been thought – is that metaphysics is the foundation of physics in the sense that from metaphysical axioms one can deduce by mathematical reasoning what in detail the world actually contains. He had a vision of physical science which was in more than one way too simple and distorted relative to what was later to prove successful, but it did not consist of identifying science totally with metaphysics, nor, again, with pure mathematics.

8. Hamelin, *Système de Descartes* (Paris, 1921), p. 340, quotes Renouvier: 'la physique de Descartes est une œuvre *philosophiquement* réussie' (his emphasis). It is not a judgement which survives much reflection.

Chapter 10

MIND AND ITS PLACE IN NATURE

I EXIST as a thinking thing; the material world exists; and there is one part of that material world which stands in a quite special relation to the thinking thing that I am – my body. What is it for a body, a certain mechanical system, to be *my* body? If I, strictly speaking, am my soul (as Descartes, against St Thomas, held) what is the relation of my soul to my body?

First Descartes insists that we must get rid of a notion which constitutes the most primitive notion of soul: that the 'presence' of soul is what makes the difference between a living thing and a dead thing – or, more generally, a non-living thing. For Descartes, unlike ancient thinkers, the difference between living bodies and dead ones is a mechanical difference which in itself has nothing to do with the soul. A living body and a dead one differ as a going watch differs from a stopped one, and we must not say that the body dies because the soul leaves it, but that the soul leaves because the body dies (*Passions of the Soul* i 6, 5). This entirely naturalistic view of the phenomenon of life is a characteristic step in the scientific revolution of the seventeenth century,[1] even though Descartes's own view about the mechanism of life in warm-blooded creatures was primitive by the most advanced standards of his own time: he held to a connection between the beating of the heart and the generation of heat, although Harvey already had considerations which refuted this.

The relation of soul and body lies not in the soul's giving life to the body or powering it, but in the double connection first that I can move my body, and second that when my body undergoes various changes (as when it is struck or comes to need food) I have experiences which register these changes. The relation, then, is an intimate one. I am, so to speak, in my body,

1. As is his determinedly naturalistic and non-teleological view of re-production: (*Primae*) *Cogitationes circa Generationem Animalium* (not published till 1701): XI 505 ff., see 524.

but not at some particular place in it; my ability to move my limbs, under normal conditions, 'reaches out' to their extremities, and an injury to my foot, for example, directly hurts *me*, and *there*. These facts of embodied experience Descartes expresses in the formula 'I am not in my body like a pilot in a ship' (*Discourse* Part v: VI 59, HR1 118; *VI Med.*: VII 81, HR1 192). In this he echoes St Thomas, who wrongly ascribes the thought to Plato.[2] A person is not just 'a mind using a body' (*IV Rep.*: VII 227–8, HR2 102). What it would be for a mind merely to use a body, to be just like a pilot in a ship, is presumably that the mind would move the body by a kind of external psychokinesis (we shall come back to this point), while, on the side of what is in fact bodily sensation, it would come to know of bodily damage without feeling or experiencing it as pain (cf. to Regius, January 1642: III 493, K 128).[3]

This intimate connection Descartes is also disposed to express, particularly in controversial connections, in terms of the traditional terminology of a 'substantial union' or a 'substantial form' (*IV Rep.*: VII 219, 227–8, HR2 97, 102; to Regius, January 1642: III 493, K 128). He objected to Regius' having baldly said that a human being was an *ens per accidens*, not essentially a unity:

It can be objected that it is not an accidental feature of the human body to be joined to a soul, but its very nature: for since the body has all the dispositions necessary to receive the soul, and without which it is not strictly a human body, it could not come about without a miracle, that a soul should not be joined to it ... These things should not be denied unqualifiedly (*prorsus*), in case the theologians take offence once more; but nevertheless one should reply, that these things can be said to be accidental in the sense that, considering the body in itself, we perceive nothing in it on account of which it has to be united to a soul; and nothing in the soul on

2. *Summa contra Gentiles* ii 57; cf. Aristotle, *De anima*, 413ᵃ8–9. For this and other material on Descartes's formulation, see Gilson, *Commentaire*, p. 430 ff.
3. Perhaps only large ships have pilots. In smaller ships, as in smaller motor cars, the famous phrase may underestimate the controller's capacity to feel the vehicle as an extension of himself.

account of which it has to be united to a body; so I said shortly before, that it was inessential *in a way*, not however *absolutely* accidental. (To Regius, December 1641: III 460–61, K 121–2.)

In the *Fourth Replies* he also says that the mind is 'substantially united' with the body (VII 228, HR2 102), but the surrounding explanations make it clear how little metaphysical weight Descartes gives to such formulations. That there must be something very flimsy about Descartes's appeal to these traditional formulations is suggested by the consideration that 'substantial union' and such expressions relate to a metaphysical doctrine, about the ontological status of soul and body, but the entire content of Descartes's denial that he is a pilot in a ship is phenomenological – it is exclusively about what the experience of being embodied is like. Further argument is needed to connect that with any ontological claims. How do we know what is metaphysically necessary to make such an experience possible?

Descartes may have a more purely metaphysical level of explanation in mind when he says occasionally that the union of soul and body is a basic and unanalysable notion: as in a letter to Elizabeth (28 June 1643: IV 691 ff., K 140) where he says that there are three basic ideas in this connection, that of the soul, that of the body, and that of the union between them (cf. also to Elizabeth, 21 May 1643: IV 664 ff., K 140; to Arnauld, 29 July 1648: V 222, K 235; *Conversation with Burman*: V 163, C p. 28). Yet while holding that the connection cannot ultimately be explained, Descartes did think that something could be said in more detail about the way in which the soul influenced the body and conversely. The developed version of this theory is to be found in his last work, the *Passions of the Soul*, but the idea occurs earlier.

The soul is 'joined to all parts of the body', but there is one place in which 'it exercises its functions more particularly than elsewhere' (*Passions of the Soul* i 30–31), and this is a structure inside the brain called the pineal gland. (For earlier reference to this identification, see *Traité de l'Homme*: XI 176–77; letter to Meysonnier, 29 January 1640: III 19, K 69; to Mersenne, 30 July 1640: III 123 ff., K 75.) In the *Principles* (iv 198) he less specifically says that the human soul 'informs' the whole body (for this traditional metaphysical expression, cf. *Reg.* xii: X 411, HR1 36), but has its 'principal seat in the brain, in which it alone not only understands and imagines, but perceives'. The theory, as developed in *Passions of the Soul*, is that there is a subtle fluid, the animal spirits, which flow through the nerves and serve to convey information to and from the gland. Perturbations in the sense organs are conveyed through the sensory nervous system by the animal spirits to the gland, which is agitated and affects the soul. Conversely, in the outward direction, when voluntary movement is in question, the soul moves the gland which affects the movement of the animal spirits (changing only their direction, not their speed, to accord with Descartes's conception of the conservation of motion[4]), and these then work the muscles. Similar, more local, transactions can involve movements of the spirits merely within the brain itself. When some visual or other sensory image is recalled, animal spirits, impelled by the gland when the recall is voluntary, search out a physical trace in the brain which has been formed there as a representation of the original stimulus.

There are insurmountable philosophical objections to any theory of this kind: I shall consider these later (see below, pp. 287 ff.). If there could conceivably have been a physical site of mind–body interaction, the pineal gland, or *Conarion*, was not, relative to the knowledge of the time, an altogether stupid suggestion. What particularly impressed Descartes was the fact that the gland appeared to be the only structure in the brain which was not duplicated, and was therefore appropriate to the

4. See Leibniz, *Explanation of the New System of the Communication of Substances;* in *Philosophical Writings of Leibniz*, Everyman edn selection (London, 1934), p. 113. See also above, p. 275. Descartes himself seems never explicitly to state this consequence of his views, but Mr J. Secada has suggested to me that it is implicit in the detailed treatment of the movement of the pineal gland in the *Traité de l'Homme*, even though that work barely deals with the interventions of the soul, a topic which was left by Descartes for the unwritten, or missing, treatise on the soul. See *René Descartes, Treatise of Man*, translated and edited by T. S. Hall (Harvard, 1972), which has in general useful information on Descartes's physiological work.

unity of the mind's operations, the synthesizing of all data into one centre of consciousness. It has been suggested that Descartes did not believe that the pineal gland occurred in animals other than man, but in fact he knew that it did; he noted that it was smaller and seemingly more mobile in man than in other animals (III 20, K 70), which he took, rather weakly, to be support for his views.[5]

Descartes took animals to have no souls, no thoughts or experiences, and to be in fact automata. This is quite certainly his view (see for example a letter to Mersenne, 30 July 1640: III 121), even though there are passages in which he expresses scepticism or takes a milder tone. More wrote to him on 11 December 1648 (V 243), in what perhaps can be seen as a particularly English spirit of outrage on this subject:

But there is nothing in your opinions that so much disgusts me, so far as I have any kindness or gentleness, as the internecine and murderous view which you bring forward in the *Method*, which snatches away life and sensibility from all the animals . . .

Descartes replies (5 February 1649: V 276–7, K 243–5) at some length, and is prepared to say that we cannot prove that there is no thought in animals, since our mind 'does not penetrate their hearts', but he does think that all their responses are purely mechanical, and that they are, as he puts it to More, 'natural automata'. His principal ground for this view, as he originally said in the fifth part of the *Discourse* (VI 56–7, HR1 117), is that animals, even higher animals such as monkeys, have no universal application of intelligence, but only limited responses or routines and, above all, have no use of language at all, as

5. The function of the pineal gland is still not wholly understood, but it is known to be a light-sensitive organ which controls the activity of various enzymes. Although it is located in the cranium, connected to the brain, and in mammals originates embryologically as part of the brain, it is not actually part of it, receiving its sole neuronal input from the peripheral autonomic nervous system. See *The Pineal Gland*, a CIBA symposium, eds. G. E. W. Wolstenholme and J. Knight (Edinburgh and London, 1971). The findings are notably distant from Descartes's understanding of its function: see e.g. J. Herbert, 'The role of the pineal gland in the control by light of the reproductive cycle of the ferret.'

opposed to a repertoire of delimited signals; and this is not because they lack the physical means of expressing themselves, since parrots and other animals are capable of making even human vocal sounds, and animals generally display behaviour which expresses their passions (cf. also a letter to the Marquis of Newcastle, 23 November 1646: IV 573–6, K 206–8).[6]

These 'passions' of animals are to be regarded as purely physical disturbances in the nervous system, which can generate behaviour, but are not associated with experiences. He says in the letter to the Marquis of Newcastle:

> So far as the movements of our passions are concerned, while in us they are accompanied by thought, because we have the faculty of thought, it is nevertheless very obvious that they do not depend on thought, since they often occur against our will (*malgré nous*), and that consequently they can occur in animals, and indeed more violently than they occur in us, without one's being able to conclude from that that animals have thoughts. (IV 573–4, K 206)

The situation is similar with the sense-perceptions of animals. I have earlier referred (see p. 225) to a passage (*IV Rep.*: VII 230, HR2 104) in which Descartes says that the flight of the sheep on 'seeing' the wolf is behaviour mechanically caused by light reflected from the body of the wolf, without what Descartes would regard as a genuinely psychological intermediate stage, that is to say, a state of consciousness.

Some human behaviour is also of this type. Quite a lot of human bodily movements and actions, in fact, are thought by Descartes to bypass the soul, and to be products of self-con-

6. The 'infinite' or 'creative' aspect of linguistic capacity as a genetic peculiarity of the human mind has been much emphasized by Noam Chomsky; both his general view of the matter, and his interpretation of historical materials, remain controversial. On the historical aspect, see particularly his *Cartesian Linguistics* (New York and London, 1966). It is perhaps worth adding that even if one accepted all Chomsky's views about both the historical questions and the issues of psycholinguistic theory, the ideological opinions which Chomsky has increasingly and famously connected with these views are very insecurely connected to them: see my review 'Where Chomsky Stands', *New York Review*, 11 November 1976, pp. 43–5.

tained mechanical cycles within the body. Such actions or movements are not just analogous to animal behaviour, but are produced in exactly the same way. However, Descartes's specification of this class of movements or actions suffers considerably from vagueness and from his appealing to what seem to be several non-equivalent criteria. In the passage from the *Fourth Replies* and in the letter to Newcastle (cf. also *Description of the Human Body*, XI 224 ff.), he variously refers to such bodily processes as heart beating and digestion; to breathing when one is asleep; to actions performed by sleep-walkers; to reflexes such as stretching out one's hand to ward off a blow; and to walking and singing that one does when awake but without thinking about it. It is obvious that no one distinction bearing on this question is marked by all these examples. Some are not actions at all. Some are actions of which the agent is aware (he monitors his behaviour in walking, for instance, though thinking of something else), but not reflexively aware. Some are actions, or again movements, of which he is even reflexively aware, but which he cannot prevent himself from performing. This last condition Descartes explicitly mentions in the *Fourth Replies* – but that, very obviously, does not apply at all to walking when one's mind is on something else.

It is hardly surprising that Descartes's account is unclear on this point, since he is engaged in an impossible task, of sorting all human movements into two sharply delimited classes, as having ultimately different causal histories, one which does, and one which does not, involve the 'intervention of the mind'. It is one product of his 'all or nothing' account of mind and consciousness: either a creature has the full range of conscious powers, and is capable of language and abstract thought as well as sensation and feelings of hunger, or it is an automaton, with no experience of any kind. This feature of the theory not only distorts, as we have just seen, the action or output side of the account. It also causes obscurity on the question of the status and nature of the conscious aspect of sensations. In a human being, who has the faculty of thought, a pain, an emotional feeling, a sensation of hunger, a visual image, perceptual experiences, all have for Descartes a purely conscious aspect; we may remember from the Doubt that we could accept these experiences just as experiences while we still doubted the body (see p. 79). Later reflection suggested that one would not have such experiences if one did not have a body, and Descartes thinks that these experiences are perceptions of states of the body, transmitted to the soul via the pineal gland. In the case of perception, and perceptual memory and imagination, the body contains some kind of corporeal representation or image (see p. 240). In performing these functions, the mind 'turns towards' or 'applies itself to' these corporeal representations (*V Rep.*: VII 387, HR2 231; *Conversation with Burman*: V 162, C p. 27).

How are we to conceive the modification of the soul that this produces?[7] Certainly 'no corporeal species can be received into the mind', as he says in the passage of the *Fifth Replies*, and nothing in the mind can have the essentially corporeal characteristic of being extended. A mental image of an extended thing is not itself extended. So much, indeed, seems to be true, and it is an important consequence of it that to say that a mental image of a square (for instance) is *like*, or resembles, a square, is either false or totally contentless. If we ask, then, what makes the mental image of a square the image of a square, we must turn away from notions of resemblance.[8] The alternative notions we must use in answering the question are not obvious, but the most promising candidates seem to be notions of intentionality, or meaning, or designation.

The paradigm of a thing that means or designates is language. Descartes himself took it that language designated only because conceptual thought, which is what is expressed in language, designates. It is possible that what he took the mental aspect of

7. Descartes is committed by his general position to the view that a purely mental *idea* is involved, which is itself the object of the mind's perception. Against this, the arguments of Kemp Smith, *New Studies in the Philosophy of Descartes* (London, 1963), are not conclusive. But whether one uses the concept 'idea' or not, something has to be said about the state of the soul in these (inwards) psychophysical transactions.

8. It is not excluded that *having* the visual image of a square may be non-vacuously like *seeing* a square.

a perceptual or sensory image to be was a confused piece of conceptual thought, which in no way resembled or pictured a corporeal thing, but had the only relation to such a thing that conceptual thought can have, that is, meaning or designation. If so, then the thought involved in such imagery is confused in more than one way: it is not obvious to unreflective consciousness that this is what the thought is, and it is not obvious what it designates. Its immediate designation is, in fact, a state of one's body. On this view, to have an image of a square is to have a confused conceptual thought about a brain-state which is a picture of a square – a picture, at least, in that it is extended and representational, though its exact degree of straightforward resemblance may not matter.

Pains, emotional disturbances, bodily sensations of pressure, and so on, will have to be treated in the same way. They will be confused conceptual thoughts about states of the body, and a pain 'in' the foot will be an unclear (or, more strictly, indistinct: see the distinction between clarity and distinctness, *Princ.* i 46) thought about there being something wrong with my foot. Although there may be something in a theory of this general type, it cannot be adequate: it does not, for instance, say enough, or anything, about why or how pains are disagreeable. Moreover, such a theory, as it stands, leads very readily to Descartes's conclusion about animals. If the conscious side of all these events is an application, even if confused, of the power of conceptual thought, then animals, who lack that power, have no conscious thought, and Descartes's all-or-nothing view of the soul becomes more comprehensible.

If Descartes was disposed to see all conscious experience as consisting of some kind of conceptual thought, this will also help to explain the notorious confusion to which he is subject between mere consciousness and reflexive consciousness: the confusion that we found him making earlier in a letter to Plempius (3 October 1637: I 413, K 36; see p. 226) between consciousness in seeing and consciousness of seeing. All conscious processes are 'accompanied' by consciousness, but Descartes was disposed to equate that truism with the falsehood that they must themselves be the objects of a reflexive consciousness.

That latter will certainly be an application of conceptual thought, and so this idea by itself will, once more, exclude the animals. If first-order and reflexive consciousness are regarded as being both of the same basic type, conceptual, then that is a factor to encourage the confusion of the two types of consciousness.

Descartes had in fact another, more external, reason or motive for denying souls to animals. For him, soul meant separable soul, and separable soul meant the possibility of immortality. Metaphysics can prove no more than the possibility – that there is actually immortality depends on God (to Mersenne, 24 December 1640: III 265, K 87; this relates to the subtitle of the *Meditations,* for which see above, p. 106). He expressly says that the idea of an animal soul would encourage the absurd idea of animal immortality, and 'it is less probable that worms, gnats, caterpillars and the rest of the animals should possess an immortal soul, than that they should move in the way machines move' (to More, 5 February 1649: V 277, K 244; cf. *Discourse* Part v: VI 59, HR1 118).

We should now turn from the details of Descartes's treatment to consider the general conception of the kind of interactionism which he introduced. It is often said, and was certainly felt by many of Descartes's contemporaries and successors, that there was something deeply mysterious about the interaction which Descartes's theory required between two items of totally disparate natures, the immaterial soul, and the gland or any other part of an extended body. 'How the body causes something to happen in the soul or vice-versa,' Leibniz wrote,[9] 'Descartes had given up the game on that point, so far as we can know from his writings.' The scandal of Cartesian interactionism helped to encourage both Malebranche's[10] 'occasionalism'

9. *New System of Nature and of the Communication of Substances* ... in *Leibniz, Selections* ed. Philip Wiener (New York, 1951), p. 113.
10. The view was that God took the 'occasion' of one change to introduce the other; Leibniz criticized it for representing God as very inefficient. Malebranche is the best-known exponent of the view, but it is to be found in other writers, such as Louis de la Forge (*Le Traité de l'esprit et de l'homme,* 1666) and Geraud de Cordemoy (*Le discernement du corps et de l'âme,*

(which had God intervening on each occasion to bring about appropriate changes in mind or body), and also the theory of the 'pre-established harmony', suggested by Arnold Guelincx and developed with much self-congratulation by Leibniz, according to which the states of mind and body unfolded harmoniously in step with one another.

Descartes's doctrine is certainly mysterious, but it is important that there are two different levels at which it is unsatisfactory. The first level, most frequently discussed, concerns the obscurity of the idea that immaterial mind could move *any* physical thing. This obscurity would be involved just as much in cases other than the workings of the embodied mind: for instance, in the supposed phenomenon of psychokinesis, in which an agent's thought allegedly influences the movement of material things quite separate from him. This conception has a characteristic property of magic, that it is the intentional significance of a symbol, rather than particular features of its physical realization, which is supposed to produce the physical effect. Thus if a gambler can affect the fall of a dice by 'willing' a certain outcome, it makes no difference whether it is in words, or in what words, that he represents the desired outcome in his thought. Experiments have in fact been conducted to test for such an influence, and to see whether it could be screened, jammed, etc. Such experiments presuppose the view, superficially plausible, that if such things as psychokinesis are impossible, they are so for empirical reasons.

I suspect that deeper consideration suggests that such an influence is not merely empirically impossible, but inconceivable, but this is not a question which should detain us here. Let us grant, generously, that whether psychokinesis is possible is an empirical issue, including in the idea of its occurring, the idea that the influence could not be affected by any physical force, and moreover, that nothing could produce the influence but conscious thought (thus printing out the desired result in a

---

1666). Guelincx was primarily an occasionalist, and although he introduced the well-known image of the two harmonized clocks, one of which strikes when the other shows the hour, it has been disputed whether he used this in the same sense as Leibniz.

near-by computer, for instance, would have no effect). With that, we have granted some approximation to the idea that it is not unintelligible for mind to influence matter separate from it. But there is a second level of difficulty which arises after this, and which is more interesting for the philosophy of mind. Even if psychokinesis were granted, it would go nowhere to explain such familiar phenomena as one's ability to move one's body at will. One's control over one's own body could not be understood as internal, localized, psychokinesis.

We can conveniently discuss this in terms of Descartes's model of the pineal gland and animal spirits, though it is important that the points at issue have nothing specially to do with that scientifically discredited model. We can substitute for Descartes's explicitly hydraulic model of nervous and muscular action (cf. *Traité de l'Homme*: XI 130–31), a contemporary one in terms of an electro-chemical system; we can imagine, in place of the pineal gland, any input point at all of the mind into the neurophysiological system (though we can presumably assume that any such point, if there could be one, would be in the brain). Now it is a notable feature of our experience that our control over our limbs is not ballistic: we do not, unless partially paralysed, throw our arm at something on a desired trajectory, but rather reach out for the thing. This, of course, is among those phenomenological facts, facts constitutive of our experience, which Descartes expressed in his formula about the pilot and the ship. We have already seen that he was tempted to read that phenomenological fact as a metaphysical one, in relation to his talk of a substantial union. Much the same occurs also with regard to the pineal gland. When he said that the soul is 'joined to all parts of the body', but that 'it exercises its functions more particularly' in the gland (*Passions of the Soul* i 30–31), his statement is in fact very confused. There is no one sense in which the soul is joined to every part of the body, but particularly connected with the gland. In the phenomenological sense in which it is joined to the whole body, it is not particularly joined to the gland: my pineal gland is not something I can move as I can move my finger (we shall come back to this), nor can I feel anything in it. In the sense in which, according to

Descartes, the soul particularly operates on the pineal gland, it does not operate on anything else; it directly moves the pineal gland, but everything else it moves by moving the pineal gland. In the supposed causal sense of 'joined', as opposed to the phenomenological, the soul is joined to the body only at the pineal gland, and not anywhere else.

Now Descartes distinguished, correctly, between changes I can bring about in my body at will, and those that I can bring about only indirectly, by bringing about some other change at will. Thus I cannot, directly, dilate or contract the pupils of my eyes, but I can look at a light, and my pupils will then contract (*Passions of the Soul* i 44). Knowing this, I can look at a light to make my pupils contract. Here there is an intentional strategy, in which the ultimate intended outcome is a result of the movement I make at will (looking at the light). But it is important that there can equally be an intentional strategy in which the ultimate intended outcome is causally related in a quite different way to the movement I bring about at will. I might find that the muscles of my forearm twitch interestingly if I contract my fingers. I might want to display this muscle movement; the way I bring it about, having learned the connection, is by contracting my fingers. But the movement of the muscle is not the result of my fingers contracting, but the cause of that contraction. Similarly, if electro-chemical changes in my brain were being monitored in some way, I might be able to bring about some state which was a causal condition of my hand's moving, by moving my hand. If Descartes had been right about the gland, and movements of my pineal gland were being monitored, I might be asked to produce a certain pattern of movement in my pineal gland. Unable to move my pineal gland at will, I could, if sufficiently informed, produce in my pineal gland, by moving my arm, whatever movement it was in the gland that produced the movement of my arm.

From this, it is clear that we must say both that the change in the brain causes *my arm to move*, and that *my moving my arm* causes the change in the brain. On the Cartesian theory, the correct understanding of this latter claim, that my moving my arm causes the change in the brain, is that my willing causes the change in the brain. Now what, on that account, is it that I will? Not, strictly speaking, *to move my arm*, or, as we may equally well put it, *that I move my arm*. My moving my arm, on Descartes's account, just is my willing, plus my willing's being effective; indeed, in the context we have just been examining, when we say that my moving my arm causes the change in the brain, the expression 'my moving my arm' refers *only* to the willing. To suppose, then, that the intentional content of the willing – what I will – refers to the action of moving my arm would be to suppose that the intentional content itself refers to an act of willing, so I will that I will, and that must be wrong. We have to say, rather, on the Cartesian account, that when I move my arm at will, what I will is *that my arm move*.

Now, as we have already seen, there are some movements that I can make at will, and others not. Thus, usually, I can move my arm at will, but never my hair. On the Cartesian account, that difference must involve this, that my willing that my arm move is usually followed by my arm moving, but my willing that my hair move is not followed by my hair moving. But to say just that is not to say enough: we have not yet characterized the difference. We must also take account of the fact that an 'external' application of willing, such as we discussed in connection with psychokinesis, is no more effective in making my arm move than it is in making my hair, or anything else, move. Put your hand next to some object, such as this book, and 'will' the book to approach your hand: nothing happens. Now 'will', *in that same way*, your hand to approach the book. Still nothing happens.[11] Direct application of psychokinesis is no more effective with my limbs than with anything else.

The only way, then, on the Cartesian theory, to get your hand to move by willing is to move your pineal gland: that is the only organ directly susceptible to psychokinesis. But if an organ is directly susceptible to psychokinesis, then that organ must be, if any is, one that I can move at will: it will be the paradigm example of my willing that something move, and its moving. So

11. I owe this idea to James Thomson. See also *Freedom and the Will*, ed. D. F. Pears (London, 1963), Chapter 2.

if the Cartesian account is correct, and I can move anything at will, I can move my pineal gland at will. But I cannot. As we have already seen, I cannot make my arm move by changing my brain-states, I can only make my brain-states change by moving my arm. The brain (for Descartes, the pineal gland) is not responsive to willing which has brain changes as intentional content, but only to willing which has movements of other parts of the body as intentional content. That is to say, the only part of my body directly responsive to my will is one which I cannot move at will.

This result seems to me enough to dispose of the idea that voluntary movement is to be explained by a kind of internalized psychokinesis. Even if causal transactions between matter and immaterial mind were possible, we cannot reasonably conceive of voluntary movement in terms of such a transaction, with a mental act as the first term of an otherwise physical causal chain originating in the brain. There are also good reasons (though I shall not try to argue it here) for denying the analogous account in the opposite direction, that perception is to be understood in terms of the occurrence of a mental event as the last step of an incoming causal chain. 'Terminal interactionism', as we might call it, must be an error. Yet it may be that many of the reasons that seem to support interactionism of any kind would support, if anything, terminal interactionism.

We should turn, finally, to the most general question left to us from Descartes's dualism: how are we to conceive of the existence of the mental? Descartes had a conception of the world containing a special kind of thing, substantial immaterial selves, and he sought to gain this conception, as we have seen, on the sole basis of the point of view of consciousness. I suggested in Chapter 3 (by an argument which is in effect only a development of Kant's in the *Paralogisms of Pure Reason*[12]) that this was not an adequate basis. Starting solely from the point of view of consciousness, one cannot gain any objective conception of there being several such selves – nor, consequently, can one gain an *objective* conception of there being even one. It is important in this connection to recall a point made in the

12. *Critique of Pure Reason*, A341–405 and (differently) B399–432.

course of that discussion (see above, p. 100): this is not a verificationist argument, resting on the idea that an observer would have no way of establishing that such selves existed. The point is that, sticking consistently to the point of view of consciousness, no coherent conception can be formed even in the abstract of what would have to obtain for a plurality of such selves to exist.

If we abandon the Cartesian conception of there being two independent kinds of object in the world, the outlook, that is to say, of *substantial* dualism, one natural recourse in looking for a coherent conception of the place of the mental in the world would be to turn to what may be called *attributive* dualism. This would concede that a thing which could be in mental states, the bearer of mental predicates, had either to be or to involve a physical thing. By introducing the term 'involve' here I mean to indicate a range of what might, crudely, be called Aristotelian theories, by which some predicates have to be true of some physical body for mental predicates to apply to anything, but nevertheless what the mental predicates apply to is some item (a *person*, for instance) which is not merely a physical body and has criteria of identity which diverge from those of a physical body.[13] This range of views, which I believe to be basically unstable, I shall leave on one side, and consider only the alternative that what mental predicates apply to are physical items such as human bodies.

The view that the bearers of mental predicates are physical things does not in itself entail that the mental predicates are reducible to, identical to, or interestingly co-extensive with, any physical properties of those things (the notion of a physical property had better be regarded as uncontentious for the pur-

13. Strawson's view in *Individuals* (London, 1959), Chapter 3, is of this kind; for a criticism of that view, and other considerations bearing on this issue, see 'Are Persons Bodies?' in my *Problems of the Self* (Cambridge, 1973). For reasons outlined in that paper, my own view is that there are only two basic possibilities: that 'person' should be a genuine particular term, in which case each person is a body; or that it should be a type term, in which case a person is, roughly, a set of bodies. There is however also a transitional conception, not clearly identified in that paper, by which a person is the unit set of a body.

poses of this discussion). Merely so far as the physical character of their bearers is concerned, the mental predicates might; it seems, be quite autonomously non-physical. The view that they are so is what we are calling 'attributive dualism'. Of course, since the bearers of these predicates would have non-physical properties, it would trivially follow that the bearers were not totally physical in character, but compatibly with that, they might be individuable only in physical terms, and would be correctly described as physical things with some non-physical properties. Attributive dualism is not merely a verbal variant on substantial dualism, and seems *prima facie* to be something of an advance on it. In particular, it seems to offer some help to the conception of a world *containing* the mental, and to the closely related task of conceiving the mental from a third-personal or objective point of view. It would remain true that to conceive of a certain thing as in a mental state – more specifically, as in a conscious state – would involve identifying with it, taking its position, conceiving of how things were for it; but the objective physical existence of the subject of the conscious state would provide me, so to speak, with the point I should imaginatively move to, the thing I should identify with, and this is certainly some advance over the immaterial points of view of substantial dualism.

But is it enough of an advance? There are reasons to think that it is not, and that attributive dualism is a superficial view, which has inherited, in a concealed way, difficulties from its substantial ancestor. I shall try to sketch, very much in outline, a reason of this sort: it is connected with a pervasive obscurity in our idea of consciousness. (I have moved from discussing the mental, to discussing the conscious: it is consciousness which is at the heart of the immediate issue. We shall come back to a broader conception of the psychological before the end.) We entertain the idea that we have some clear conception of what we are including in the world when we include in it conscious states; and attributive dualism needs us to have such a conception, since autonomous conscious states are, on that view, just what we are attributing to the physical subjects of mental predicates. But on reflection it looks less and less plausible that we have a clear conception of this.

We can say that the general form of a question about someone's conscious state is *how is it for A?* Wondering whether *A* is in pain, I take up in imagination *A*'s point of view, and encounter from that point of view the possibilities that there is pain or not, that it does or does not hurt. Let us call this conception of how things are from *A*'s point of view the conception of the *content* of *A*'s experience (while being aware that the notion of content so introduced is entirely schematic and certainly contains large problems). If I then revert to the third-personal or objective point of view, and try to form a conception from there of just what is in the world when *A* is in pain, the temptation is to try to write into the world, in some hazy way, the appropriate content of *A*'s experience – as we might naturally, but too easily, say: the pain. But in taking the content of *A*'s experience, and putting it into the world as a thing we can conceive of as there, we are in effect trying to abstract from *how it is for A*, the *how it is* and leave it as a fact on its own, which however has the mysterious property that it is available only to *A*, and can only be known directly to *A*, though it can be conceived of, guessed at, and so on by others. But there must be a misconception here. The *only* perspective on the contents of *A*'s consciousness is the perspective of *A*'s consciousness. When *it is so for A* (e.g. *it hurts for A*), the only way of one's conceiving the appropriate *it is so* at all is that of adopting once more *A*'s point of view and putting oneself imaginatively in a state which one expresses (if it can be verbally expressed) by saying, as *A*, *it is so* (e.g. *it hurts*).

What we need as an objective fact in the world, conceivable from a third-personal point of view, is not the *it is so* of *it is so for A*, but *it is so for A* itself. But we are naturally disposed to conceive of this fact in a way which puts into the world, as an autonomous but hidden item, the content of *A*'s consciousness. It may seem a platitude that the contents of consciousness can be conceived only from the point of view of that consciousness, but if it is, it is not one that we think through consistently in trying to conceive what is in the world when there are conscious states. Rather, we are subject to an illusion on that score, an illusion generated by our capacity for reflexive consciousness of our own conscious states, and our ability to project ourselves imaginatively into another's point of view – capacities which are necessary to our raising any of these problems at all, and also essentially connected with each other.

The illusion involved here harmonizes with a mistaken model of self-knowledge. It is widely agreed that the privacy of pains (for instance) is necessary: it is not merely a contingent fact that I alone can feel my pains, as it is a contingency that I alone can read my diary, if I carefully lock it up. Yet there remains something incurably mysterious about this privacy so long as an objective, third-personal, conception of the content of mental states is thought possible, since that conception must be of an object or state which is 'there', but somehow can announce itself only to the subject. The puzzling nature of this necessity, together with the obscurity of the way in which these supposed facts can be related to genuinely third-personal facts of speech and behaviour, and also to neurophysiological and similar data, then generates the sceptical problem of other minds: if there are these autonomous objects or facts, how can any general correlation of them with the public phenomena be known?

As against this model, if we hold firmly to the platitude, as it is, that there can be no third-personal perspective on the contents of consciousness, we should be less surprised to find that a third-personal conception of the world which contains only the genuinely third-personal facts of behaviour, speech, and physiology, can *already* determine the existence of consciousness in the world. If there were a class of autonomous items in the world which were the contents of consciousness, then there would have to be a coherent conception of the world from which just those items had been removed, leaving all those other facts as they were. But, if we conceive a world determined just as ours is with regard to all the physical facts, then surely we have already included the facts of persons having pains and thoughts and being in other conscious states? (If not, then indeed it is obscure why, even as things are, we have any reason to believe in the general occurrence of these things.)[14] So perhaps facts of the form *it is so for A* can, in some way or other, be included in the world just by including all the physic.l facts in it; that is to say, some version of physicalism is true. It is not clear to me how that may be so, and none of the current theories on these matters seems to me to make it adequately clear how this may be so. It may even be – though there is nothing to force one to the conclusion – that we do not yet possess the concepts that we shall need to make these matters clear to ourselves. But at any rate many of the most immediate and seemingly overwhelming objections to physicalism stem from the thought that there is no way to incorporate into the physicalist picture of things the existence of the contents of consciousness. There is not, but that is no objection, if there is no coherent way of regarding the contents of consciousness from an objective or third-personal point of view at all. If any version of physicalism is true, then attributive dualism is mistaken; and indeed the previous line of discussion does suggest that it rests, with regard to the contents of consciousness, on much the same sort of illusion as that from which substantial dualism formed its conception of conscious subjects.

If we give up a Cartesian conception of self-knowledge and of the status of the mental in the world, we shall have reason to give up a related idea, also deeply lodged in our thought, that the mental is fully determinate. Descartes construed first-personal psychological certainty as the intimate presence to the subject of a certain class of facts, and also conceived of those facts as being as fully determinate as the facts of physical reality. In rejecting such a picture, we have to think anew about the whole question of the determinateness of our experience. However, in turning briefly to this area, I shall leave phenomena such as pains, feelings and images, and turn to the case of verbal thoughts. This will serve to bring in another and different

14. On this, see James Hopkins, 'Wittgenstein and Physicalism', *Proceedings of the Aristotelian Society* LXXV (1974–5), 121–46, which illuminatingly connects physicalism and Wittgenstein's critique of our illusory models of self-knowledge.

dimension of indeterminacy, which will be important in taking a rather broader view of the place of the psychological.

In one way, we seem to have a more determinate conception of the nature and content of someone else's verbal thought than of, say, his visual images. Indeed, the more that a thought approximates to the condition of a private speech-act, the closer its content comes to being a public thing. I suggested in Chapter 3 (p. 85) that there were two different paradigms of privacy with regard to the mental: the pain case, where the notion centres on the marked difference between having the sensation oneself and thinking about someone else's having it; and the case of episodic thought in words or images, where the notion centres on the entirely voluntary character of any expression of the thought. I remarked that in this latter case, the contrast between having the thought and thinking about someone else's having it is less dramatic, and can vanish. It totally vanishes where the thought is entirely verbal, and the one who conceives it has a thought with exactly the same verbal content. In this ultimate case, thinking, speaking, hearing and understanding are entirely homogeneous in their content. A person can actually be in doubt whether he thought or spoke, or again whether he spoke or heard, and yet be in no doubt what it was that he spoke or thought or heard. There is no analogy for this with sensations, or even with images (though I can doubt whether I am imaging or seeing, that gives an analogy only to the link between thinking and hearing, not to the link between speaking and hearing). Although it can be entirely and indeed paradigmatically private, episodic thought which is totally verbal is nevertheless the nearest thing in the inner life to public thought.

What this means is that a totally verbal thought-occurrence can be as fully determinate as a public utterance in its intentional aspects; and that means that it can be fully determinate *relative to a shared understanding of the language*. If *A*'s thought is just these words, then we can be given the words, and being given them, we shall be given his thought just to the extent that we understand the words. The thought which we then all have will be determinate to the extent that the meanings we all ascribe to those words are determinate. But recent work, particularly by Quine,[15] on the 'indeterminacy of translation' has raised serious questions about how determinate that may be. For the present purpose, we may leave the question of our understanding of a thinker who shares, as we would naturally suppose, a language with us: in a favourable case, of one from whom we have learned our language, say, or one to whom we have taught it, let us accept for the present argument that no question of indeterminacy arises between him and ourselves. Relative to some other linguistic scheme, however, what we mean may be indeterminate in the sense that two sentences not equivalent in that language may equally serve as translations of some sentence of ours, and the choice between them be undetermined by everything we do or say. In such a case, what we mean is, relative to that other language, indeterminate, just as what they mean may be indeterminate relative to our language. In such a case, it is not that there is some ultimate truth, hidden from these parties: there is in Quine's phrase, 'no fact of the matter about it'. Granted that, fully determinate meanings of what we and these others say cannot figure in the absolute conception of things, that conception which is neutral between all observers; consequently fully determinate content for verbal thoughts cannot figure there either.

Rather similar considerations lead us to another domain of indeterminacy which presents itself when we turn from both pains and episodic verbal thoughts to psychological phenomena which are not episodic – phenomena such as desires, beliefs and intentions. Descartes thought that the subject had incorrigible knowledge of these as of all mental states, a view which I rejected in Chapter 3. He took the expressions of such states in episodic thought as totally revelatory of them. We should rather say that there are indeed such expressions, and that they do make an essential contribution to interpretation of thought, action and behaviour, yet it is, all the same, interpretation which is in question, and the subject's interpretation is not necessarily incontestable. We may for recognizable reasons know more, each of us, about what we want or believe or intend than others know, but there is nothing in the inner life to give us

15. See in particular his *Word and Object* (New York and London, 1960).

answers to these questions which are indubitable. When we give interpretations in terms of belief, desire and intention, it is possible that we should be confronted by alternative and conflicting schemata of interpretation, and the choice between them be underdetermined by the facts, including among the facts the subject's verbal expressions, if any. This is because of the holistic character of the interpretative framework, and an ineliminable looseness of fit of these interpretative concepts to behaviour, even when behaviour has already been characterized in terms of action, a process which itself involves interpretation. It can be so, moreover, even if we assume determinacy about what the subject's verbal declarations mean: if we add the possibility of indeterminacy there as well, as already discussed, then we have two layers of indeterminacy in the present connection. Davidson, in particular,[16] has stressed the need to adopt methodological principles of a strongly pragmatic kind, such as principles of 'charity' concerning the agent's rationality, in order to arrive at interpretations of this kind. If we accept this kind of view, then at the end of this line, too, there can be conflicting interpretations about which there is no fact of the matter.

If the various sorts of consideration which have been summarily sketched here are correct, then we have to give up not just dualism but the belief in the determinacy of the mental. These considerations converge on the conclusion that there are no fully determinate contents of the world which are its psychological contents.

What effects will this kind of conclusion have on the idea of an absolute conception of reality? We may recall in particular two demands which that conception seemed to make: that we should at least show the possibility of explanations of the place in the world of psychological phenomena such as the perception of secondary qualities, and, further, of cultural phenomena

16. See for instance his 'Psychology as Philosophy', reprinted in *The Philosophy of Mind*, ed. J. Glover (Oxford, 1976) and 'The Material Mind', in *Logic, Methodology and Philosophy of Science IV*, ed. P. Suppes *et al.* (North-Holland, 1973). Davidson has argued, e.g. in the latter piece, that there could never be tight or effective psycho-physical laws, a position which he calls 'anomalous monism'.

such as the local non-absolute conceptions of the world, and of the absolute conception itself, including in that the possibility of physical science. No one is yet in a position to meet those demands; to do so is a programme for philosophy, one in which (if not necessarily under that specification) many philosophers are engaged. But on the first question, it can at least be said that there is nothing in these last reflections about the indeterminacy of the mental which increases the onus on those who deny that perceived secondary qualities would figure, as such, in the absolute conception of things. The chief obstacle to explaining perceptual experience in a broadly physicalist framework has seemed to be the inexpressible content of that experience, but if the line suggested earlier can be followed, then this will be, here as more generally, no objection. To the extent, certainly, that psycho-physical science can succeed in explaining any non-verbal conscious states at all (including those which have always been regarded as 'subjective' in their content), there is no reason in the present arguments to make us suppose that it will have less success in explaining perceptual states.

The demand in the second area may be much harder to meet, or to evade. The requirement was that we should be able to overcome relativism in our view of reality through having a view of the world (or at least the coherent conception of such a view) which contains a theory of error: which can explain the existence of rival views, and of itself. But this conception involves a dimension not just of physical explanation, but of social explanation as well. We have to explain the emergence of physical science as something which is indeed knowledge. This entails, if we are to sustain the realist outlook which is essential to the idea of the absolute conception, that physical theory and the interpretation of nature should not suffer from the same kind of ultimate indeterminacy that may affect translation and the interpretation of the mental. We have to explain, further, how psychological, social and other theories, and also less theoretical views of the world, can be related to the world as we understand it in terms of physical theory. In these philosophical and social scientific tasks, we are not only explaining, but ourselves giving examples of, theories which we have no reason to suppose will ever yield very strong decision procedures, and which deal with just the kind of subject matter which may be liable to radical indeterminacy of interpretation.

In face of such considerations, the most ambitious ideas that have been entertained of the absolute conception must fail: the idea, for instance, of a cumulative, convergent, self-vindicating unified science of man and nature. How much less than this positivist fantasy will do? What is the minimum? Perhaps just this: that we should make sense of how natural science can be absolute knowledge of reality, and of why we cannot even agree how much else is absolute knowledge of reality. There is no obvious impossibility in the idea that the natural sciences should be able to give absolute explanations of a determinate and realistically conceived world, while the social sciences could not do this and should not be expected to. On such a scheme, philosophy will belong, presumably, with the social sciences. Since, unlike the results and methods of the natural sciences, it hardly transcends the local interpretative predispositions of various cultural communities on earth, there is not much reason to think that it could transcend the peculiarities of humanity as a whole.

It may seem, however, that there will have to be at least one piece of philosophy which has absolute status: that, namely, which makes clear why natural science can be absolute knowledge of how things are, while social science, common perceptual experience and so forth, cannot (with the result that we cannot even agree how much other knowledge we have). But that piece of philosophy would constitute almost all of philosophy. So does not even this minimum hope for an absolute conception end, as other more ambitious hopes have ended, in the conclusion that philosophy itself is absolute knowledge – perhaps even the highest form of absolute knowledge? And that is a conclusion which we, unlike those earlier philosophers, must reasonably see as a *reductio ad absurdum*. But we are not forced to that result. The absolute status of philosophy would not be required just by there being some absolute conception of the world, but rather by our knowing that there was, and what it was. We have agreed all along that we should need some reasonable idea of what such a conception would be like, but we have not agreed that if we have that conception, we have to know that we have it. The absolute conception was taken to be a presupposition of knowledge about the world, and it is knowledge about the world that is our objective. To ask not just that we should know, but that we should know that we know, is (as we remarked a long time ago) to ask for more – very probably for too much.

In holding on, if rather grimly, to Descartes's aspiration for an absolute conception which abstracts from local or distorted representations of the world, we have left behind his transcendental guarantee of knowledge, his project of pure and solitary enquiry, and his picture of the enquiring mind as transparent rationality. We left behind also, and importantly so, the demand that the conception be grounded in certainty – we have separated the demand that the conception be absolute from the requirement that it be indubitable. It is one consequence of this last point, that we have just encountered. More generally, we can perhaps glimpse, in these last considerations, ways in which these various rejections of Descartes turn out to be deeply connected with one another. This only reflects something which this study has, at more than one point, tried to bring out – the extent to which Descartes's remarkable project, its conception and its execution, were all of a piece.

Appendix 1

EPISTEMOLOGICAL CONCEPTS

1. In the expressions that follow, '*P*' stands in for what in the text are called 'propositions'. There are various complications, some trivial, that arise in the handling of notions such as *proposition, sentence,* etc. in epistemological connections. To avoid repeated qualifications, we adopt a set of conventions to govern the use of *proposition*. (By these conventions, a proposition is roughly equivalent to a synonymy-class of sentences.)

(a) A given proposition is tied to a grammatical person: 'I am in pain' is a different proposition from 'he is in pain'.

(b) A given proposition is tied to tense: 'I was in pain' is a different proposition from 'I am in pain'.

(c) A given proposition is not tied to a given occasion or subject: 'I am in pain' is the same proposition whoever asserts it on whatever occasion (it follows that one and the same proposition can be sometimes true, sometimes false).

(d) A given proposition is not tied to a given language or form of words: any sentence synonymous with 'I am in pain' expresses the same proposition.

(e) The formula '*A* believes *P*' is to be read as e.g. '*A* believes "I am in pain" ', where (i) this is not tied to any particular sentence of any particular language – in this respect it is like the indirect speech formula '*A* believes that . . .'; (ii) the 'I' is taken as referring to *A*: thus the indirect speech version of 'Descartes believes "I am in pain" ' is not 'Descartes believes that I am in pain' (something he had no opportunity to do) but 'Descartes believes that he is in pain'. Similar considerations apply to 'knows', 'doubts', and 'thinks of'.

2. '*A*' can be taken as referring to the Pure Enquirer, but the Pure Enquirer can be anyone, and we are concerned with general properties of the propositions in question, so the formulae

can equally be taken as universally quantified with respect to '*A*'.

3. For a point about the meaning of 'believe', see p. 201 and note.

Definitions

D1 *S–V* P is *self-verifying*: P is not a necessary truth, and if P is asserted, P is asserted truly.

D2 *INC* P is *incorrigible*: if A believes P, P is true.

D3 *EV* P is *evident*: if P is true, A believes P.

D4 *StEV* P is *strongly evident*: if P is true, A knows P.

D5 *IRR* P is *irresistible*: if A thinks of P, A believes P.

D6 *SOL* P is *solid*: if A believes P, A knows P.

D7 *OInd* P is *objectively indubitable*: if A thinks of P, A knows P.

　　D1 and D2 are to be understood as though 'necessarily' occurred before 'if': P will not be *S-V* or *INC* just because it is true.

Axioms

A1 If A believes P, A asserts P.

A2 If A doubts P, A thinks of P.

A3 If A doubts P, A does not believe P.

Consequences

C1 If P is *INC* and *StEV*, P is *SOL*.

C2 If P is *IRR* and *SOL*, P is *OInd*.

The proofs of C1 and C2 are obvious.

C3 If P is true and EV, P is *IRR*.

For: Suppose that if P is true, A believes P (that is, P is *EV*); then it follows that if P is true, then if A thinks of P, A believes P: that is, if P is true, P is *IRR*. So, if P is *EV*, then if P is true, P is *IRR*. So, C3.

C4 If P is *OInd*, A cannot doubt P.

If P is *OInd*, P is *IRR*. We can either derive this using the premiss that knowledge implies belief; or else just note that all the *OInd* conclusions the Pure Enquirer arrives at (see Appendix 2) he arrives at via their being *IRR*. The reassuring conclusion C4 is then reached straightforwardly from A2, A3 and D5, as on pp. 184–5.

Appendix 2

WHAT THE PURE ENQUIRER KNOWS

THIS can be taken as a retrospective assessment by the Pure Enquirer, A, of the objectively indubitable pieces of information he has acquired: not all of the considerations used here will be available to A until he has reached the view of his situation considered in Chapter 7. The assumptions employed are, of course, Descartes's and not necessarily ours. The claim is that, granted his general assumptions and the apparatus of Appendix 1, a clear account can be given of the various ways in which the conclusions he basically needs emerge as objectively indubitable. In some cases, they are only relatively so, in a (harmless) sense which will become clear.

First, an additional consequence:
C5 If P is EV and INC, P is $StEV$.
Consider some proposition P which is EV. Suppose it true. Then

1	If P, A believes P	(D3)
2	P	
3	P and A believes P.	(1, 2)

Suppose P is also INC. Since it is EV and INC, A believes P just in case it is true. Such a belief must surely possess in the highest degree the property of being reliably acquired: it is so reliably acquired that beliefs so acquired are exceptionlessly true. Call this property of being acquired in a way which is exceptionlessly reliable, '*E': *E is a stronger version of the property E discussed on pp. 39 ff.

Then   4 $*E(A$'s belief in $P)$
So, by the most demanding standards,

	5	A knows P	(3, 4)
So	6	P is $StEV$	(2–5)

Cogito 'Cogito' itself is EV. It is also $S–V$, hence INC (by D1 and the strongly Cartesian assumption A1). It is thus $StEV$ (C5).

The other first-person psychological extensions of the *cogito* (see pp. 78 ff.) are *INC* (though not *S–V*: see p. 80). They are also *EV*, hence (C5) *StEV*.

So in all forms the propositions associated with the *cogito* are *INC* and *StEV*, and so (C1) SOL. 'Cogito' itself is unqualifiedly *IRR*; since it is *SOL*, it is thus (C3) *OInd*. The other *cogito* propositions are *IRR* relative to their being true (cf. p. 186); since they are *SOL*, they are, relative to their being true, *OInd*. (This includes 'I am doubting', which Descartes needs for the premiss of his own imperfection, used in the first proof of God's existence: see p. 142).

Eternal truths, simple necessary truths etc. These are *IRR* (when properly 'thought of'), but not *EV*. They are, trivially, *INC*.

Suppose that such a proposition is carefully considered (the sense of 'thought of' relevant to D5 and D7, see p. 185).

Then	1	*A* believes *P*	(*P* is *IRR*)
	2	*P*	(it is a necessary truth)

But there is no better way of coming to believe such a proposition than carefully considering it: e.g. any attempt to prove such a proposition could only rely, at best, on premisses which were no more evident. So

	3	**E(A*'s belief in *P*)	
So	4	*A* knows *P*	(1, 2, 3)

Thus, relative to its being closely considered, *P* is *SOL*. (The qualification is inserted to allow for the possibility that someone might believe *P* without ever closely considering it, and that Descartes might deny that state the title of knowledge. The proposition is, however, unqualifiedly *IRR*, because 'thought of' is just defined to imply careful consideration.)

It follows that, relative to its being closely considered, *P* is *OInd*.

'I have the idea of God'. This is not *S–V*, see p. 88, nor is it unqualifiedly *IRR*, see p. 185. But it is *IRR* relative to its being true; and relative to its being carefully considered, it is *StEV* and *INC* – hence (C1) *SOL*. Thus (C2) it is, relative to its being true and its being carefully considered, *OInd*.

DREAMING

DESCARTES takes dreaming to consist of experiences we have when asleep, accompanied very often by judgements, usually false. He writes, moreover, at least sometimes, as though the power of the will could be exercised even during a dream to withhold one's assent, so that one will not make false judgements.

This conception of what dreaming is has been attacked by Norman Malcolm in his book *Dreaming* (London, 1959), in which he denies that it is possible to believe anything, or to have any experiences, while asleep. The theory of meaning on which this view rests is open to fatal objections: see, in particular, Hilary Putnam, 'Dreaming and "Depth Grammar" ', now in his *Mind, Language and Reality* (Cambridge, 1975), pp. 304–24. I shall not discuss this view. It is worth noting, though, that it might be the case, quite independently of Malcolm's kind of position, that dreams turned out not to be experiences; thus there might in principle be experimental evidence that they were not, as D. C. Dennett has suggested in an argument quite contrary in spirit to Malcolm's ('Are Dreams Experiences?', *Philosophical Review* LXXXV (1976), 151–71).

However, there is another argument in Malcolm's book, taken up by him from Margaret Macdonald (see her 'Sleeping and Waking', *Mind* LXII (1953), 202–15), according to which there cannot be a criterion of whether one is awake or dreaming, as Descartes and many others have supposed there to be, since whatever the supposed criterion might be, one could always dream that it was satisfied. Thus it could not put you in a position to tell whether it was satisfied or you were dreaming that it was satisfied; so it could not be a criterion. This argument itself is independent of Malcolm's theory about the nature of dreaming (though of course the way in which he uses this argument himself is not). It is the area of this argument that I shall discuss. If it is right, then Descartes must be wrong in his well-known claim at the very end of the *Sixth Meditation* (VII 89–90, HR1 199) that, after dismissing the hyperbolical doubt, he has a perfectly good way of distinguishing between waking and dreaming, which consists in the coherence of his waking experience, relative to natural regularities. More generally, if the argument is right, it seems that it must be wrong to say that there is some way of telling that one is awake rather than dreaming. This seems counter-intuitive. I shall suggest that while there is something in the considerations that the argument deploys, we do not have to accept the counter-intuitive conclusion.

'Criterion' is a term of art, but I take it that one has a criterion for the state of affairs S obtaining, only if there are some features of the world or of one's experience by observing, noting, etc. which, one can tell whether S obtains or not. We should add some further condition about its being necessary that the features in question are so related to S: criteria have to be better than mere evidence. But the exact form or strength of this condition need not bother us here.

The idea of one's being able to tell *whether* S seems to entail the conjunction of two things:

(a) one can tell that S when S;

(b) one can tell that not-S when not-S.

We may be tempted to think that (a) and (b) must go together. The vital point, for the present question, is that they do not necessarily go together. One can of course decide to use the word 'criterion' only in cases where (a) and (b) both obtain, but that is uninteresting. The important point is that for many values of 'S', (b) can obtain without (a) obtaining.

We are concerned with states of the subject (whether one is dreaming or awake), so let us replace the formula 'one's being able to tell that S (not-S)' with the formula 'A's being able to tell that $F(A)$ (not-$F(A)$)', where 'being able to tell' means 'being able rationally to tell'. Now there are many values of '$F(\ )$' for which it is obviously not possible for A to tell that $F(A)$ when $F(A)$, though it looks as though A can tell that not-$F(A)$ when not-$F(A)$ – where '$F(\ )$' is 'being dead', for instance, or 'being in a dreamless sleep'. An example nearer the present question might be (under rather idealized assumptions) anoxia. I recall a lecture on the symptoms of anoxia (lack of oxygen), against which high-altitude pilots have to be on their guard. One symptom was blue finger-nails; another was over-confidence, which led one to neglect such things as blue finger-nails. On a rather idealized version of this phenomenon, it might well be that A could not tell that he was anoxic when he was; but it would surely be paradoxical to suggest that therefore A could not tell that he was not anoxic when he was not (for instance, A is you, now).

Consider an ordering, from more drastic to less drastic, of different sorts of reasons why A might not be able to tell that $F(A)$ when $F(A)$:

(1) A does not exist to judge anything. (Death)

(2) A cannot do anything, or more particularly cannot do anything of which he is conscious. (Dreamless sleep)

(3) (a) A cannot *tell that* anything, come to any conclusion about anything, make any judgement. (Some kinds of drugged condition)

(b) A cannot rationally *tell that* anything, come to any rational conclusion about anything. (Idealized anoxia; severe drunkenness)

It seems that Descartes did not assign dreaming to any of these classes. His picture of what obtains when one is dreaming seems rather to be something like this:

(4) A can rationally decide, come to rational conclusions, etc., but his experience is such as to lead rational decision to the wrong conclusion.

Class (4) naturally covers cases of illusion (refracted sticks, Gestalt figures, good forgeries etc.). But is it true in cases of that sort that A cannot tell that $F(A)$ when $F(A)$? Here it matters how '$F(\ )$' is specified. It is of course a necessary truth that A cannot tell that he is deceived when he is deceived, but this is trivial. If some specification of '$F(\ )$' is given which is not question-begging in that way, such as 'confronted with a straight stick which looks bent in water', A may well be able to tell that this is true of him when it is true of him, for instance by being familiar with such cases and deploying his information in relation to features of the present case. But in the case of dreaming, it does look much more plausible to say that one cannot tell that one is dreaming when one is dreaming – or at least only rarely and randomly so, if at all. In the ordinary illusion cases, it is often true (as we saw in contrasting the two things: see pp. 51–2) that there is both something about the situation to arouse a doubt, and something you can do to settle the doubt when aroused. These conditions do not obtain with dreaming. Moreover, if the question does come up when you are dreaming, and you try to settle it when dreaming, you will reach no answer, or not any well-grounded answer, since *every* consideration that one might deploy is liable to be distorted when one is dreaming, so, unlike the particular illusion cases, rational judgement gets no leverage. This, however, does seem to cast doubt on the idea that there is a set of considerations one could deploy when *not* dreaming to show that one was *not* dreaming. For, granted this picture, one should be able to start on the question just from the standpoint of rational enquiry – if we assign dreaming to (4), the standpoint of rational enquiry is neutral between dreaming and not dreaming. So one will expect it to be a property of the reasons that one can deploy from that standpoint that they distinguish between its being the case now that one is dreaming, and its being the case now that one is not, and if all features of the situation as experienced when one is dreaming can be such as to ground rationally the judgement that one is not dreaming, it really is obscure how one can ever tell which obtains.

But all of this arises only if dreaming is to be assigned to (4), and in fact it is absurd to assign it to (4). It belongs in either (3a) or (3b). With these classes, as with (1) and (2), where A cannot (rationally) tell that $F(A)$ when $F(A)$, because A cannot (rationally) tell *anything* when $F(A)$, how could it be a consequence that A could not rationally tell that not-$F(A)$ when not-$F(A)$? The point about (3) cases is not of course that when $F(A)$, A can detect the absence of (rational) decision and use that as his way of telling that $F(A)$. The point is that in (3) cases, there is no question of there being a (rational) way of telling anything when $F(A)$, so it cannot be a complaint against a suggested rational way of telling something (in particular, that not-$F(A)$), that it cannot be used in circumstances in which necessarily no way of rationally telling anything can be used.

Of course, there are important differences between (3) cases, such as dreaming, and (1) and (2). Thus in (3) cases, A may have false beliefs. So not surprisingly there is a sceptical problem about dreaming, but not about dreamless sleep. But this difference does not merely return us to scepticism. The assignment of dreaming to (3) is not just a classification in the abstract: it reflects features of dreaming, features which cannot of course be appealed to when we are dreaming, for no features can be rationally appealed to when dreaming, but which can (*contra* Malcolm) be rationally appealed to at the only time when we can rationally appeal to anything, viz. when we are awake.

What we can deploy when we are awake are certain considerations about what dreaming is like and what waking is like. Very importantly, we do not just have an asymmetry of coherence, but also have a perspective in which we can place dreaming in relation to waking. From the perspective of waking we can *explain* dreaming, and this is an important asymmetry. Such features are part of our way of telling, when we are awake, that we are awake. Of course it is true that we cannot make rational reference to these features, or to anything else, to decide that we are dreaming when we are dreaming, but that is itself a consequence of things we understand when we are awake, about dreaming.

The claim that Descartes saw dreaming in the light of (4) rather than (3) is based on the consideration, which I take to be true, that he thought that one could *at any moment* withhold assent from one's experience and stand back from it in the critical spirit of the Doubt. This does imply that rational decision is a power which is not vitiated in dreaming. Yet it is a notable fact that the passage in the *Sixth Meditation* is entirely from the perspective of waking, and is, as it should be, only about how we can, when we are awake, tell that we are awake.

INDEX

References to Descartes's *works* in this index are solely to passages of the text in which their history or general character are discussed. References to Descartes's contemporaries include passages in which they are mentioned only as recipients of letters from him.